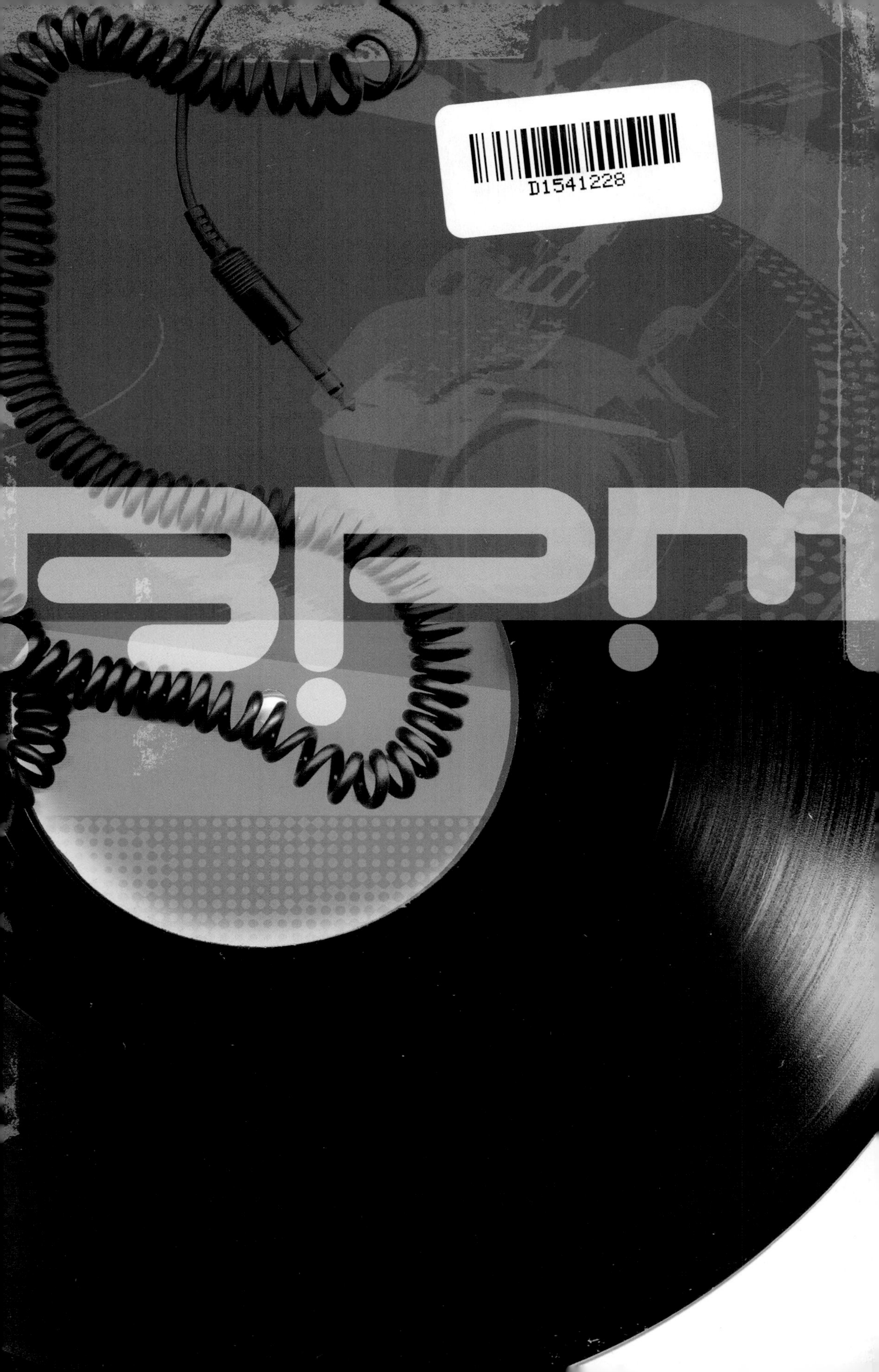

PRODUCTION CREDITS

PAUL SIZER
STORY, PENCILS, INKS, DIGITAL COLOR, DIGITAL COMPOSITING, GRAPHIC DESIGN, ORIGINAL PHOTOGRAPHY, MUSIC SEQUENCING AND SELECTION

WITH

JANE IRWIN
DATA ENTRY, WEBWORK, BETA EDITOR

JOHANNA DRAPER CARLSON

DAN TRAEGER
BETA EDITORS

KAREN (DJ JACKALOPE) MAEDA
TECHNICAL D.J. CONSULTANT, BETA EDITOR

TRACK LISTING

⟨⟩CAFE DIGITAL

B.P.M. (Beats Per Minute) (FIRST PRINTING, AUGUST 2008) Published by CAFE DIGITAL STUDIOS
P.O. Box 51595, Kalamazoo, Michigan 49005 USA.
Printed in Malaysia at Times International Printing. FIRST EDITION: 2008 $15.99 US
ISBN-10# 0-9768565-6-5 ISBN-13# 978-0-9768565-6-6

(FAST) FOREWORDS

KAREN (DJ JACKALOPE) MAEDA

DJ/COMIC BOOK FAN

I'm sure like BPM's comic book heroine, Roxy, I have found myself seated in too many 24-hour diners having pancakes and french fries and maybe a chocolate shake all at the same time cuz I'd been up for 24 hours after throwing a rave or deejaying at a club and couldn't decide on what to eat. It's usually around 7 a.m., after a night of sheer chaos and carefully constructed fun. Fun such as rocking the room, testing a crowd (or even the sound system for that matter) to see how much they will take or carefully finding the right moments to back off, throw some vocals in, and give everyone a short rest before decimating the room with bass. These are things that all DJs can identify with whether if they are in a comic book or in real life. I wish I could live in both worlds!

Deejaying is way too much fun. It's something I've been doing for the past 12 years, spent countless dollars on when I could have been out buying groceries, but instead would come home with the newest record by my favorite producer. And besides, what other jobs give you an excuse to dye your hair blue and rock out at earth shattering volume to your favorite music?

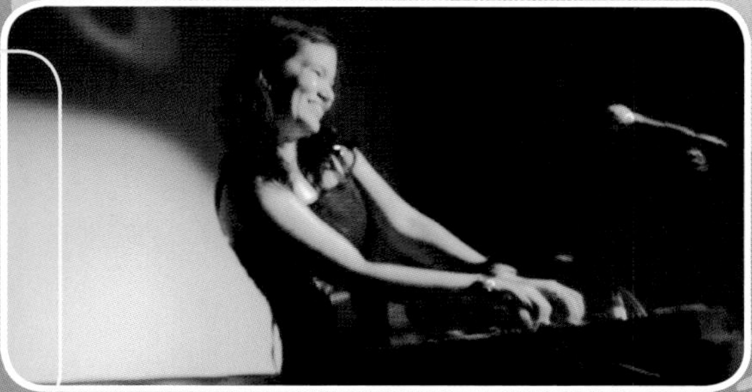

Miss Jackalope been playing records for 12 years and has played almost every electronic genre you can think of. Somehow, over time, the breakbeats stuck, and she stayed with jungle and electrobreaks. Her dedication to hard beats has her opening for the likes of NYC's pH10, Ming+FS, Reid Speed, DRC, and a variety of other DJs and live performers. She is the resident DJ for some of the largest computer security conferences in the world. Her website is located at www.dj-jackalope.com where she sells cds and has some mp3s to download. She has a little grey cat, a car in need of selling, and she also has an army.

MIKE PFIEFFER

PODCASTER, "MOST PEOPLE ARE DJ'S"

I don't have the data, but I have a theory it's not until the teen years, people start developing their own taste in music. Up until that point it's all guided by what our parents are listening to. I got the short end of that stick. My parents were country-western lovers. Is it any wonder then the music we listen to as teens tends to be rebellious? It's our chance to announce to our parents (as well as the world) this is what separates "me" from "you."

As a person who always felt somewhat removed or on the outside looking in at the various "clicks" and groups at school. My self-identification with music came with Gary Numan's groundbreaking album "The Pleasure Principle." At the time, I couldn't put words around it, but something about the texture of the music, the flatness of the vocals and the themes of alienation and machines appealed to my love of science fiction as well as my self-imposed isolation. From Gary Numan to Kraftwerk to the beginnings of techno, the themes and melodies of electronic music continued to pique my interest. Moreover, I started to discover something else about electronic music. How when weaved together from track to track it creates an atmosphere of sound that just can't be matched with any other genre of music.

Similarly, Roxy, Atsuko, and Dominic, the DJs from BPM understand how music informs, guides and exists as the soundtrack to our mostly mundane lives. However, as Paul so masterfully tells it in BPM, their comprehension runs deeper. As a DJ they construct patterns of sound that cause movement and thought to a crowd, resulting in shaping their identity and life choices for years to come. They'll never get the recognition they deserve for giving more meaning to life. The most recognition they get is a "nod" and a "thanks" for providing the crowd with something to move to. But, the DJ doesn't need recognition.

They just need music, preferably with a good beat.

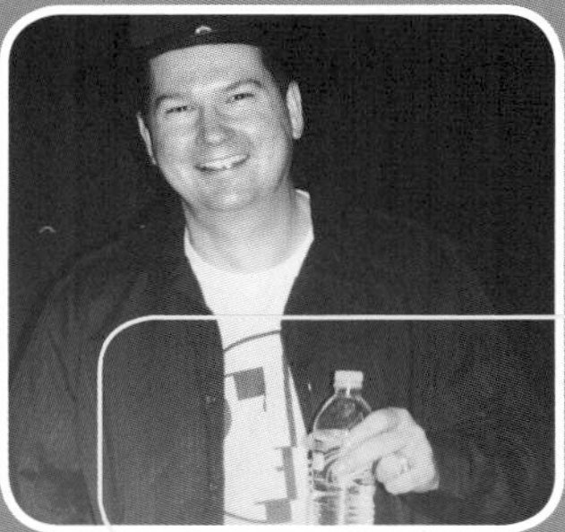

Mike Pfeiffer aka Mikel O.D. is a freelance Journalist and the host of Most People Are DJs, a music show available on the internet at www.mostpeoplearedjs.com. Mike believes traditional radio is inherently evil and any band that charges more than $50 to see them should be boycotted.

REMIX AND REWIND

"Dear Comics,

I felt I needed to write you this note. I've been spending time with someone else. It's been going on since high school, and I feel as strongly about this other person as I do you, so I felt it would be good to get this all out in the open and talk about it. I don't want to lose either of you. Isn't there some way the two of you can get along together and maybe learn from one another?

All my love, Paul"

Wow, my first "Dear John" letter. Not my first "It's not you, it's me" line. Ridiculous, but true.

With equal importance and involvement in my life, my love of music, and especially electronic dance music, has been as much as a constant as comics and drawing. From as early as high school, music and comics began to vie for space in my life, and being the negotiator that I am, I always worked to pursue them both equally.

Tenth grade was when I really feel I first realized music was something for me to learn about, research and become a geek about. My friends who got me cool new music would give me tapes with hardcore punk on one side, and icy gothic Euro synthpop on the other, and let me fill in the blanks. I grew up in a really great time; the early 80's were a time when punk and new wave were fighting for the spotlight, and across the ocean, people were making music with synthesizers and drum machines. The future was so close, and this music was grabbing at it, either to embrace it or shake it by the throat. Anything went, and there was a very genuine sense of crashing into unknown frontiers, for either good or bad. It was happening, and I decided to grab hold and listen.

It wasn't enough for me to just listen to the music, I had to know as much as I could about it. Who was the producer? Who were the band members? Which 12" British import single had the non-LP version of "Pedestrian Walkway" with Thomas Dolby still playing synthesizers as part of the Camera Club? Suddenly, knowing the names of every X-Man ever didn't seem so weird. But the stuff I liked was still off the beaten path, and that made it all the more fun to hoard, discover and share.

In college, I was in the middle of the 80's and working at Believe In Music, the first music store in my town to rent videos (VHS AND Beta!) and to stock CDs when they first came out. Working there meant all my spare cash went to making my record collection go from "modest" to "insane" in just a few short years. I had a hunger for this stuff, and getting discounts on it was the key I had been looking for. I met one of my best friends because we were both trying to purchase the same 12" single. After that we began a musical journey that included renting drum machines, chasing Arthur Baker remixes and travelling to Chicago to see equal amounts of Ministry and Pet Shop Boys concerts and hanging out at Wax Trax Records. Music was my full time squeeze.

The early 90's came around, and comics came knocking at my door again. So for the next few years, I was "double dating", spending equal amounts of times learning about the power of comics and the power of music. Both were satisfying, but both were demanding. I was making decisions to take a serious stab at making comics professionally, being inspired by people like Geof Darrow, Terry Moore, Frank Miller, Mike Mignola, and Paul Chadwick. I was also hanging around a dance club called the Warehouse in Kalamazoo. I ended up doing design work for them, and when they told me they couldn't pay me very much, I told them they could pay me by letting me learn how to beatmix and eventually spin at the club. Three weeks later, I was in the booth, learning on the fly and helping out on "College Night", taking over when the head DJ wanted to take a piss or get a beer. Eventually I got to solo on "Techno Night" and every once in a while on "Industrial Night". During one of those nights, I needed to use the bathroom and cued up an 11 minute Nine Inch Nails "mega-mix" on CD, plenty of time for me to descend the rickety stairs and take a pee. As I got to the bottom of the stairway, the CD began skipping during "Head Like A Hole", and the club was filled with "I'd rather die than give you con-trol-trol-trol-trol-trol-trol..." As I shot back into the booth to cue up another song, from the darkened cavernous club came a lone voice: "Fix it, fuck-up!" At that moment, I became a DJ.

So, in a way, "B.P.M." was inevitable; a story that had to happen, a subject way too close to my heart to ignore. This is my love letter to the two things I've loved since I was a kid. What I was waiting for was the ability to be able to do it justice, to have the tools to talk about music and show what music looks like, on the comic page. Have I succeeded? I'll let you be the judge of that. Thanks for reading and dancing (and not throwing bottles at me).

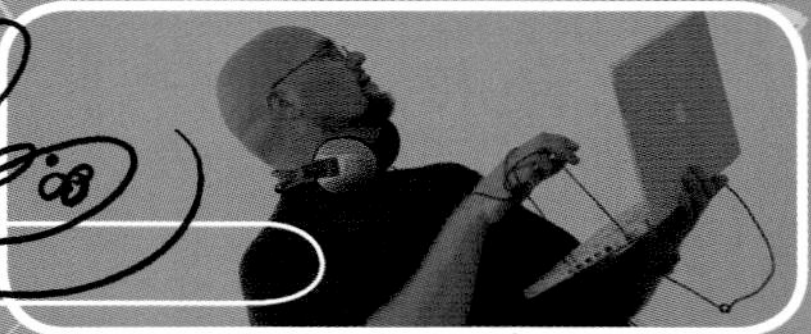

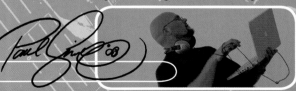

PAUL SIZER, MAY 2008

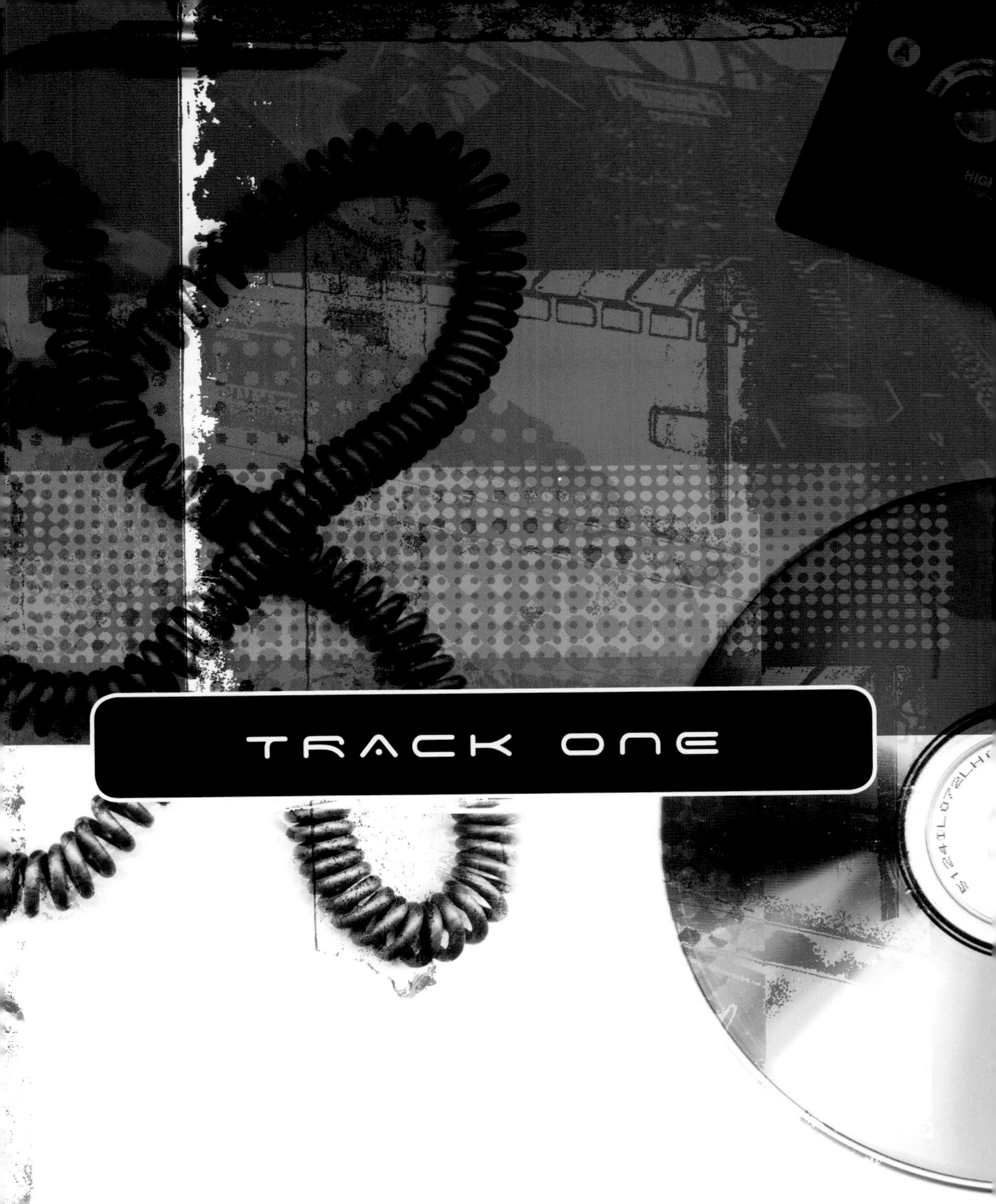

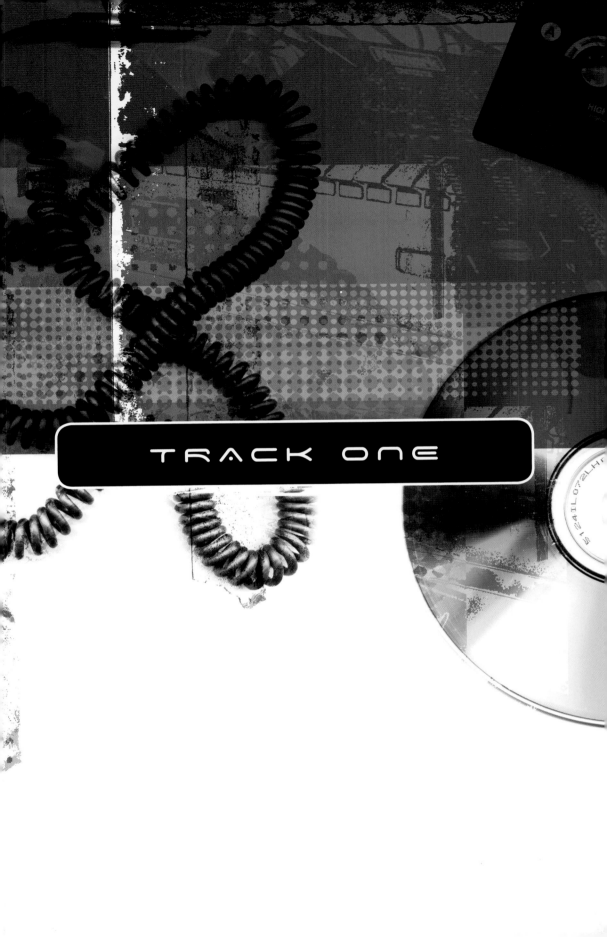

TRACK ONE

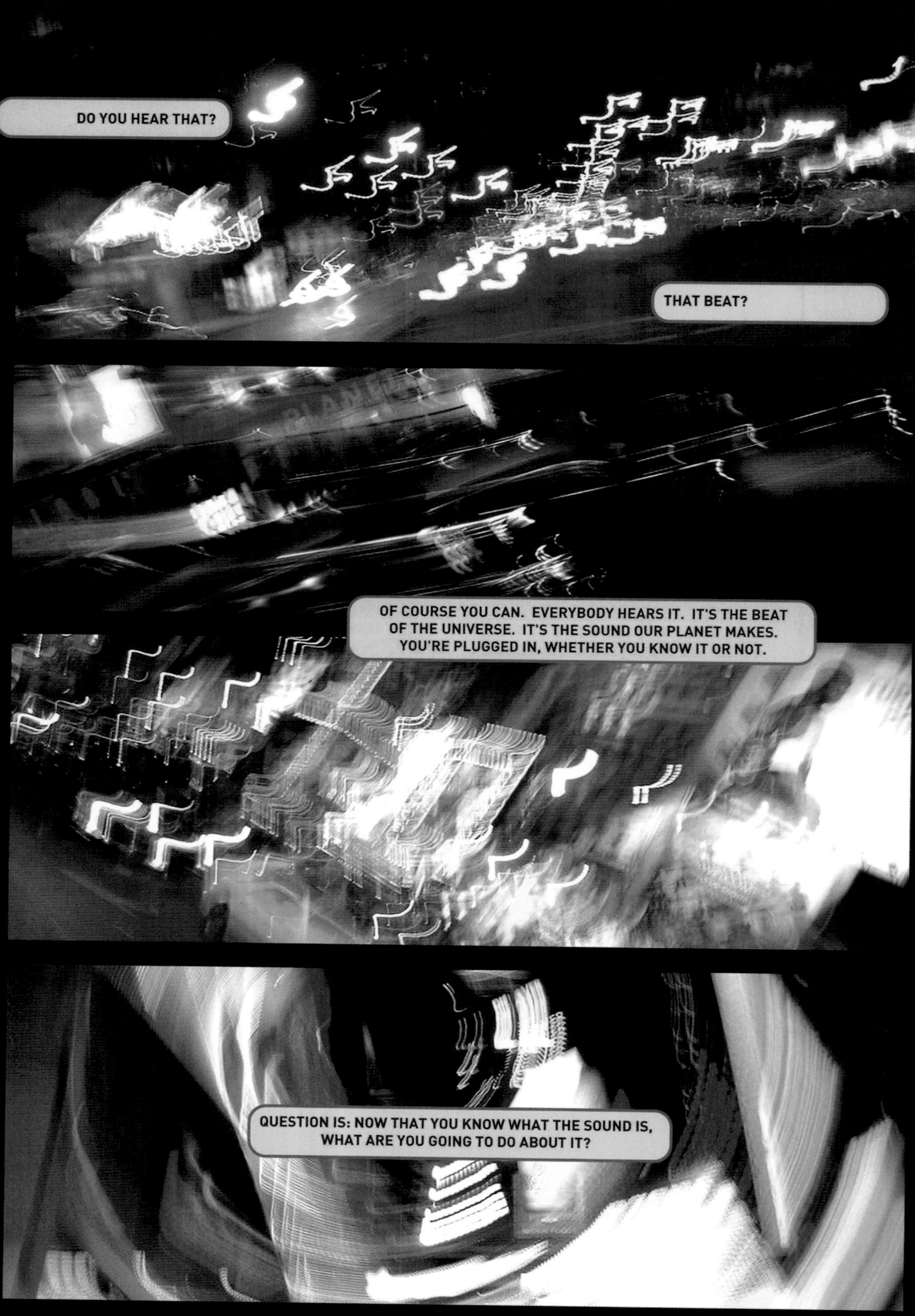
DO YOU HEAR THAT?
THAT BEAT?
OF COURSE YOU CAN. EVERYBODY HEARS IT. IT'S THE BEAT OF THE UNIVERSE. IT'S THE SOUND OUR PLANET MAKES. YOU'RE PLUGGED IN, WHETHER YOU KNOW IT OR NOT.
QUESTION IS: NOW THAT YOU KNOW WHAT THE SOUND IS, WHAT ARE YOU GOING TO DO ABOUT IT?

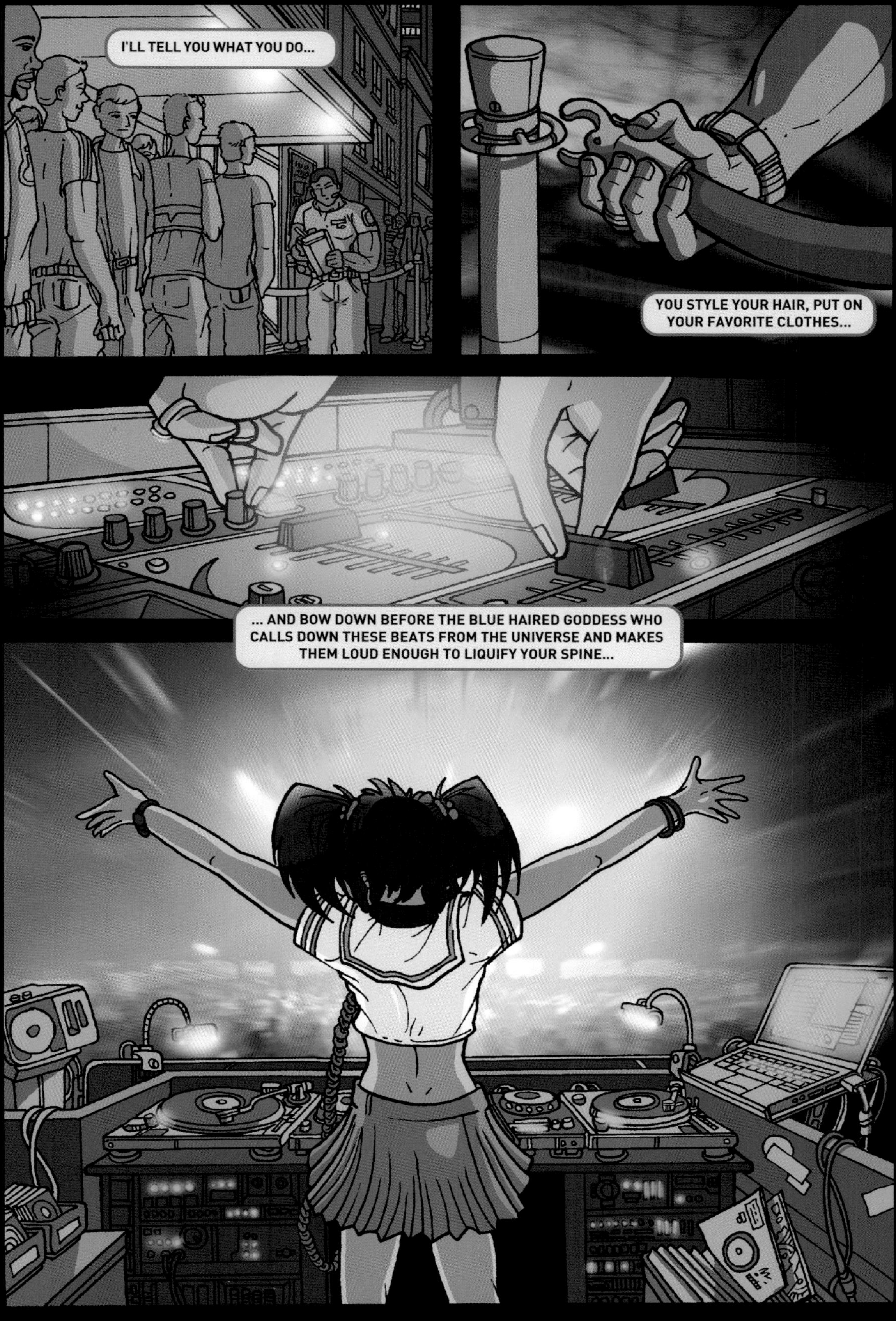
I'LL TELL YOU WHAT YOU DO...
YOU STYLE YOUR HAIR, PUT ON YOUR FAVORITE CLOTHES...
... AND BOW DOWN BEFORE THE BLUE HAIRED GODDESS WHO CALLS DOWN THESE BEATS FROM THE UNIVERSE AND MAKES THEM LOUD ENOUGH TO LIQUIFY YOUR SPINE...

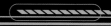

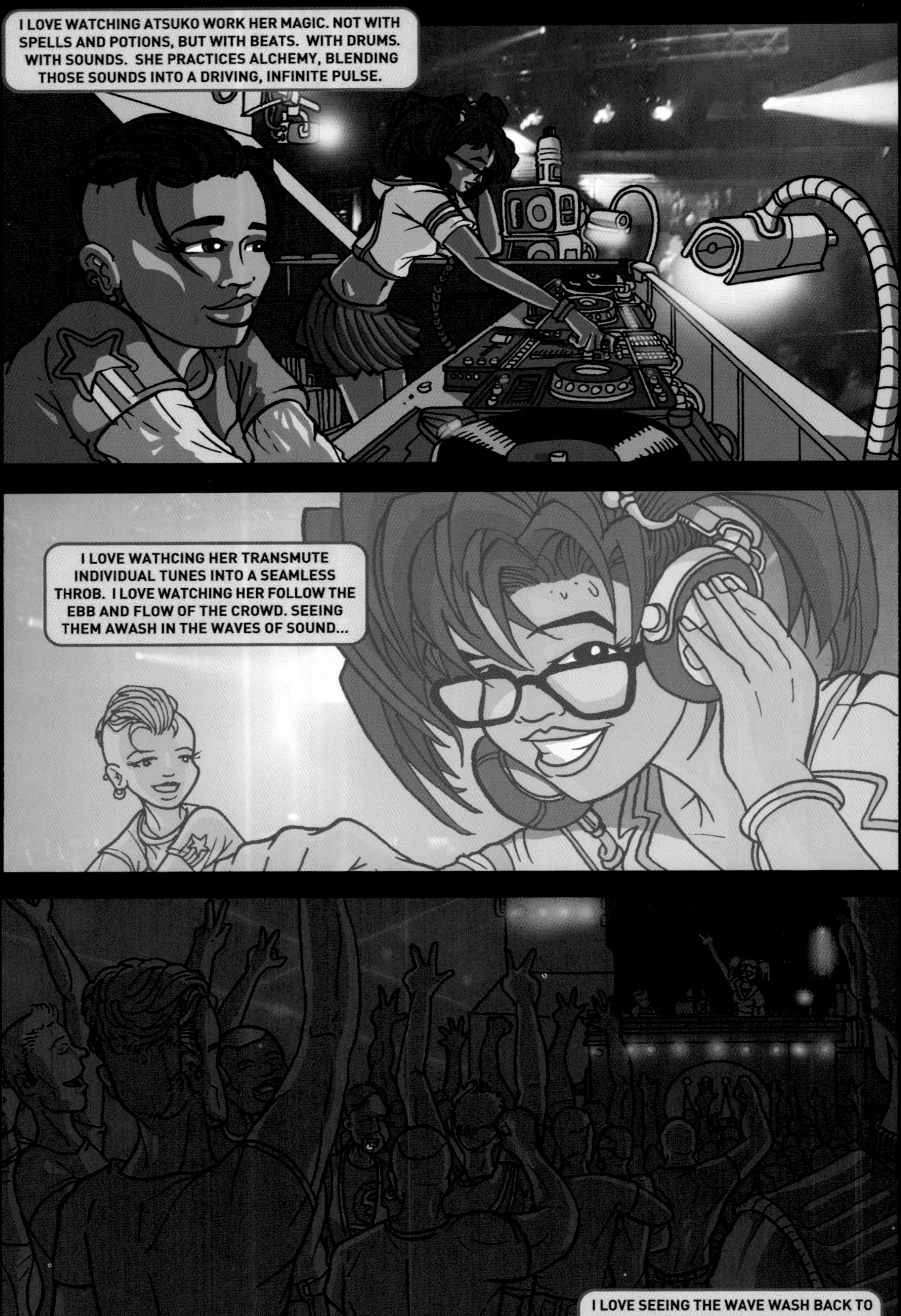
I LOVE WATCHING ATSUKO WORK HER MAGIC. NOT WITH SPELLS AND POTIONS, BUT WITH BEATS. WITH DRUMS. WITH SOUNDS. SHE PRACTICES ALCHEMY, BLENDING THOSE SOUNDS INTO A DRIVING, INFINITE PULSE.
I LOVE WATHCING HER TRANSMUTE INDIVIDUAL TUNES INTO A SEAMLESS THROB. I LOVE WATCHING HER FOLLOW THE EBB AND FLOW OF THE CROWD. SEEING THEM AWASH IN THE WAVES OF SOUND...
I LOVE SEEING THE WAVE WASH BACK TO HER. A SEA OF ARMS. GIVING BACK THE LOVE SHE'S GIVING TO THEM.

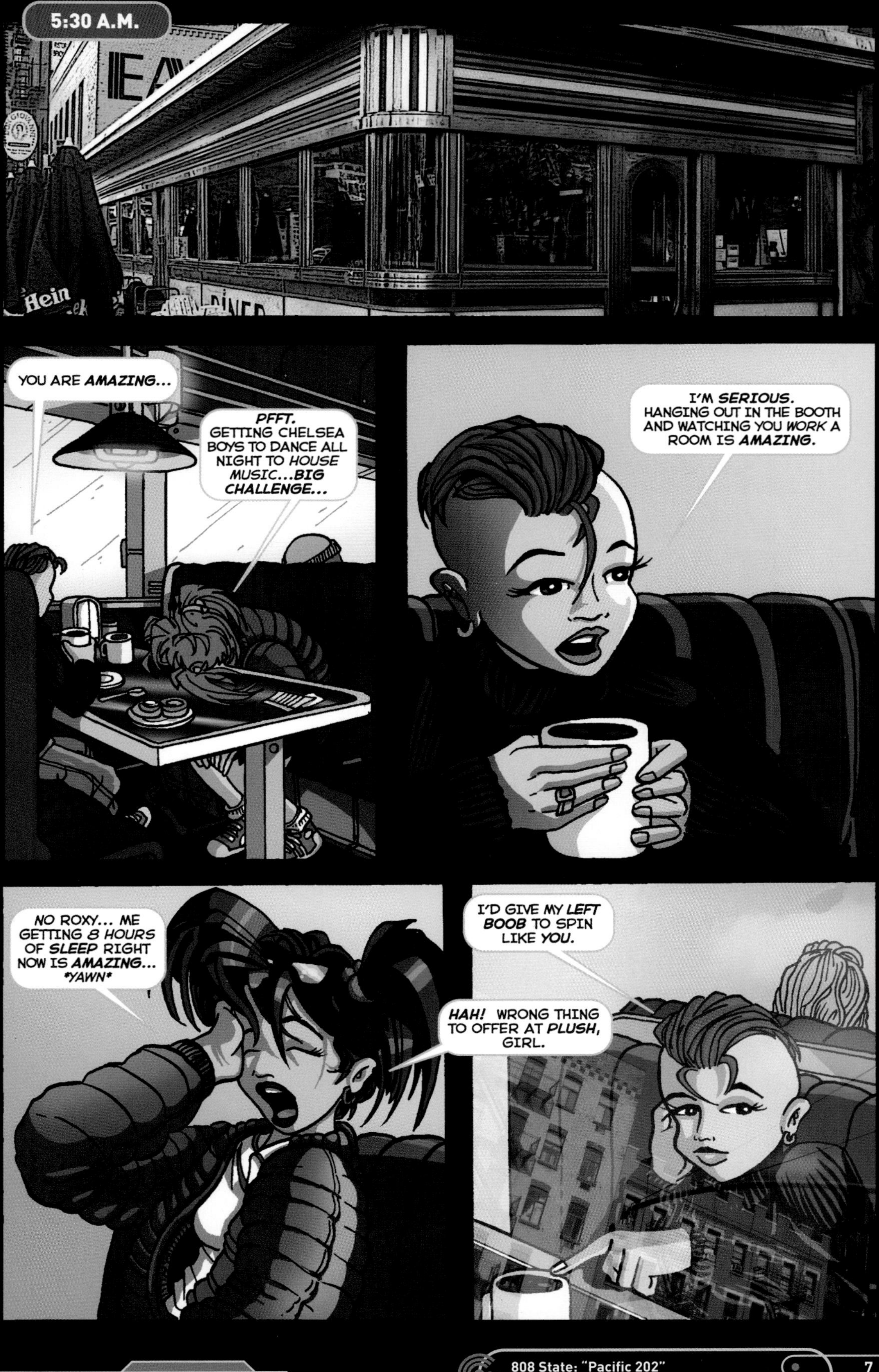
5:30 A.M.
YOU ARE AMAZING...
PFFT. GETTING CHELSEA BOYS TO DANCE ALL NIGHT TO HOUSE MUSIC...BIG CHALLENGE...
I'M SERIOUS. HANGING OUT IN THE BOOTH AND WATCHING YOU WORK A ROOM IS AMAZING.
NO ROXY... ME GETTING 8 HOURS OF SLEEP RIGHT NOW IS AMAZING... *YAWN*
I'D GIVE MY LEFT BOOB TO SPIN LIKE YOU.
HAH! WRONG THING TO OFFER AT PLUSH, GIRL.

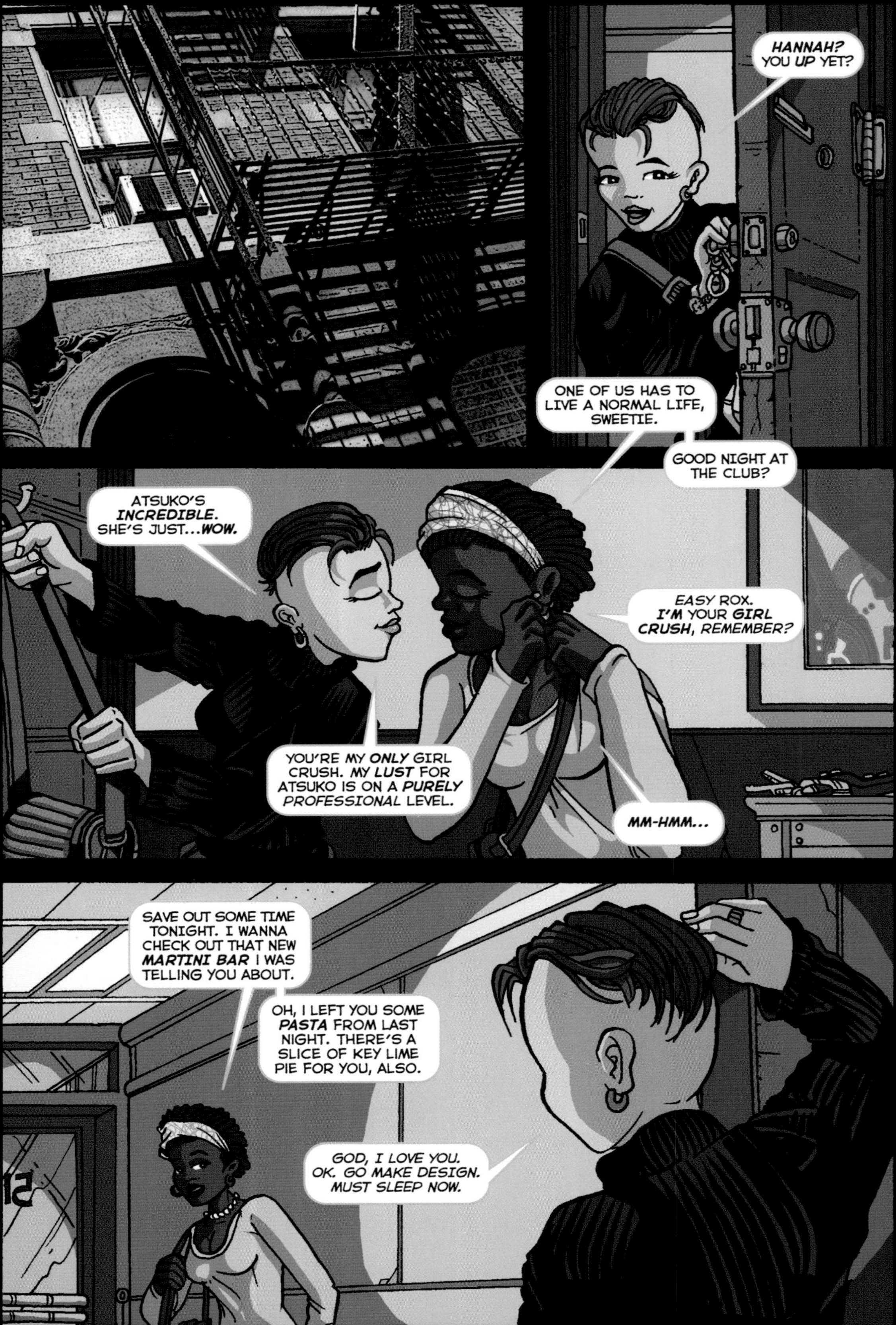
HANNAH? YOU UP YET?
ONE OF US HAS TO LIVE A NORMAL LIFE, SWEETIE.
GOOD NIGHT AT THE CLUB?
ATSUKO'S INCREDIBLE. SHE'S JUST...WOW.
EASY ROX. I'M YOUR GIRL CRUSH, REMEMBER?
YOU'RE MY ONLY GIRL CRUSH. MY LUST FOR ATSUKO IS ON A PURELY PROFESSIONAL LEVEL.
MM-HMM...
SAVE OUT SOME TIME TONIGHT. I WANNA CHECK OUT THAT NEW MARTINI BAR I WAS TELLING YOU ABOUT.
OH, I LEFT YOU SOME PASTA FROM LAST NIGHT. THERE'S A SLICE OF KEY LIME PIE FOR YOU, ALSO.
GOD, I LOVE YOU. OK. GO MAKE DESIGN. MUST SLEEP NOW.

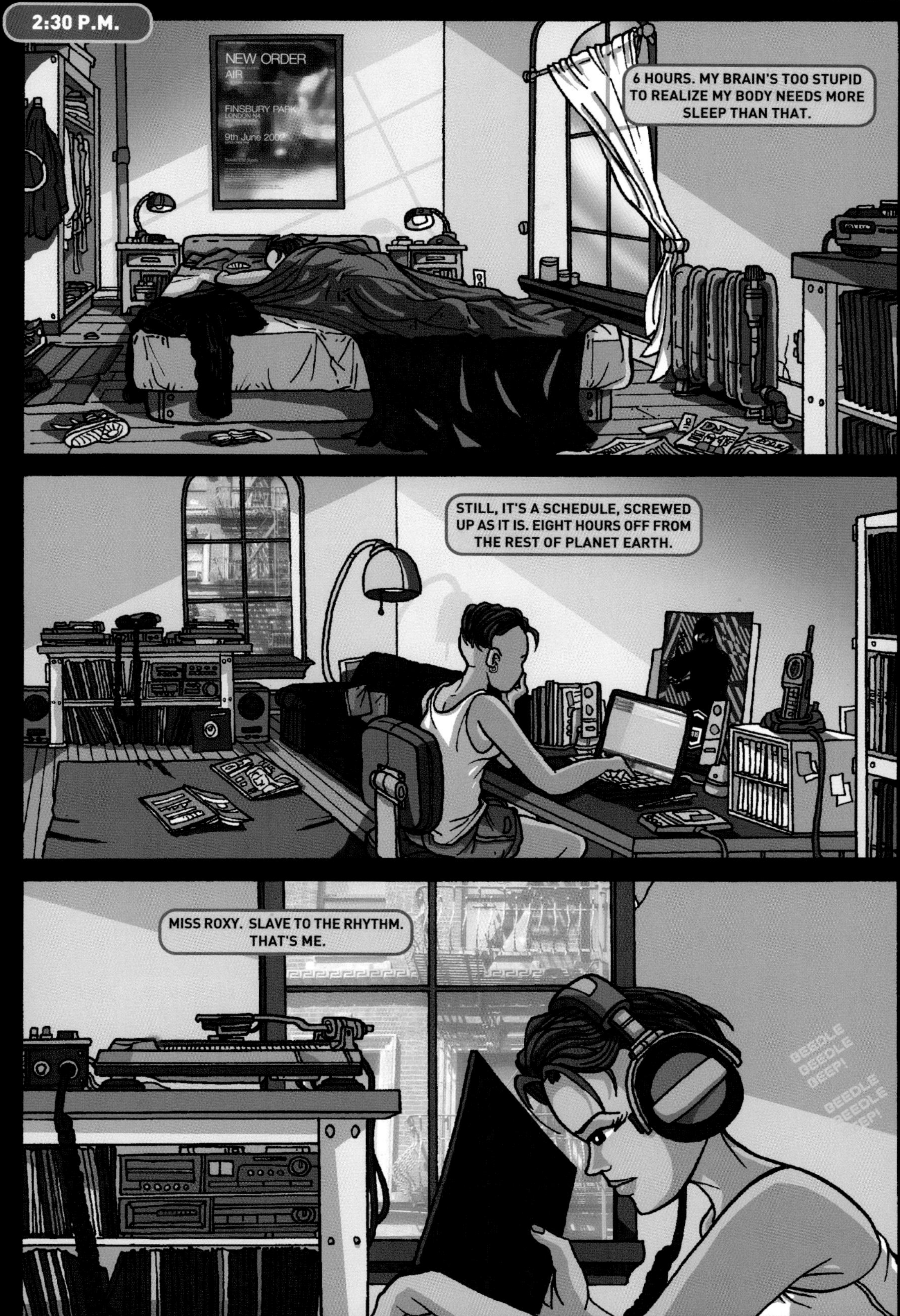
2:30 P.M.
NEW ORDER
AIR
FINSBURY PARK
LONDON N4
9th June 2002
6 HOURS. MY BRAIN'S TOO STUPID TO REALIZE MY BODY NEEDS MORE SLEEP THAN THAT.
STILL, IT'S A SCHEDULE, SCREWED UP AS IT IS. EIGHT HOURS OFF FROM THE REST OF PLANET EARTH.
MISS ROXY. SLAVE TO THE RHYTHM. THAT'S ME.
BEEDLE BEEDLE BEEP!

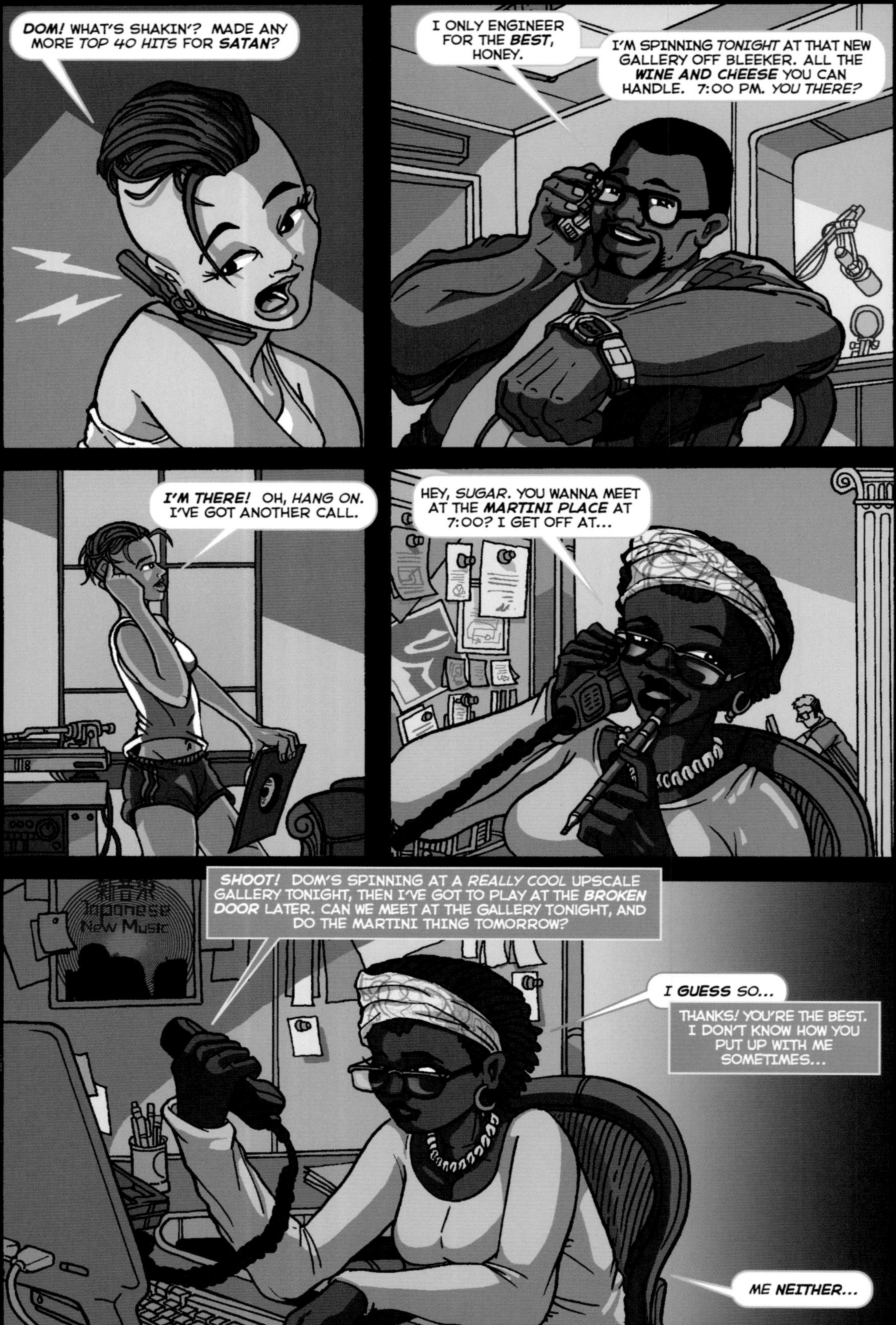
DOM! WHAT'S SHAKIN'? MADE ANY MORE TOP 40 HITS FOR SATAN?
I ONLY ENGINEER FOR THE BEST, HONEY.
I'M SPINNING TONIGHT AT THAT NEW GALLERY OFF BLEEKER. ALL THE WINE AND CHEESE YOU CAN HANDLE. 7:00 PM. YOU THERE?
I'M THERE! OH, HANG ON. I'VE GOT ANOTHER CALL.
HEY, SUGAR. YOU WANNA MEET AT THE MARTINI PLACE AT 7:00? I GET OFF AT...
SHOOT! DOM'S SPINNING AT A REALLY COOL UPSCALE GALLERY TONIGHT, THEN I'VE GOT TO PLAY AT THE BROKEN DOOR LATER. CAN WE MEET AT THE GALLERY TONIGHT, AND DO THE MARTINI THING TOMORROW?
Japanese New Music
I GUESS SO...
THANKS! YOU'RE THE BEST. I DON'T KNOW HOW YOU PUT UP WITH ME SOMETIMES...
ME NEITHER...

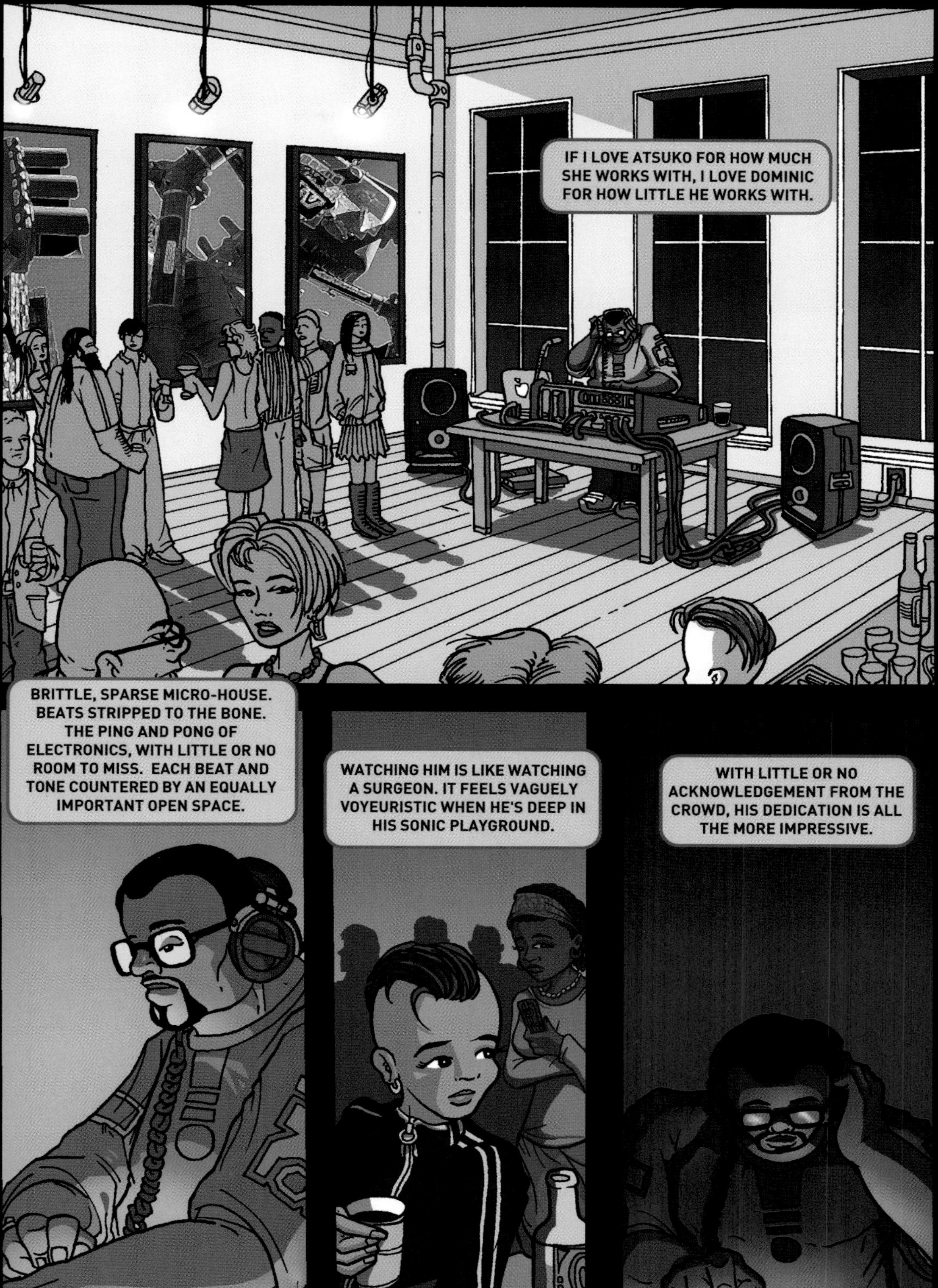
IF I LOVE ATSUKO FOR HOW MUCH SHE WORKS WITH, I LOVE DOMINIC FOR HOW LITTLE HE WORKS WITH.
BRITTLE, SPARSE MICRO-HOUSE. BEATS STRIPPED TO THE BONE. THE PING AND PONG OF ELECTRONICS, WITH LITTLE OR NO ROOM TO MISS. EACH BEAT AND TONE COUNTERED BY AN EQUALLY IMPORTANT OPEN SPACE.
WATCHING HIM IS LIKE WATCHING A SURGEON. IT FEELS VAGUELY VOYEURISTIC WHEN HE'S DEEP IN HIS SONIC PLAYGROUND.
WITH LITTLE OR NO ACKNOWLEDGEMENT FROM THE CROWD, HIS DEDICATION IS ALL THE MORE IMPRESSIVE.

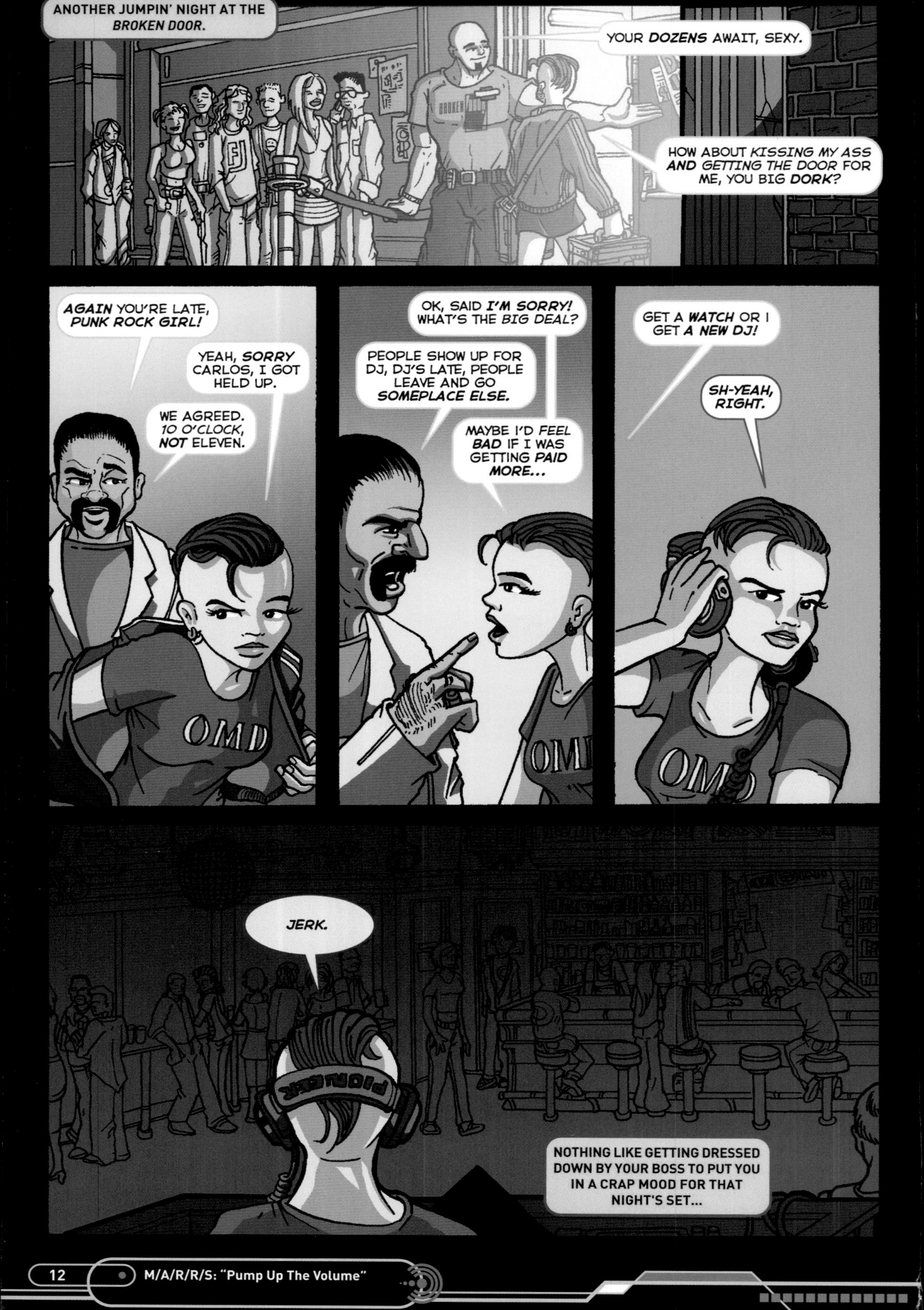
ANOTHER JUMPIN' NIGHT AT THE BROKEN DOOR.
YOUR DOZENS AWAIT, SEXY.
HOW ABOUT KISSING MY ASS AND GETTING THE DOOR FOR ME, YOU BIG DORK?
AGAIN YOU'RE LATE, PUNK ROCK GIRL!
YEAH, SORRY CARLOS, I GOT HELD UP.
WE AGREED. 10 O'CLOCK, NOT ELEVEN.
OK, SAID I'M SORRY! WHAT'S THE BIG DEAL?
PEOPLE SHOW UP FOR DJ, DJ'S LATE, PEOPLE LEAVE AND GO SOMEPLACE ELSE.
MAYBE I'D FEEL BAD IF I WAS GETTING PAID MORE...
GET A WATCH OR I GET A NEW DJ!
SH-YEAH, RIGHT.
JERK.
NOTHING LIKE GETTING DRESSED DOWN BY YOUR BOSS TO PUT YOU IN A CRAP MOOD FOR THAT NIGHT'S SET...

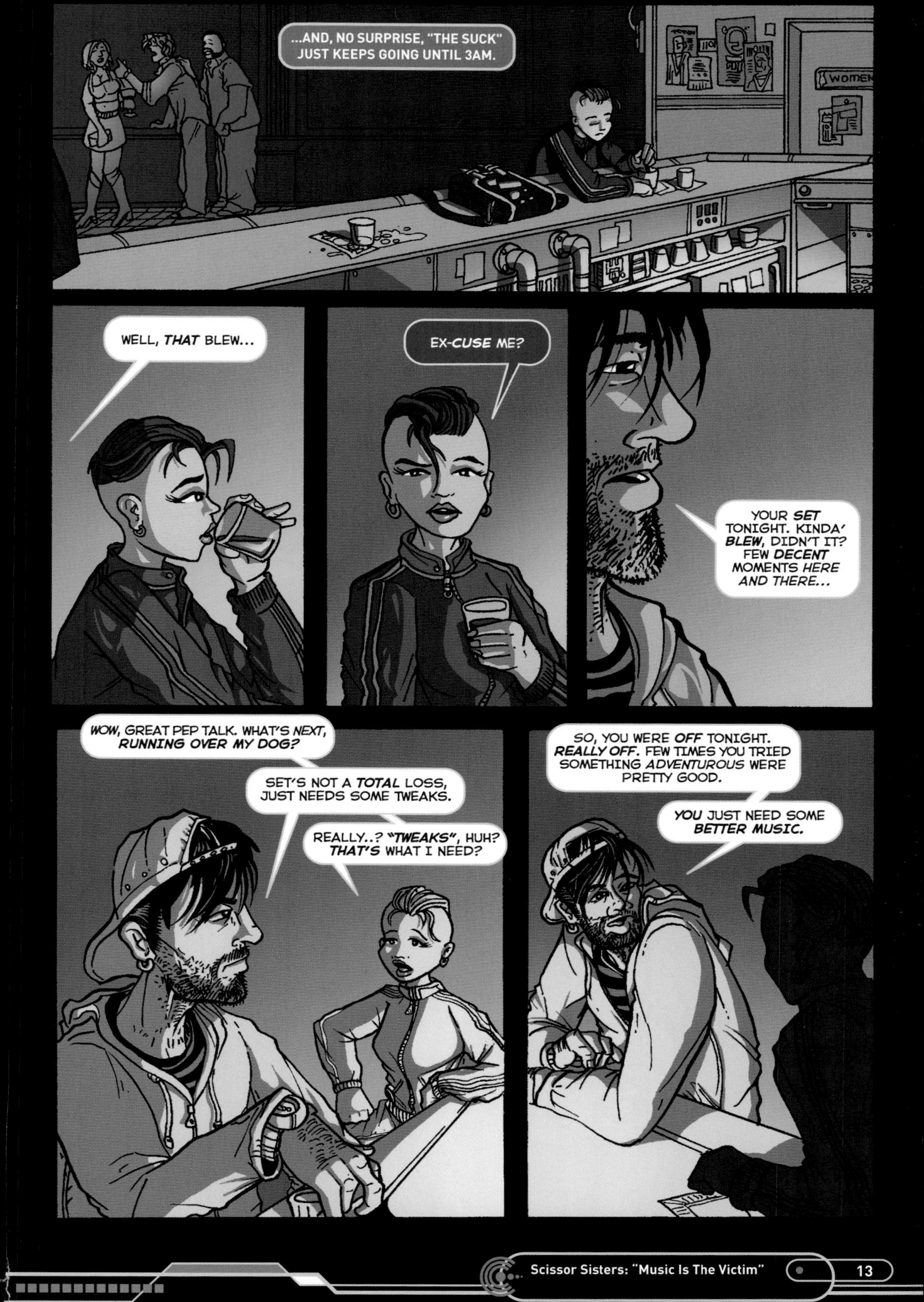
...AND, NO SURPRISE, "THE SUCK" JUST KEEPS GOING UNTIL 3AM.
WOMEN
WELL, THAT BLEW...
EX-CUSE ME?
YOUR SET TONIGHT. KINDA' BLEW, DIDN'T IT? FEW DECENT MOMENTS HERE AND THERE...
WOW, GREAT PEP TALK. WHAT'S NEXT, RUNNING OVER MY DOG?
SET'S NOT A TOTAL LOSS, JUST NEEDS SOME TWEAKS.
REALLY..? "TWEAKS", HUH? THAT'S WHAT I NEED?
SO, YOU WERE OFF TONIGHT. REALLY OFF. FEW TIMES YOU TRIED SOMETHING ADVENTUROUS WERE PRETTY GOOD.
YOU JUST NEED SOME BETTER MUSIC.

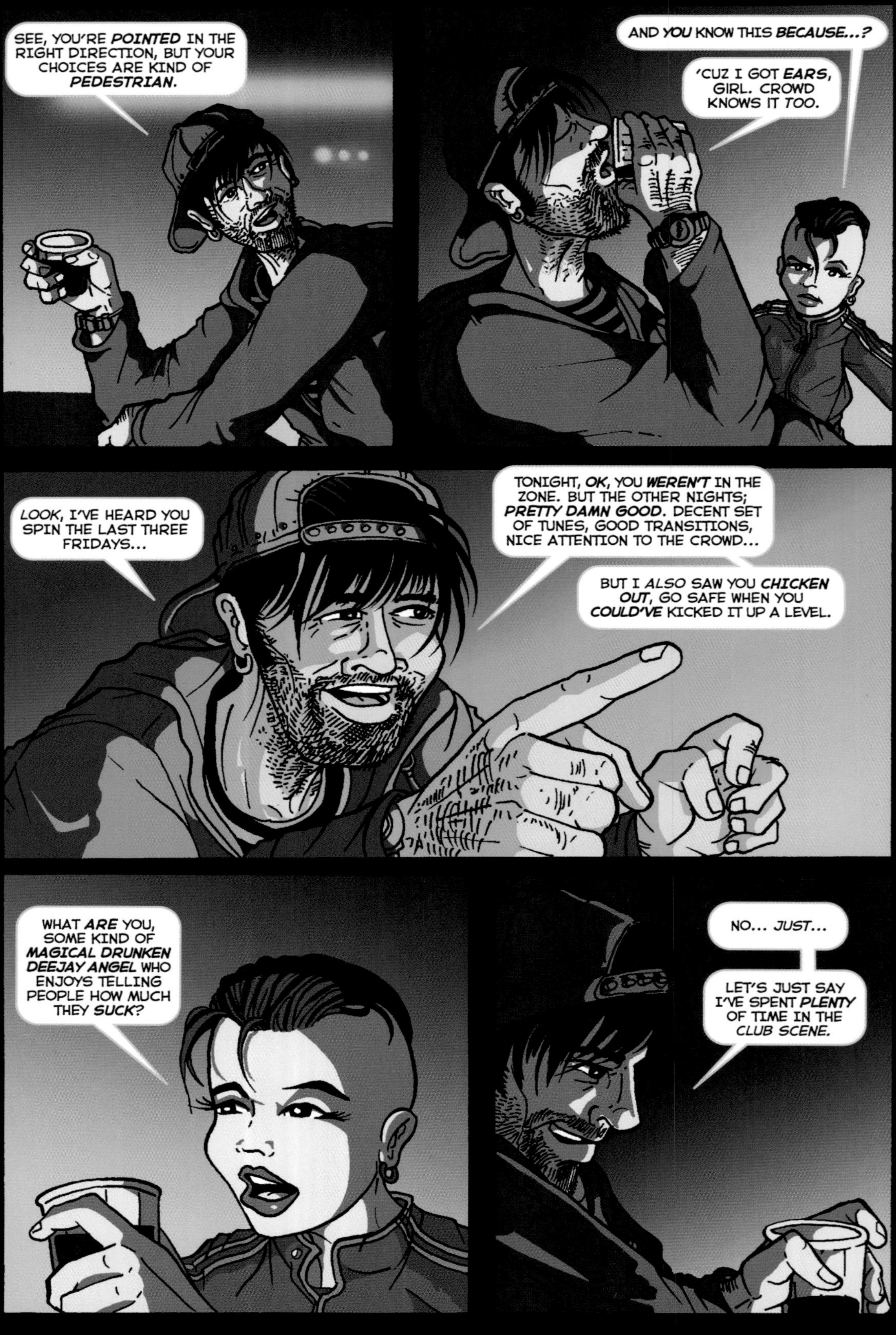
SEE, YOU'RE *POINTED* IN THE RIGHT DIRECTION, BUT YOUR CHOICES ARE KIND OF *PEDESTRIAN.*
AND *YOU* KNOW THIS *BECAUSE...?*
'CUZ I GOT *EARS*, GIRL. CROWD KNOWS IT *TOO.*
LOOK, I'VE HEARD YOU SPIN THE LAST THREE FRIDAYS...
TONIGHT, *OK*, YOU *WEREN'T* IN THE ZONE. BUT THE OTHER NIGHTS; *PRETTY DAMN GOOD.* DECENT SET OF TUNES, GOOD TRANSITIONS, NICE ATTENTION TO THE CROWD...
BUT I *ALSO* SAW YOU *CHICKEN OUT*, GO SAFE WHEN YOU *COULD'VE* KICKED IT UP A LEVEL.
WHAT *ARE* YOU, SOME KIND OF *MAGICAL DRUNKEN DEEJAY ANGEL* WHO ENJOYS TELLING PEOPLE HOW MUCH THEY *SUCK?*
NO... *JUST...*
LET'S JUST SAY I'VE SPENT *PLENTY* OF TIME IN THE *CLUB SCENE.*

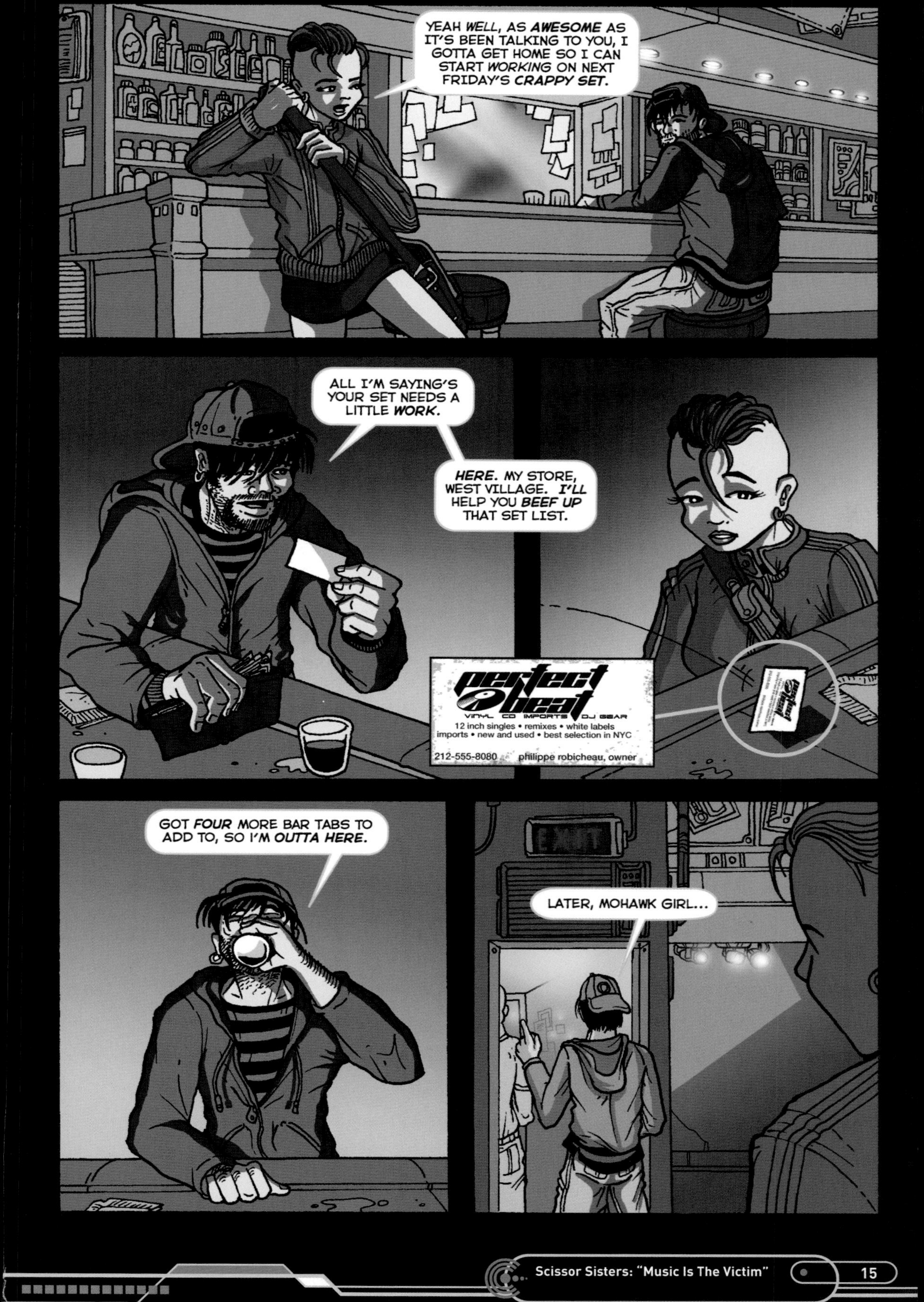
YEAH WELL, AS AWESOME AS IT'S BEEN TALKING TO YOU, I GOTTA GET HOME SO I CAN START WORKING ON NEXT FRIDAY'S CRAPPY SET.
ALL I'M SAYING'S YOUR SET NEEDS A LITTLE WORK.
HERE. MY STORE, WEST VILLAGE. I'LL HELP YOU BEEF UP THAT SET LIST.
perfect beat
VINYL CD IMPORTS DJ GEAR
12 inch singles • remixes • white labels
imports • new and used • best selection in NYC
212-555-8080 philippe robicheau, owner
GOT FOUR MORE BAR TABS TO ADD TO, SO I'M OUTTA HERE.
LATER, MOHAWK GIRL...

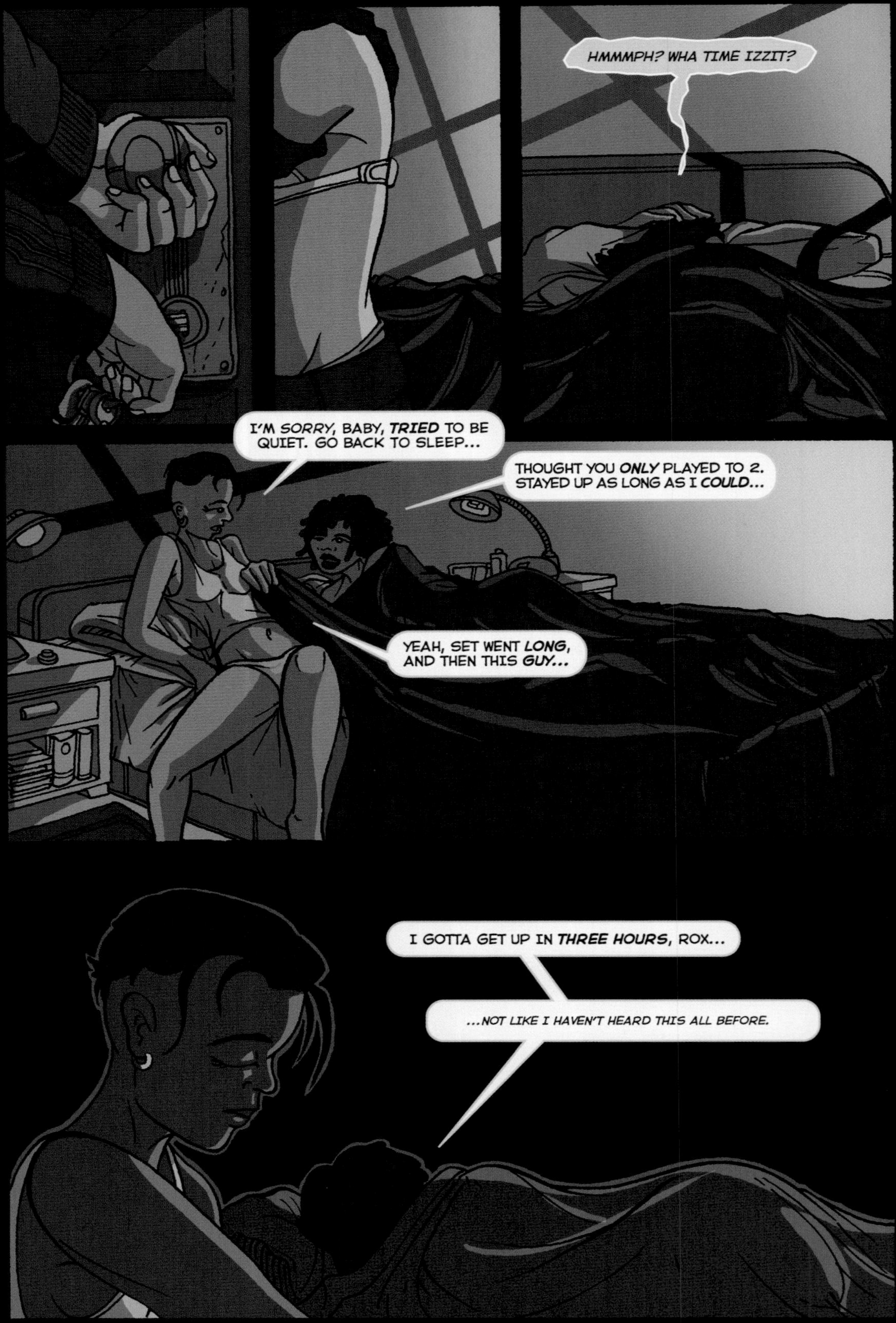
HMMMPH? WHA TIME IZZIT?
I'M SORRY, BABY, TRIED TO BE QUIET. GO BACK TO SLEEP...
THOUGHT YOU ONLY PLAYED TO 2. STAYED UP AS LONG AS I COULD...
YEAH, SET WENT LONG, AND THEN THIS GUY...
I GOTTA GET UP IN THREE HOURS, ROX...
...NOT LIKE I HAVEN'T HEARD THIS ALL BEFORE.

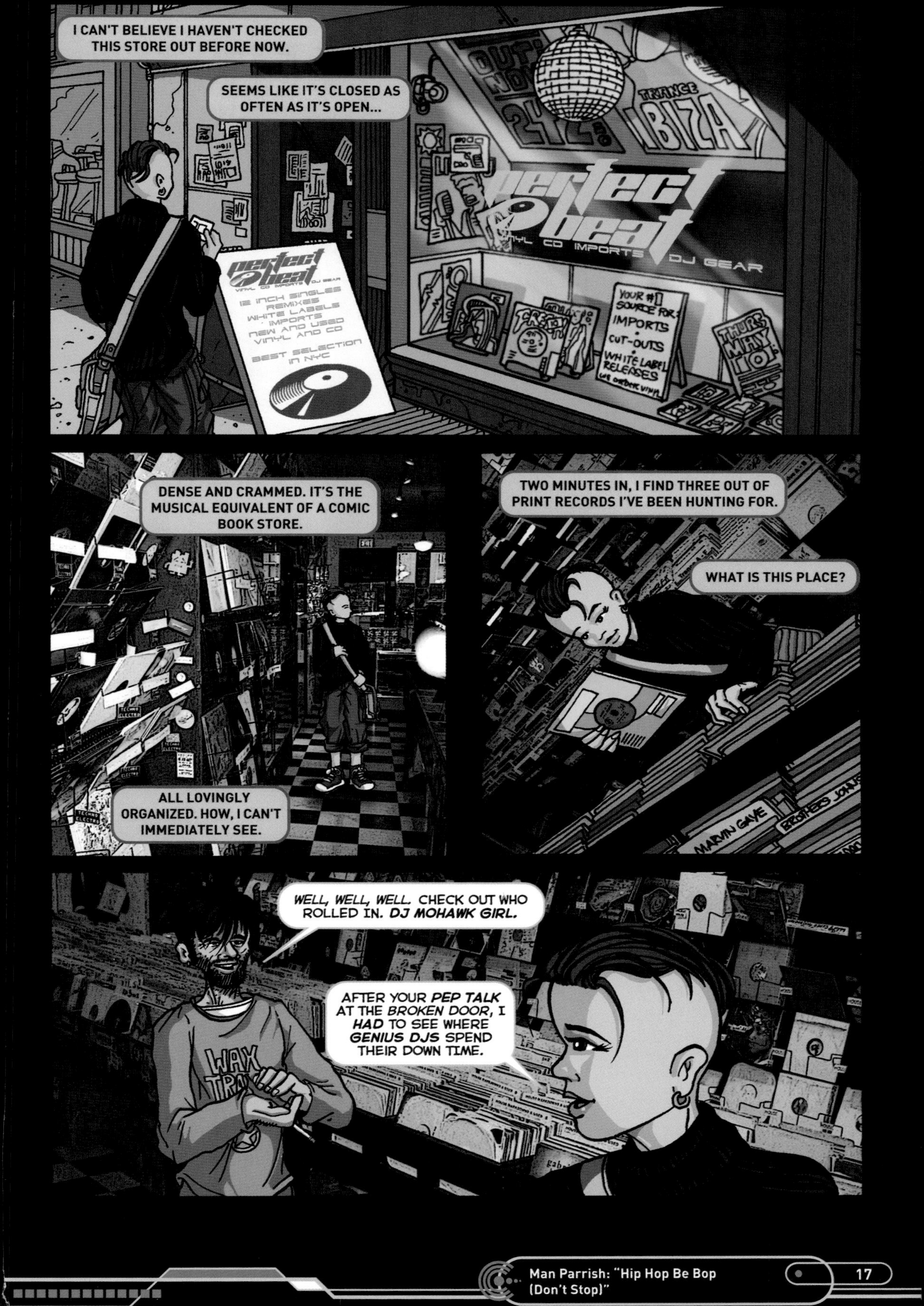
I CAN'T BELIEVE I HAVEN'T CHECKED THIS STORE OUT BEFORE NOW.
SEEMS LIKE IT'S CLOSED AS OFTEN AS IT'S OPEN...
TRANCE IBIZA
perfect beat
VINYL CD IMPORTS DJ GEAR
12 INCH SINGLES
REMIXES
WHITE LABELS
IMPORTS
NEW AND USED
VINYL AND CD
BEST SELECTION IN NYC
YOUR #1 SOURCE FOR: IMPORTS • CUT-OUTS • WHITE LABEL RELEASES
DENSE AND CRAMMED. IT'S THE MUSICAL EQUIVALENT OF A COMIC BOOK STORE.
ALL LOVINGLY ORGANIZED. HOW, I CAN'T IMMEDIATELY SEE.
TWO MINUTES IN, I FIND THREE OUT OF PRINT RECORDS I'VE BEEN HUNTING FOR.
WHAT IS THIS PLACE?
MARVIN GAYE
BROTHERS JOHNSON
WELL, WELL, WELL. CHECK OUT WHO ROLLED IN. DJ MOHAWK GIRL.
AFTER YOUR PEP TALK AT THE BROKEN DOOR, I HAD TO SEE WHERE GENIUS DJS SPEND THEIR DOWN TIME.

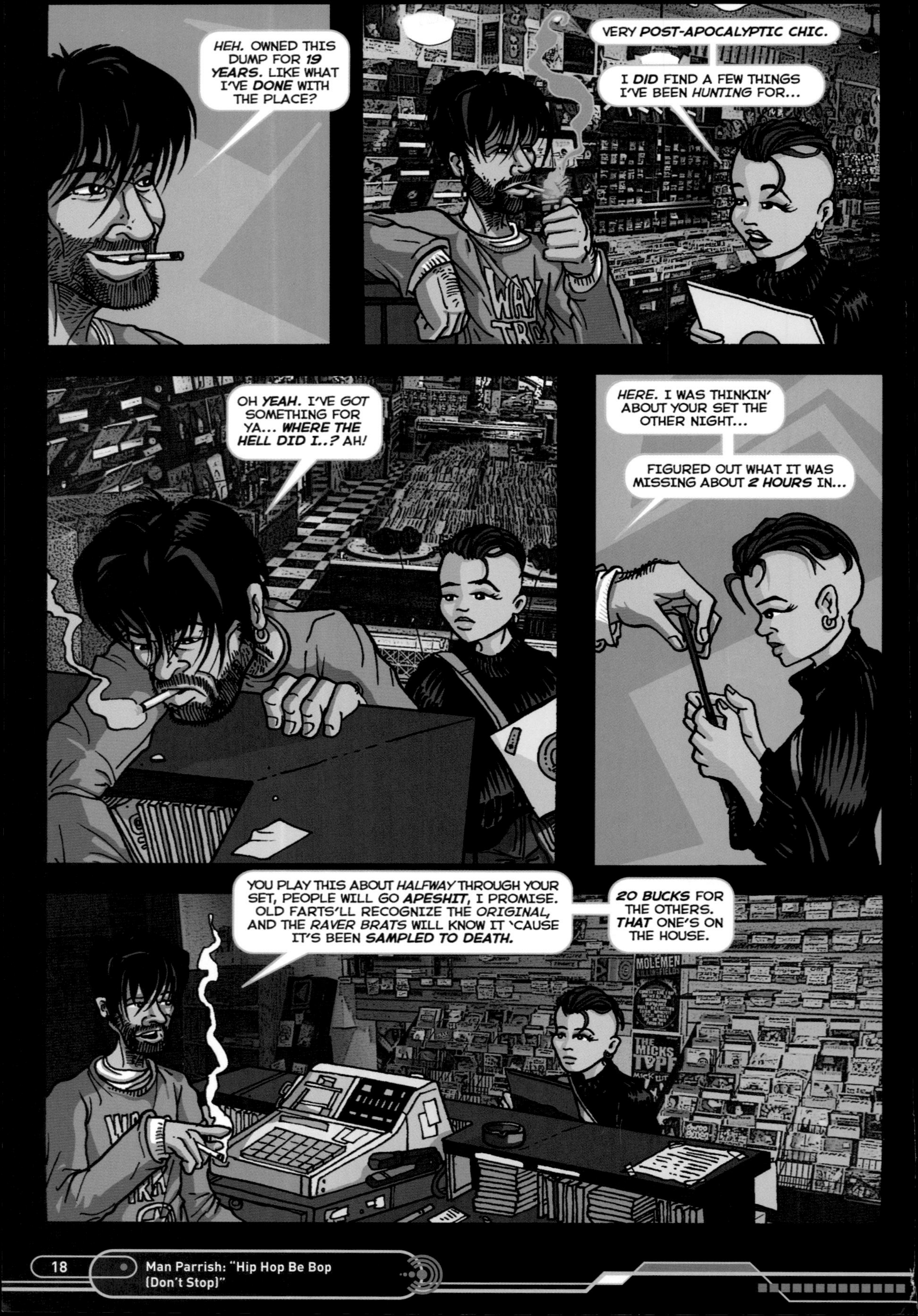
HEH. OWNED THIS DUMP FOR 19 YEARS. LIKE WHAT I'VE DONE WITH THE PLACE?
VERY POST-APOCALYPTIC CHIC.
I DID FIND A FEW THINGS I'VE BEEN HUNTING FOR...
OH YEAH. I'VE GOT SOMETHING FOR YA... WHERE THE HELL DID I..? AH!
HERE. I WAS THINKIN' ABOUT YOUR SET THE OTHER NIGHT...
FIGURED OUT WHAT IT WAS MISSING ABOUT 2 HOURS IN...
YOU PLAY THIS ABOUT HALFWAY THROUGH YOUR SET, PEOPLE WILL GO APESHIT, I PROMISE. OLD FARTS'LL RECOGNIZE THE ORIGINAL, AND THE RAVER BRATS WILL KNOW IT 'CAUSE IT'S BEEN SAMPLED TO DEATH.
20 BUCKS FOR THE OTHERS. THAT ONE'S ON THE HOUSE.

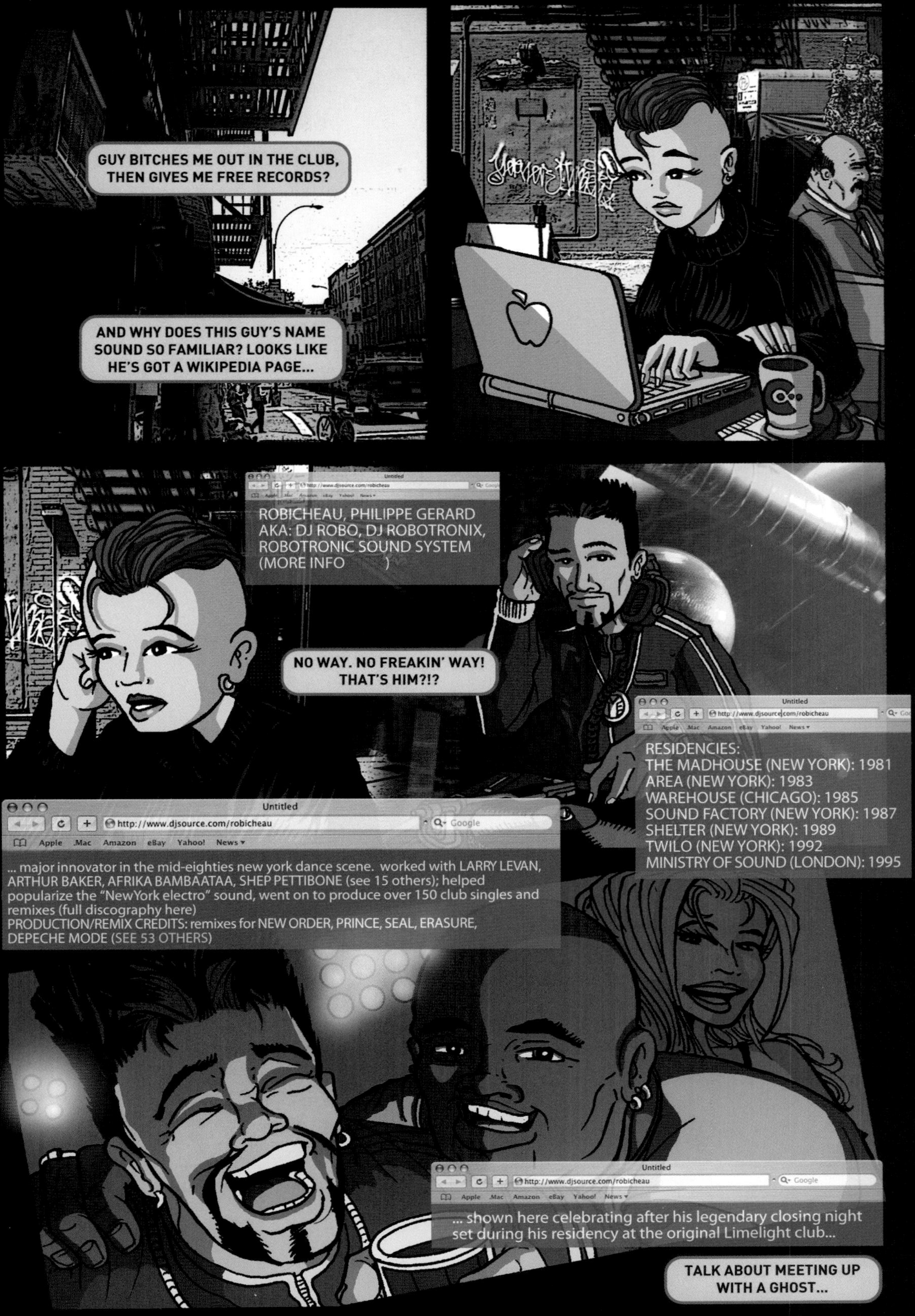
GUY BITCHES ME OUT IN THE CLUB, THEN GIVES ME FREE RECORDS?
AND WHY DOES THIS GUY'S NAME SOUND SO FAMILIAR? LOOKS LIKE HE'S GOT A WIKIPEDIA PAGE...
ROBICHEAU, PHILIPPE GERARD
AKA: DJ ROBO, DJ ROBOTRONIX, ROBOTRONIC SOUND SYSTEM
(MORE INFO)
NO WAY. NO FREAKIN' WAY! THAT'S HIM?!?
Untitled
http://www.djsource.com/robicheau
RESIDENCIES:
THE MADHOUSE (NEW YORK): 1981
AREA (NEW YORK): 1983
WAREHOUSE (CHICAGO): 1985
SOUND FACTORY (NEW YORK): 1987
SHELTER (NEW YORK): 1989
TWILO (NEW YORK): 1992
MINISTRY OF SOUND (LONDON): 1995
Untitled
http://www.djsource.com/robicheau
Google
Apple .Mac Amazon eBay Yahoo! News
... major innovator in the mid-eighties new york dance scene. worked with LARRY LEVAN, ARTHUR BAKER, AFRIKA BAMBAATAA, SHEP PETTIBONE (see 15 others); helped popularize the "NewYork electro" sound, went on to produce over 150 club singles and remixes (full discography here)
PRODUCTION/REMIX CREDITS: remixes for NEW ORDER, PRINCE, SEAL, ERASURE, DEPECHE MODE (SEE 53 OTHERS)
Untitled
http://www.djsource.com/robicheau
... shown here celebrating after his legendary closing night set during his residency at the original Limelight club...
TALK ABOUT MEETING UP WITH A GHOST...

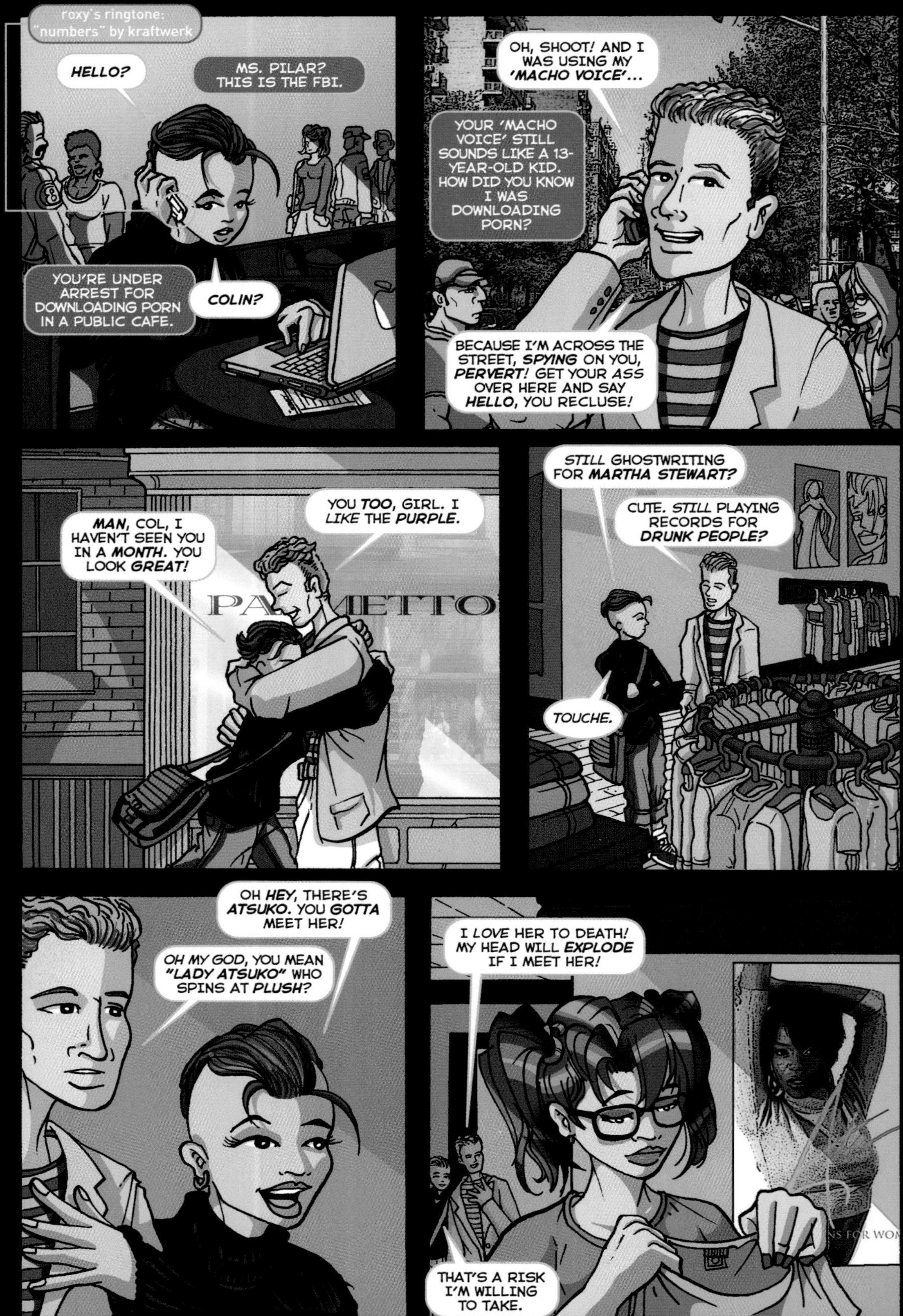
roxy's ringtone: "numbers" by kraftwerk
HELLO?
MS. PILAR? THIS IS THE FBI.
YOU'RE UNDER ARREST FOR DOWNLOADING PORN IN A PUBLIC CAFE.
COLIN?
OH, SHOOT! AND I WAS USING MY 'MACHO VOICE'...
YOUR 'MACHO VOICE' STILL SOUNDS LIKE A 13-YEAR-OLD KID. HOW DID YOU KNOW I WAS DOWNLOADING PORN?
BECAUSE I'M ACROSS THE STREET, SPYING ON YOU, PERVERT! GET YOUR ASS OVER HERE AND SAY HELLO, YOU RECLUSE!
MAN, COL, I HAVEN'T SEEN YOU IN A MONTH. YOU LOOK GREAT!
YOU TOO, GIRL. I LIKE THE PURPLE.
STILL GHOSTWRITING FOR MARTHA STEWART?
CUTE. STILL PLAYING RECORDS FOR DRUNK PEOPLE?
TOUCHE.
OH HEY, THERE'S ATSUKO. YOU GOTTA MEET HER!
OH MY GOD, YOU MEAN "LADY ATSUKO" WHO SPINS AT PLUSH?
I LOVE HER TO DEATH! MY HEAD WILL EXPLODE IF I MEET HER!
THAT'S A RISK I'M WILLING TO TAKE.

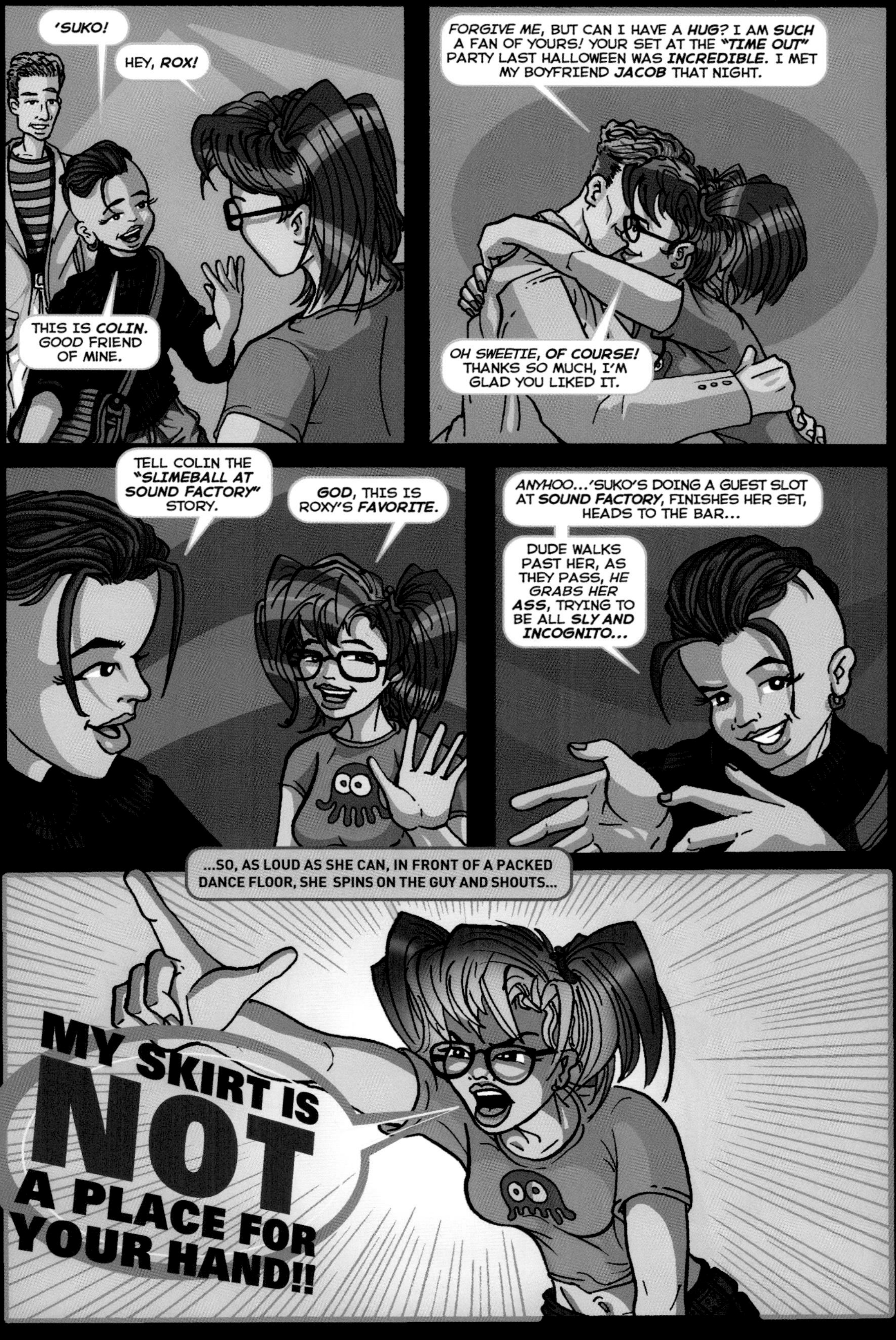
'SUKO!
HEY, ROX!
THIS IS COLIN. GOOD FRIEND OF MINE.
FORGIVE ME, BUT CAN I HAVE A HUG? I AM SUCH A FAN OF YOURS! YOUR SET AT THE "TIME OUT" PARTY LAST HALLOWEEN WAS INCREDIBLE. I MET MY BOYFRIEND JACOB THAT NIGHT.
OH SWEETIE, OF COURSE! THANKS SO MUCH, I'M GLAD YOU LIKED IT.
TELL COLIN THE "SLIMEBALL AT SOUND FACTORY" STORY.
GOD, THIS IS ROXY'S FAVORITE.
ANYHOO...'SUKO'S DOING A GUEST SLOT AT SOUND FACTORY, FINISHES HER SET, HEADS TO THE BAR...
DUDE WALKS PAST HER, AS THEY PASS, HE GRABS HER ASS, TRYING TO BE ALL SLY AND INCOGNITO...
...SO, AS LOUD AS SHE CAN, IN FRONT OF A PACKED DANCE FLOOR, SHE SPINS ON THE GUY AND SHOUTS...
MY SKIRT IS NOT A PLACE FOR YOUR HAND!!

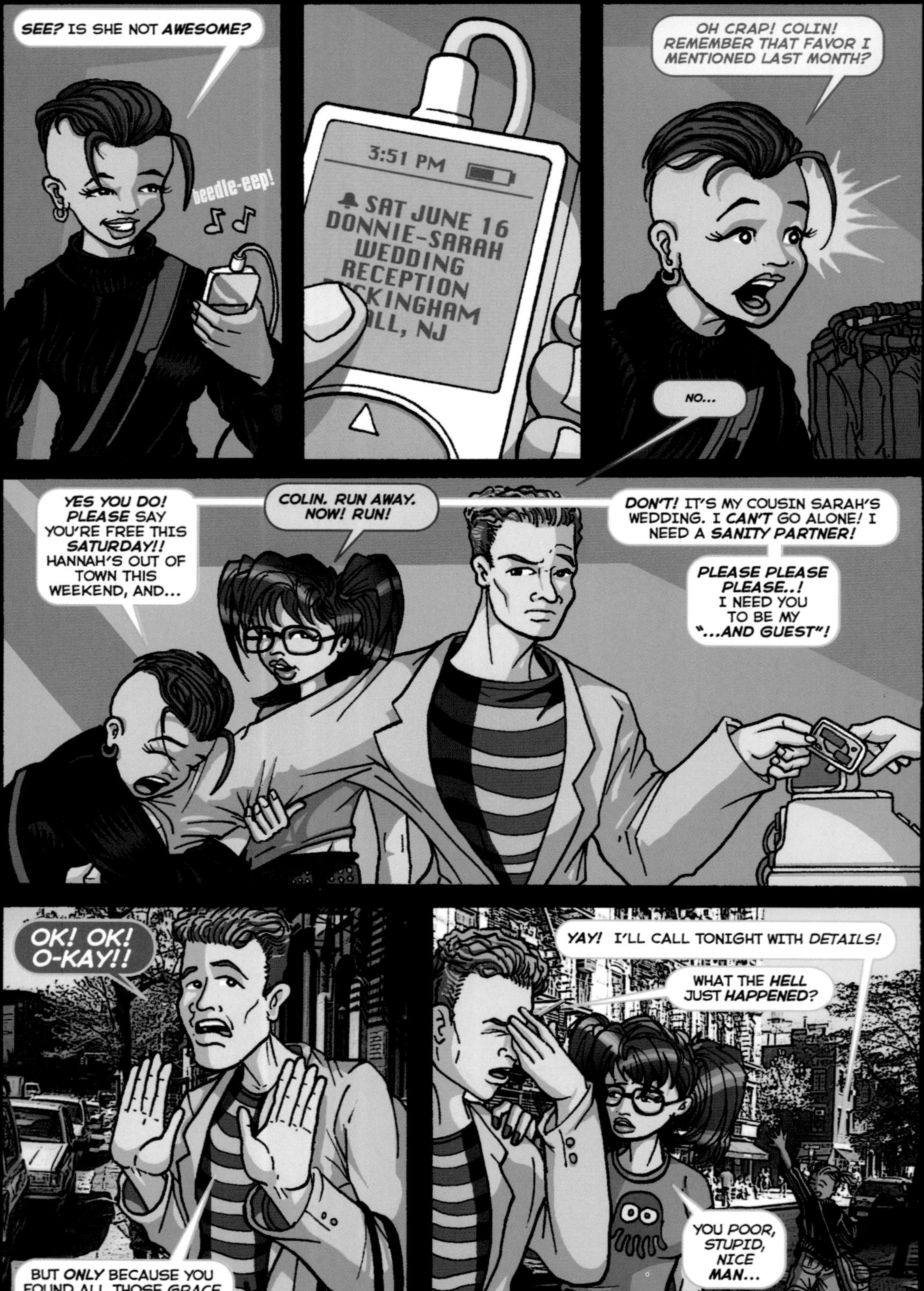
SEE? IS SHE NOT AWESOME?
beedle-eep!
3:51 PM
SAT JUNE 16
DONNIE-SARAH
WEDDING
RECEPTION
OH CRAP! COLIN! REMEMBER THAT FAVOR I MENTIONED LAST MONTH?
NO...
YES YOU DO! PLEASE SAY YOU'RE FREE THIS SATURDAY!! HANNAH'S OUT OF TOWN THIS WEEKEND, AND...
COLIN. RUN AWAY. NOW! RUN!
DON'T! IT'S MY COUSIN SARAH'S WEDDING. I CAN'T GO ALONE! I NEED A SANITY PARTNER!
PLEASE PLEASE PLEASE..! I NEED YOU TO BE MY "...AND GUEST"!
OK! OK! O-KAY!!
BUT ONLY BECAUSE YOU FOUND ALL THOSE GRACE JONES ALBUMS FOR ME.
YAY! I'LL CALL TONIGHT WITH DETAILS!
WHAT THE HELL JUST HAPPENED?
YOU POOR, STUPID, NICE MAN...

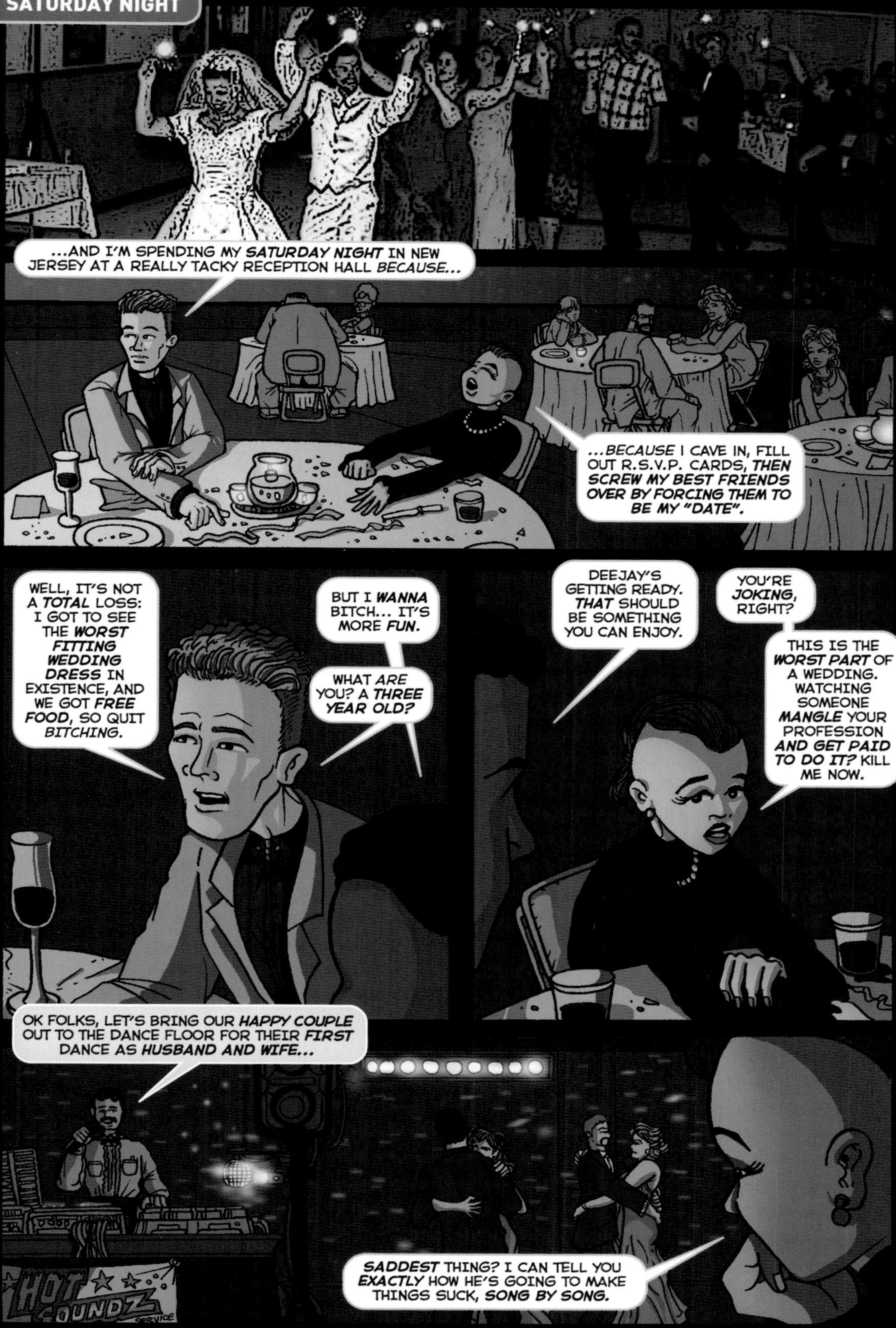
...AND I'M SPENDING MY SATURDAY NIGHT IN NEW JERSEY AT A REALLY TACKY RECEPTION HALL BECAUSE...
...BECAUSE I CAVE IN, FILL OUT R.S.V.P. CARDS, THEN SCREW MY BEST FRIENDS OVER BY FORCING THEM TO BE MY "DATE".
WELL, IT'S NOT A TOTAL LOSS: I GOT TO SEE THE WORST FITTING WEDDING DRESS IN EXISTENCE, AND WE GOT FREE FOOD, SO QUIT BITCHING.
BUT I WANNA BITCH... IT'S MORE FUN.
WHAT ARE YOU? A THREE YEAR OLD?
DEEJAY'S GETTING READY. THAT SHOULD BE SOMETHING YOU CAN ENJOY.
YOU'RE JOKING, RIGHT?
THIS IS THE WORST PART OF A WEDDING. WATCHING SOMEONE MANGLE YOUR PROFESSION AND GET PAID TO DO IT? KILL ME NOW.
OK FOLKS, LET'S BRING OUR HAPPY COUPLE OUT TO THE DANCE FLOOR FOR THEIR FIRST DANCE AS HUSBAND AND WIFE...
HOT SOUNDZ SERVICE
SADDEST THING? I CAN TELL YOU EXACTLY HOW HE'S GOING TO MAKE THINGS SUCK, SONG BY SONG.

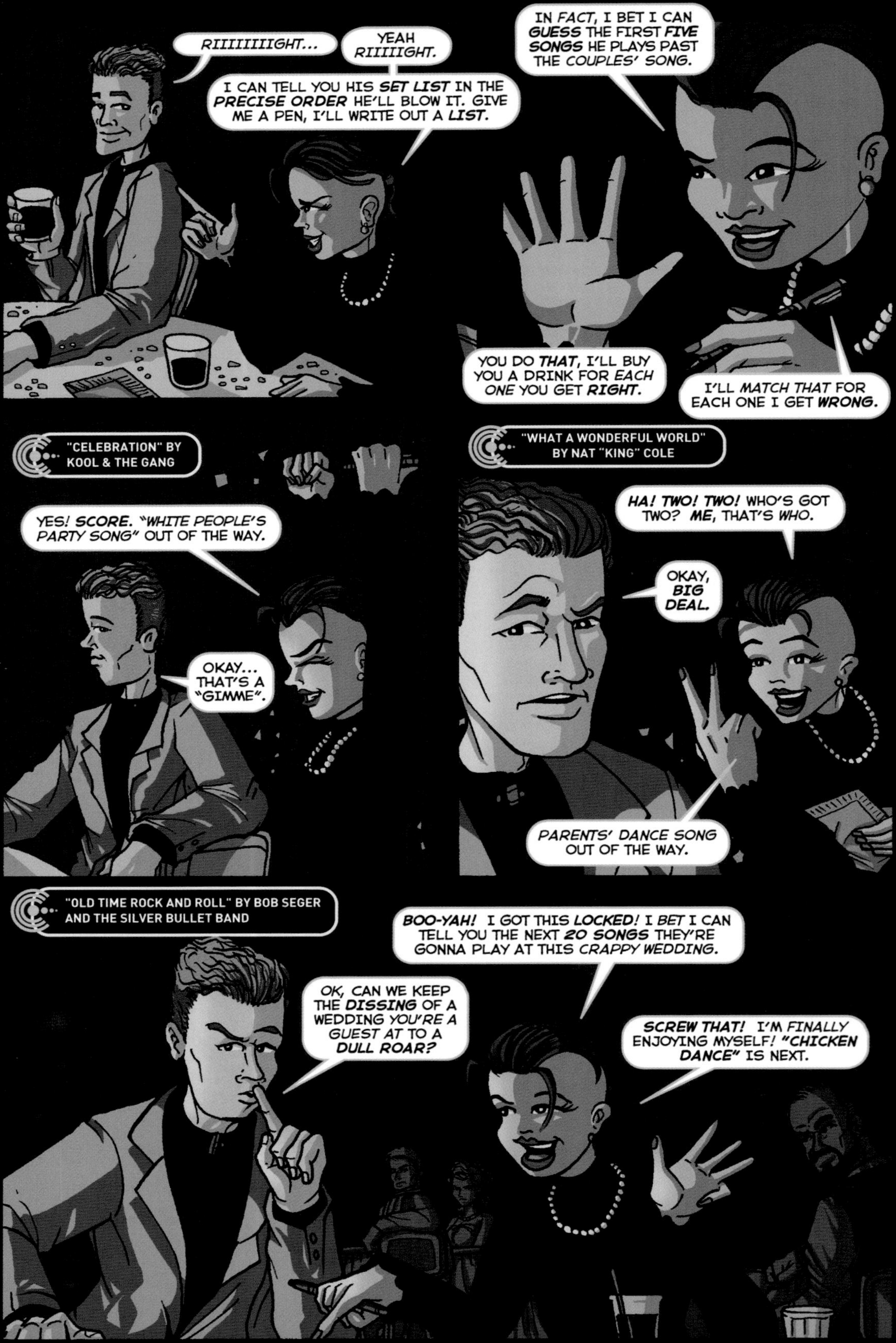
RIIIIIIIGHT...
YEAH RIIIIIGHT.
I CAN TELL YOU HIS SET LIST IN THE PRECISE ORDER HE'LL BLOW IT. GIVE ME A PEN, I'LL WRITE OUT A LIST.
IN FACT, I BET I CAN GUESS THE FIRST FIVE SONGS HE PLAYS PAST THE COUPLES' SONG.
YOU DO THAT, I'LL BUY YOU A DRINK FOR EACH ONE YOU GET RIGHT.
I'LL MATCH THAT FOR EACH ONE I GET WRONG.
"CELEBRATION" BY KOOL & THE GANG
YES! SCORE. "WHITE PEOPLE'S PARTY SONG" OUT OF THE WAY.
OKAY... THAT'S A "GIMME".
"WHAT A WONDERFUL WORLD" BY NAT "KING" COLE
HA! TWO! TWO! WHO'S GOT TWO? ME, THAT'S WHO.
OKAY, BIG DEAL.
PARENTS' DANCE SONG OUT OF THE WAY.
"OLD TIME ROCK AND ROLL" BY BOB SEGER AND THE SILVER BULLET BAND
BOO-YAH! I GOT THIS LOCKED! I BET I CAN TELL YOU THE NEXT 20 SONGS THEY'RE GONNA PLAY AT THIS CRAPPY WEDDING.
OK, CAN WE KEEP THE DISSING OF A WEDDING YOU'RE A GUEST AT TO A DULL ROAR?
SCREW THAT! I'M FINALLY ENJOYING MYSELF! "CHICKEN DANCE" IS NEXT.

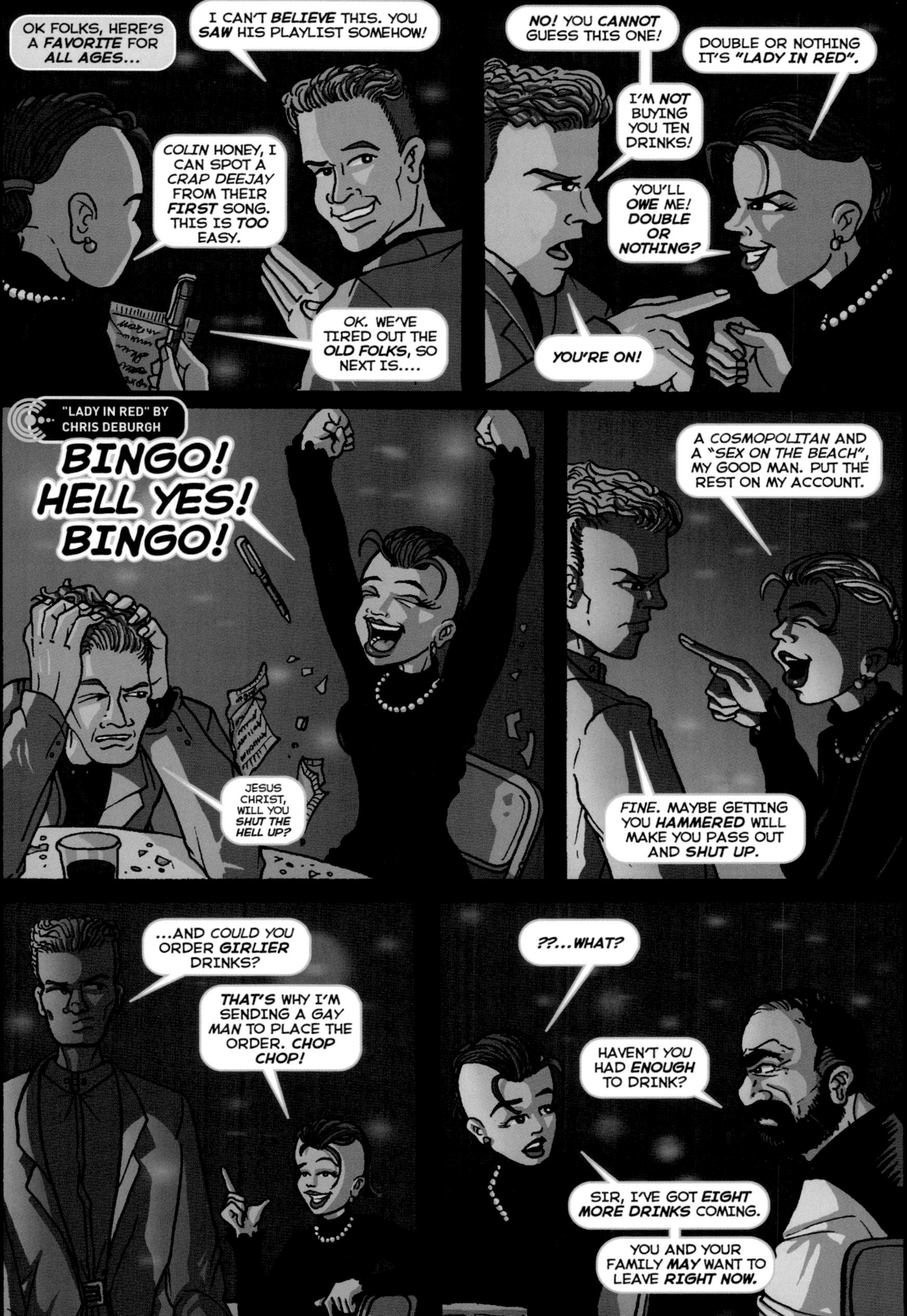
OK FOLKS, HERE'S A FAVORITE FOR ALL AGES...
I CAN'T BELIEVE THIS. YOU SAW HIS PLAYLIST SOMEHOW!
COLIN HONEY, I CAN SPOT A CRAP DEEJAY FROM THEIR FIRST SONG. THIS IS TOO EASY.
OK. WE'VE TIRED OUT THE OLD FOLKS, SO NEXT IS....
NO! YOU CANNOT GUESS THIS ONE!
DOUBLE OR NOTHING IT'S "LADY IN RED".
I'M NOT BUYING YOU TEN DRINKS!
YOU'LL OWE ME! DOUBLE OR NOTHING?
YOU'RE ON!
"LADY IN RED" BY CHRIS DEBURGH
BINGO! HELL YES! BINGO!
JESUS CHRIST, WILL YOU SHUT THE HELL UP?
A COSMOPOLITAN AND A "SEX ON THE BEACH", MY GOOD MAN. PUT THE REST ON MY ACCOUNT.
FINE. MAYBE GETTING YOU HAMMERED WILL MAKE YOU PASS OUT AND SHUT UP.
...AND COULD YOU ORDER GIRLIER DRINKS?
THAT'S WHY I'M SENDING A GAY MAN TO PLACE THE ORDER. CHOP CHOP!
??...WHAT?
HAVEN'T YOU HAD ENOUGH TO DRINK?
SIR, I'VE GOT EIGHT MORE DRINKS COMING.
YOU AND YOUR FAMILY MAY WANT TO LEAVE RIGHT NOW.

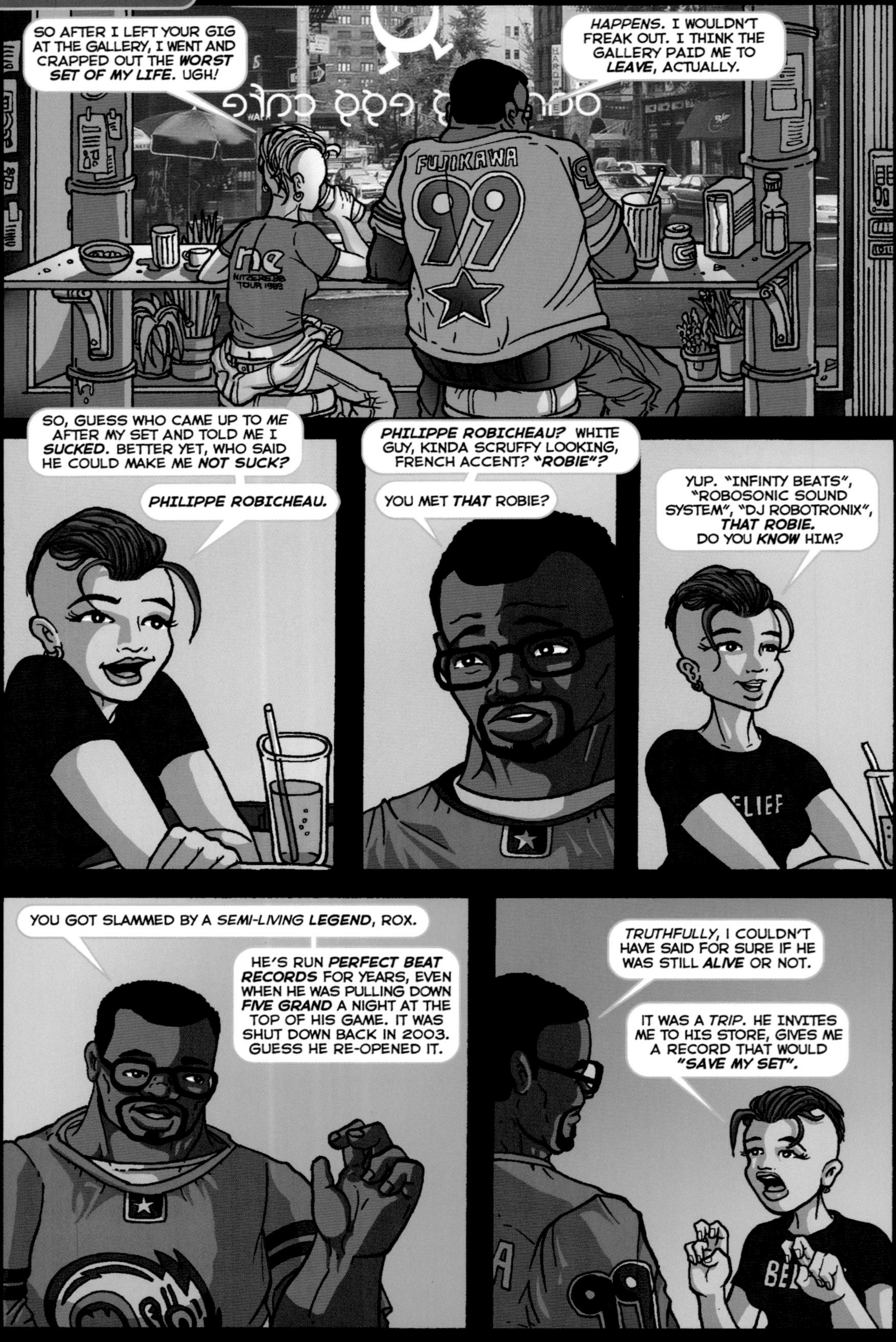
SO AFTER I LEFT YOUR GIG AT THE GALLERY, I WENT AND CRAPPED OUT THE WORST SET OF MY LIFE. UGH!
HAPPENS. I WOULDN'T FREAK OUT. I THINK THE GALLERY PAID ME TO LEAVE, ACTUALLY.
FUJIKAWA
99
SO, GUESS WHO CAME UP TO ME AFTER MY SET AND TOLD ME I SUCKED. BETTER YET, WHO SAID HE COULD MAKE ME NOT SUCK?
PHILIPPE ROBICHEAU.
PHILIPPE ROBICHEAU? WHITE GUY, KINDA SCRUFFY LOOKING, FRENCH ACCENT? "ROBIE"?
YOU MET THAT ROBIE?
YUP. "INFINTY BEATS", "ROBOSONIC SOUND SYSTEM", "DJ ROBOTRONIX", THAT ROBIE. DO YOU KNOW HIM?
YOU GOT SLAMMED BY A SEMI-LIVING LEGEND, ROX.
HE'S RUN PERFECT BEAT RECORDS FOR YEARS, EVEN WHEN HE WAS PULLING DOWN FIVE GRAND A NIGHT AT THE TOP OF HIS GAME. IT WAS SHUT DOWN BACK IN 2003. GUESS HE RE-OPENED IT.
TRUTHFULLY, I COULDN'T HAVE SAID FOR SURE IF HE WAS STILL ALIVE OR NOT.
IT WAS A TRIP. HE INVITES ME TO HIS STORE, GIVES ME A RECORD THAT WOULD "SAVE MY SET".

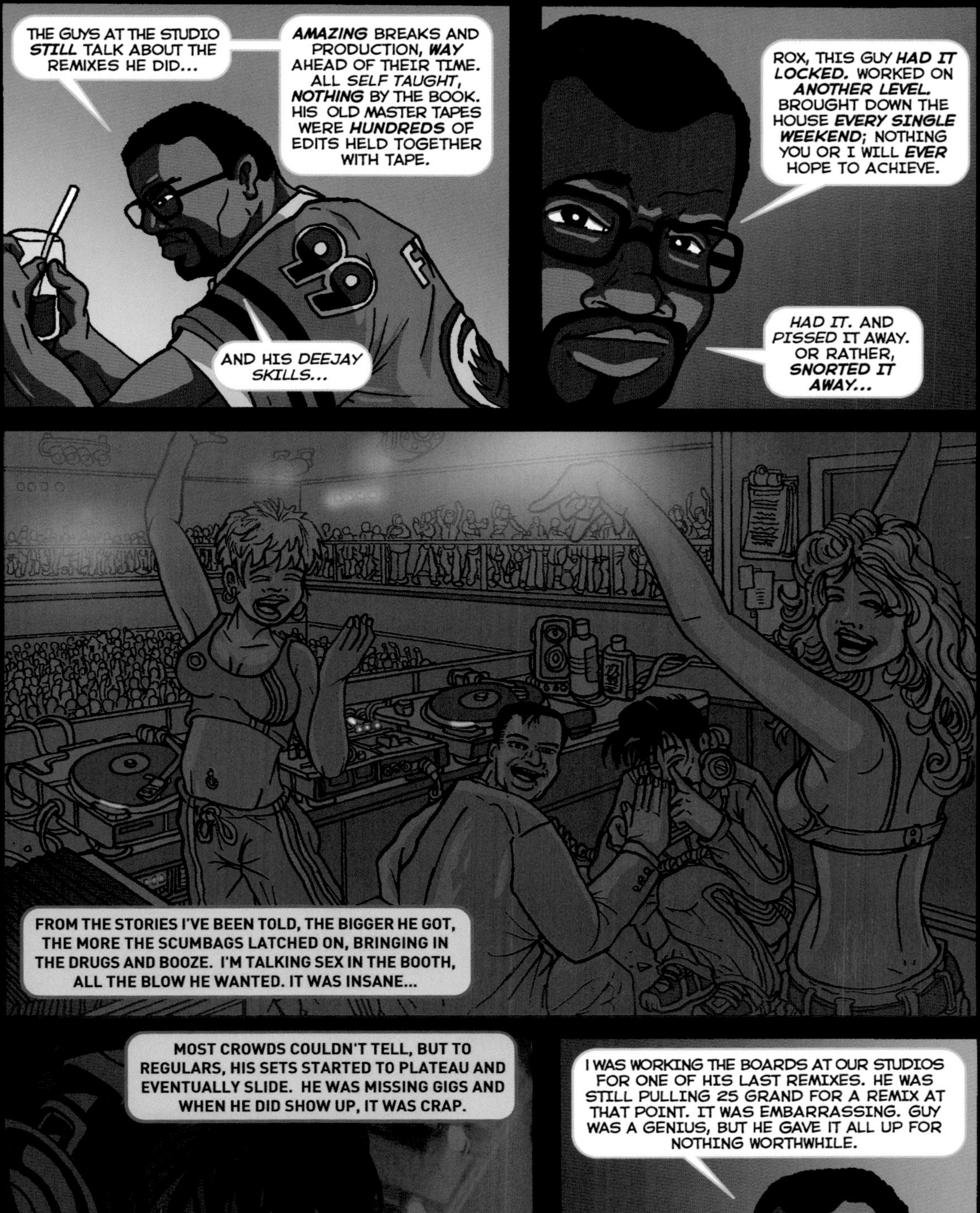
THE GUYS AT THE STUDIO *STILL* TALK ABOUT THE REMIXES HE DID...
AMAZING BREAKS AND PRODUCTION, ***WAY*** AHEAD OF THEIR TIME. ALL *SELF TAUGHT*, ***NOTHING*** BY THE BOOK. HIS OLD MASTER TAPES WERE ***HUNDREDS*** OF EDITS HELD TOGETHER WITH TAPE.
AND HIS *DEEJAY SKILLS...*
ROX, THIS GUY ***HAD IT LOCKED.*** WORKED ON ***ANOTHER LEVEL.*** BROUGHT DOWN THE HOUSE ***EVERY SINGLE WEEKEND;*** NOTHING YOU OR I WILL ***EVER*** HOPE TO ACHIEVE.
HAD IT. AND *PISSED* IT AWAY. OR RATHER, ***SNORTED IT AWAY...***
FROM THE STORIES I'VE BEEN TOLD, THE BIGGER HE GOT, THE MORE THE SCUMBAGS LATCHED ON, BRINGING IN THE DRUGS AND BOOZE. I'M TALKING SEX IN THE BOOTH, ALL THE BLOW HE WANTED. IT WAS INSANE...
MOST CROWDS COULDN'T TELL, BUT TO REGULARS, HIS SETS STARTED TO PLATEAU AND EVENTUALLY SLIDE. HE WAS MISSING GIGS AND WHEN HE DID SHOW UP, IT WAS CRAP.
I WAS WORKING THE BOARDS AT OUR STUDIOS FOR ONE OF HIS LAST REMIXES. HE WAS STILL PULLING 25 GRAND FOR A REMIX AT THAT POINT. IT WAS EMBARRASSING. GUY WAS A GENIUS, BUT HE GAVE IT ALL UP FOR NOTHING WORTHWHILE.
STILL PISSES ME OFF.

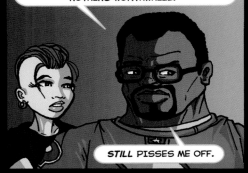

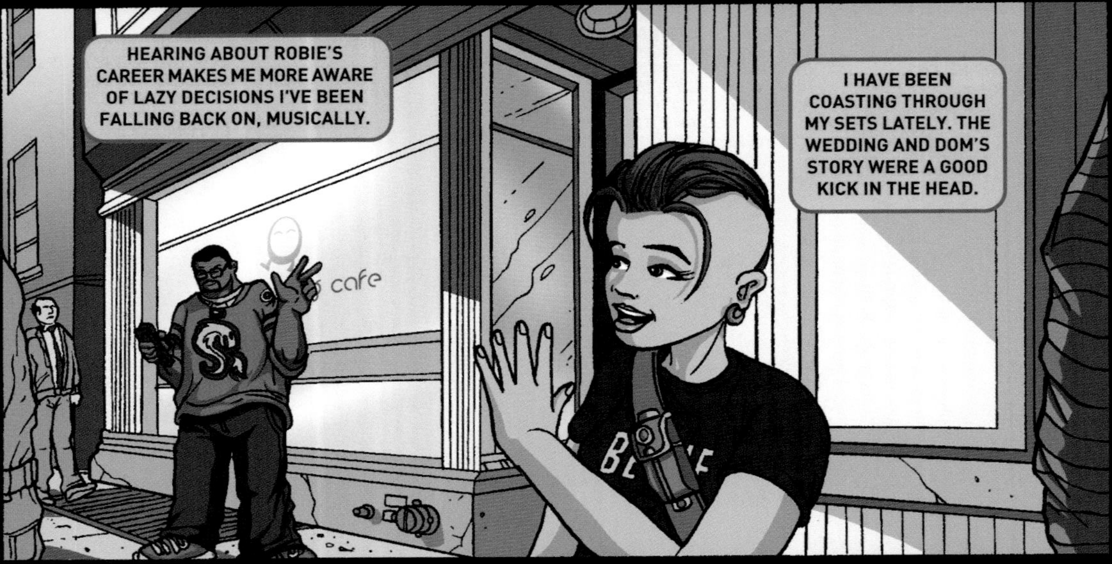
HEARING ABOUT ROBIE'S CAREER MAKES ME MORE AWARE OF LAZY DECISIONS I'VE BEEN FALLING BACK ON, MUSICALLY.
I HAVE BEEN COASTING THROUGH MY SETS LATELY. THE WEDDING AND DOM'S STORY WERE A GOOD KICK IN THE HEAD.
cafe

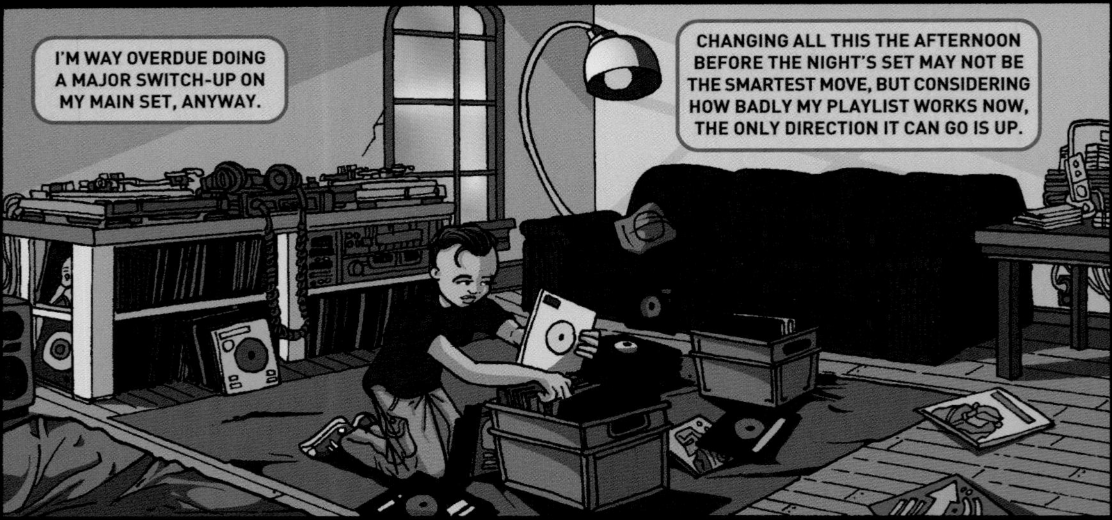
I'M WAY OVERDUE DOING A MAJOR SWITCH-UP ON MY MAIN SET, ANYWAY.
CHANGING ALL THIS THE AFTERNOON BEFORE THE NIGHT'S SET MAY NOT BE THE SMARTEST MOVE, BUT CONSIDERING HOW BADLY MY PLAYLIST WORKS NOW, THE ONLY DIRECTION IT CAN GO IS UP.

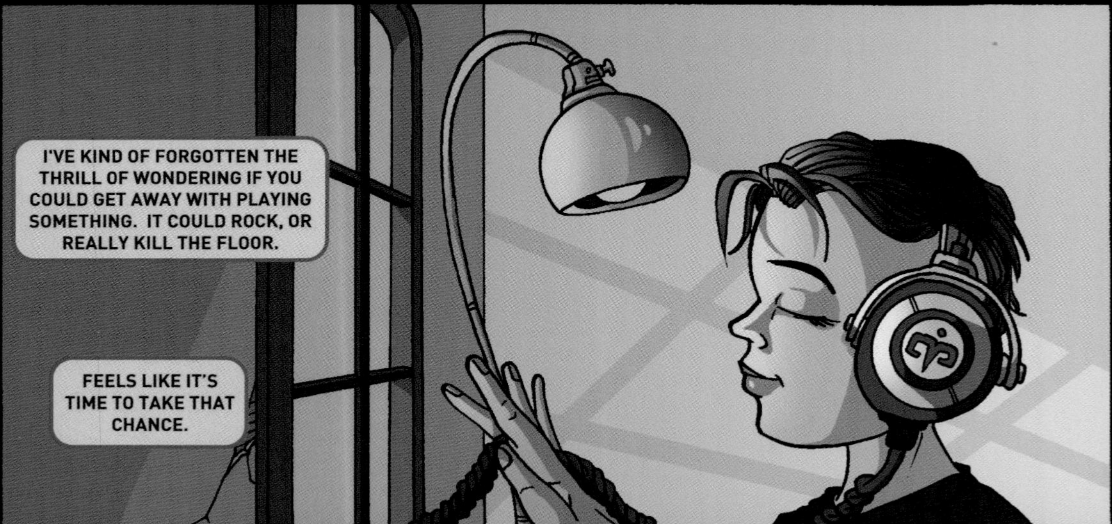
I'VE KIND OF FORGOTTEN THE THRILL OF WONDERING IF YOU COULD GET AWAY WITH PLAYING SOMETHING. IT COULD ROCK, OR REALLY KILL THE FLOOR.
FEELS LIKE IT'S TIME TO TAKE THAT CHANCE.

TRACK TWO

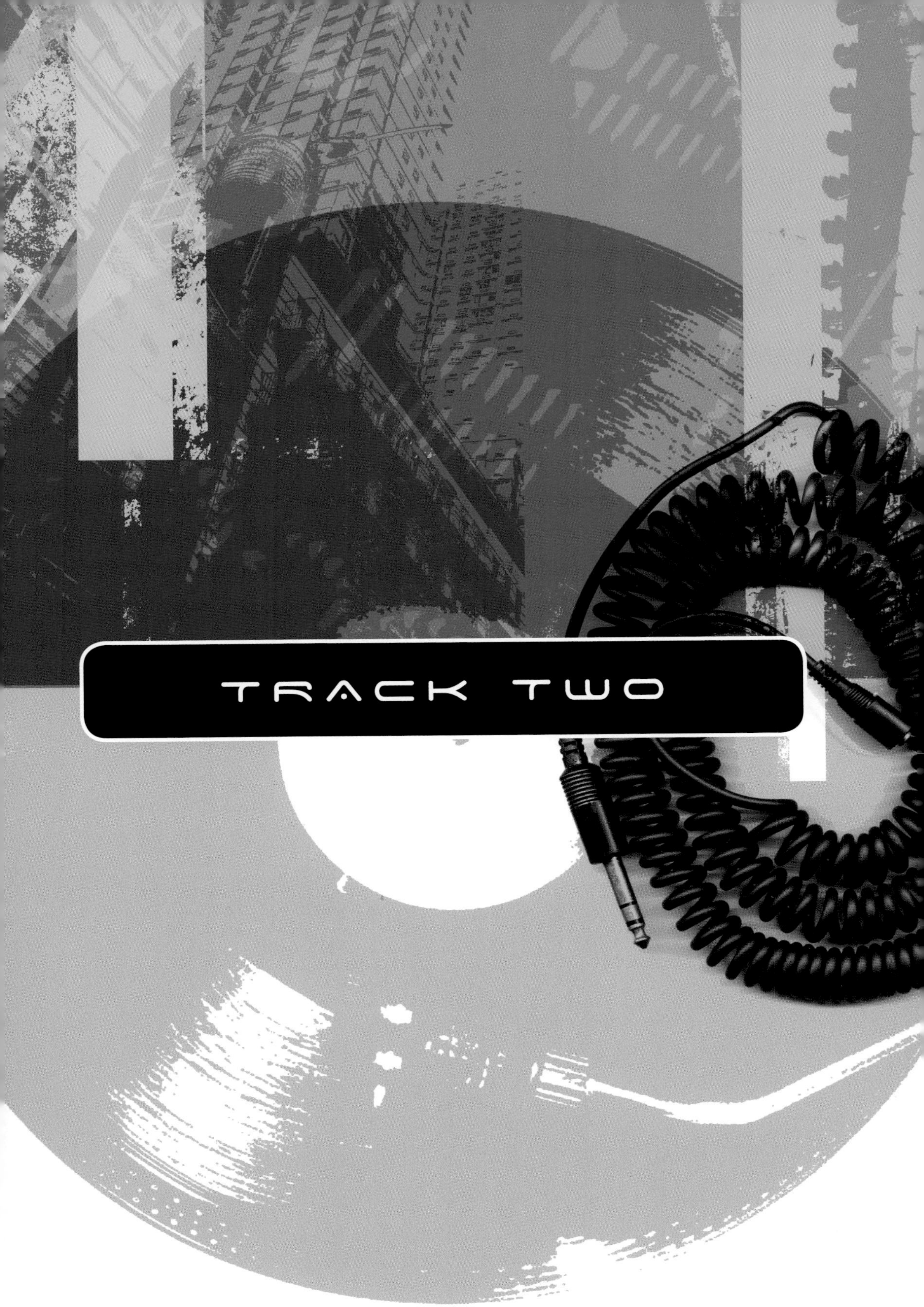

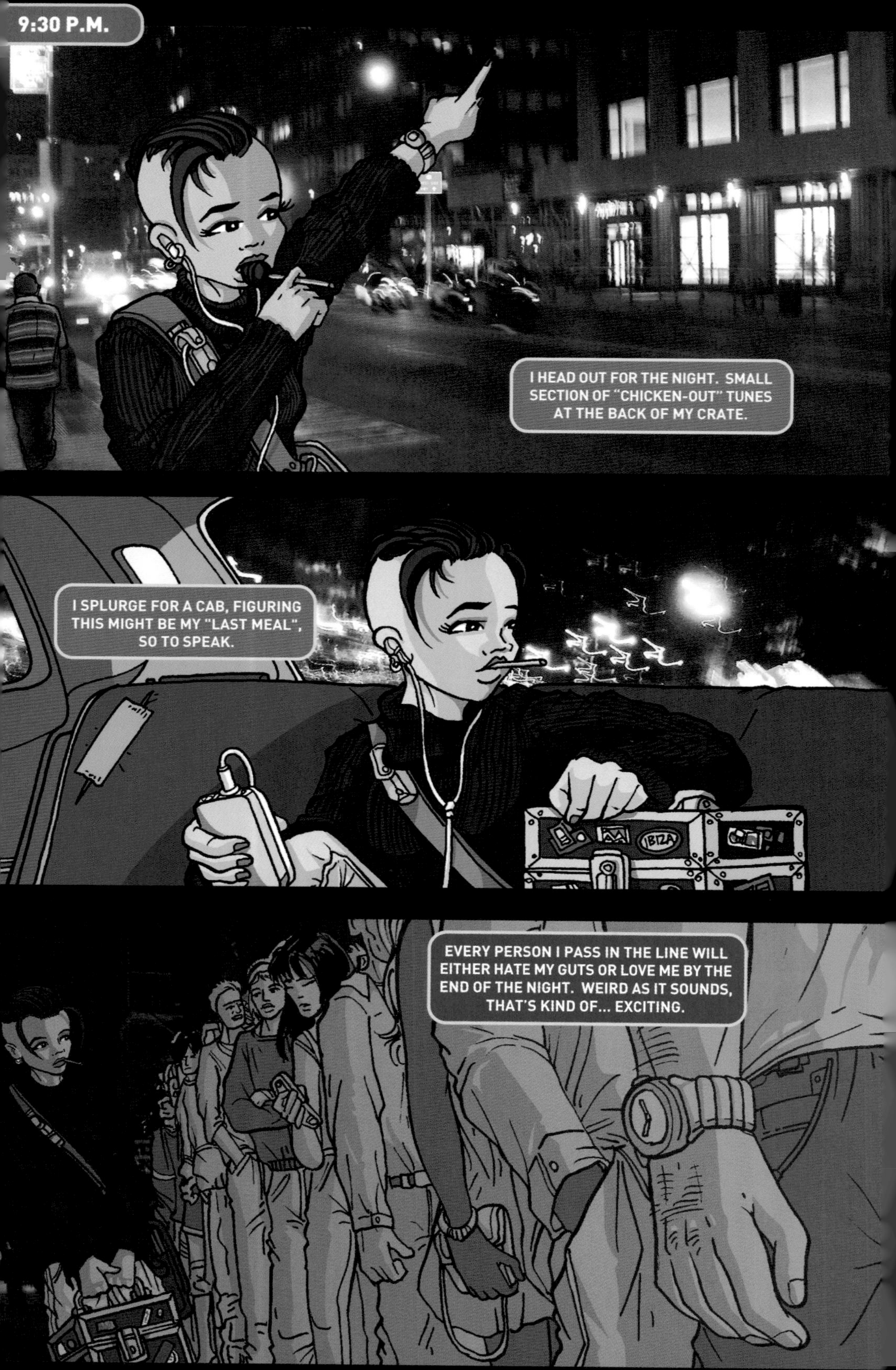
9:30 P.M.
I HEAD OUT FOR THE NIGHT. SMALL SECTION OF "CHICKEN-OUT" TUNES AT THE BACK OF MY CRATE.
I SPLURGE FOR A CAB, FIGURING THIS MIGHT BE MY "LAST MEAL", SO TO SPEAK.
IBIZA
EVERY PERSON I PASS IN THE LINE WILL EITHER HATE MY GUTS OR LOVE ME BY THE END OF THE NIGHT. WEIRD AS IT SOUNDS, THAT'S KIND OF... EXCITING.

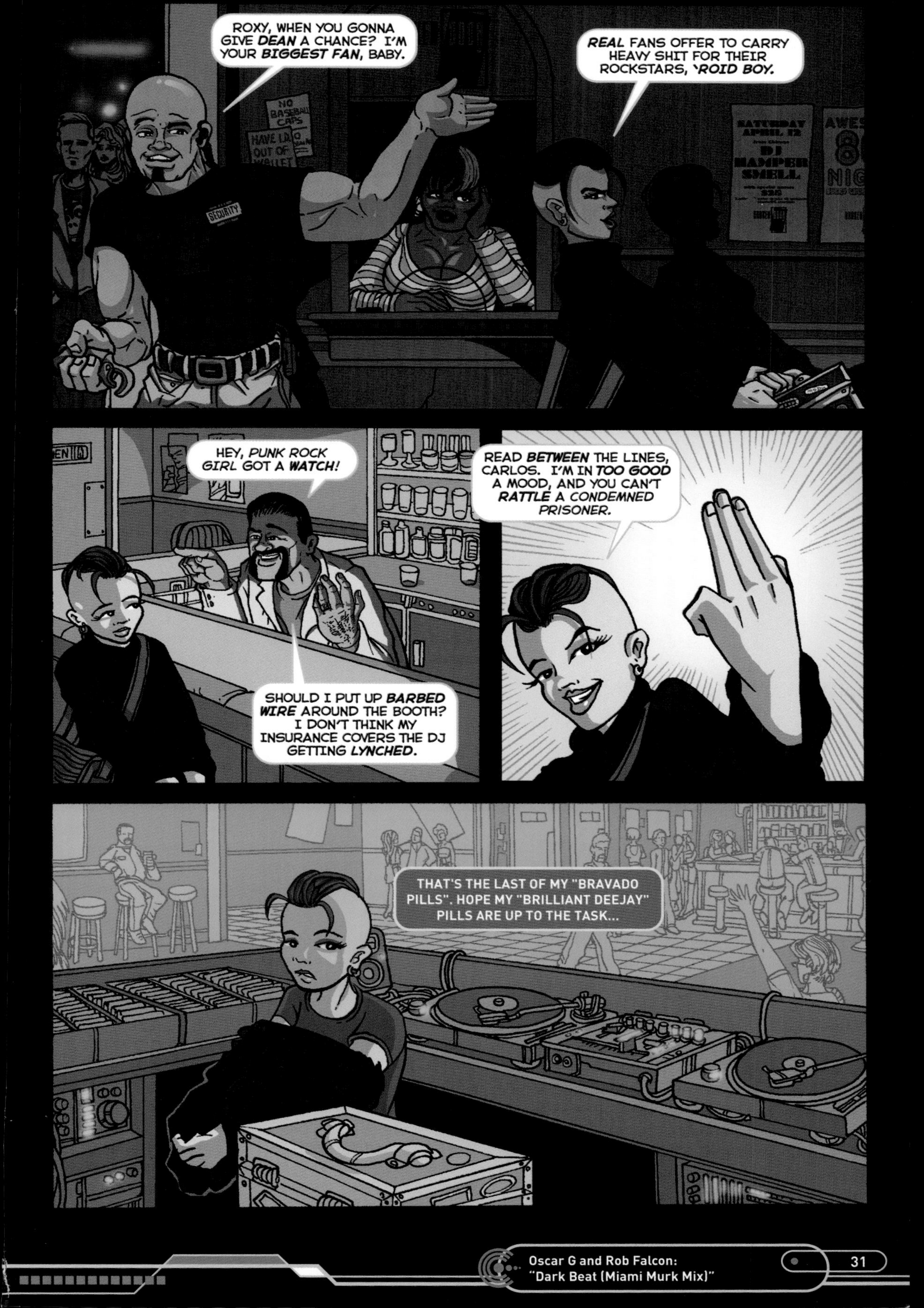

ROXY, WHEN YOU GONNA GIVE DEAN A CHANCE? I'M YOUR BIGGEST FAN, BABY.
NO BASEBALL CAPS
SECURITY
REAL FANS OFFER TO CARRY HEAVY SHIT FOR THEIR ROCKSTARS, 'ROID BOY.
SATURDAY APRIL 12
DJ HAMPER SMELL
HEY, PUNK ROCK GIRL GOT A WATCH!
SHOULD I PUT UP BARBED WIRE AROUND THE BOOTH? I DON'T THINK MY INSURANCE COVERS THE DJ GETTING LYNCHED.
READ BETWEEN THE LINES, CARLOS. I'M IN TOO GOOD A MOOD, AND YOU CAN'T RATTLE A CONDEMNED PRISONER.
THAT'S THE LAST OF MY "BRAVADO PILLS". HOPE MY "BRILLIANT DEEJAY" PILLS ARE UP TO THE TASK...

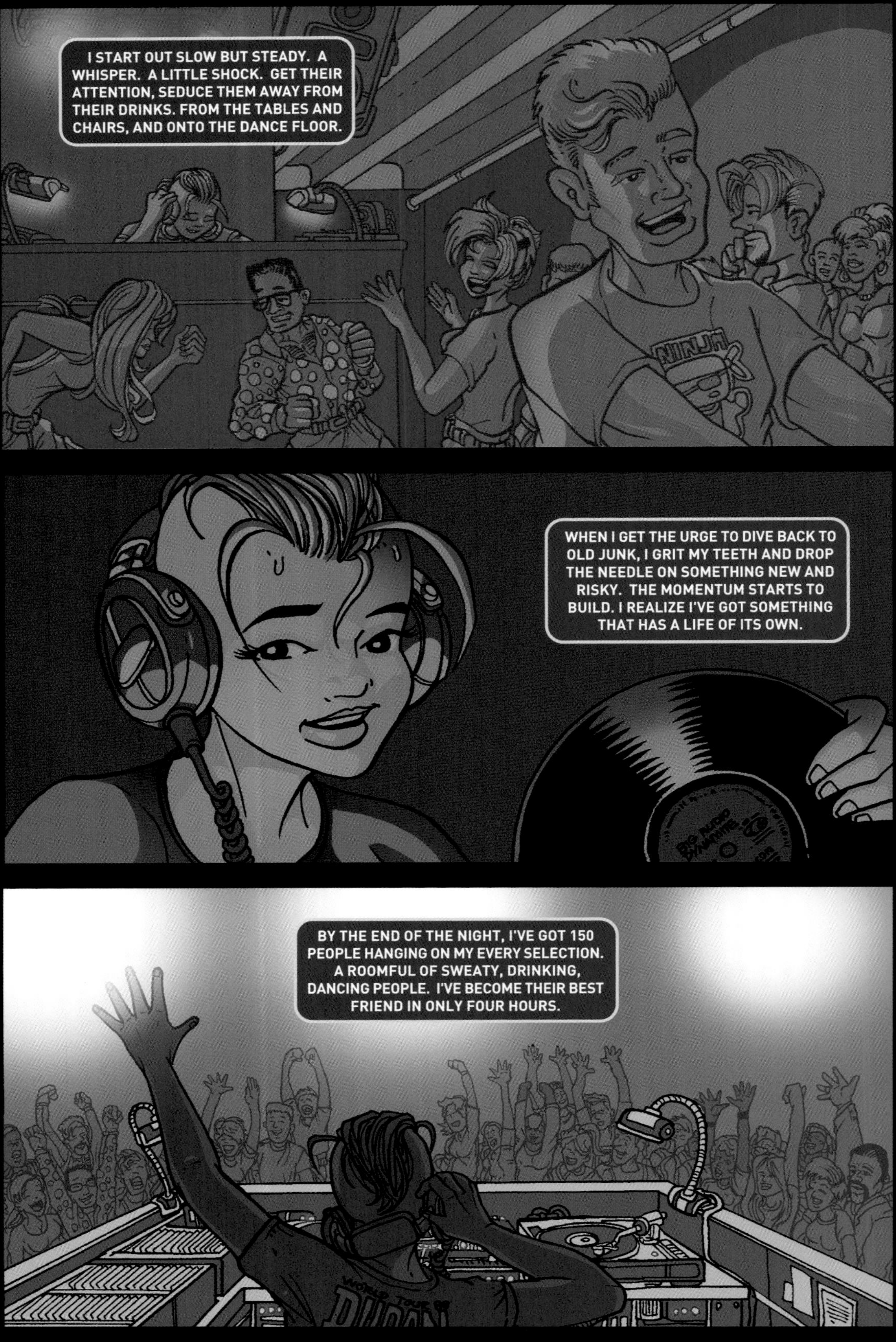
I START OUT SLOW BUT STEADY. A WHISPER. A LITTLE SHOCK. GET THEIR ATTENTION, SEDUCE THEM AWAY FROM THEIR DRINKS. FROM THE TABLES AND CHAIRS, AND ONTO THE DANCE FLOOR.
NINJA
WHEN I GET THE URGE TO DIVE BACK TO OLD JUNK, I GRIT MY TEETH AND DROP THE NEEDLE ON SOMETHING NEW AND RISKY. THE MOMENTUM STARTS TO BUILD. I REALIZE I'VE GOT SOMETHING THAT HAS A LIFE OF ITS OWN.
BY THE END OF THE NIGHT, I'VE GOT 150 PEOPLE HANGING ON MY EVERY SELECTION. A ROOMFUL OF SWEATY, DRINKING, DANCING PEOPLE. I'VE BECOME THEIR BEST FRIEND IN ONLY FOUR HOURS.

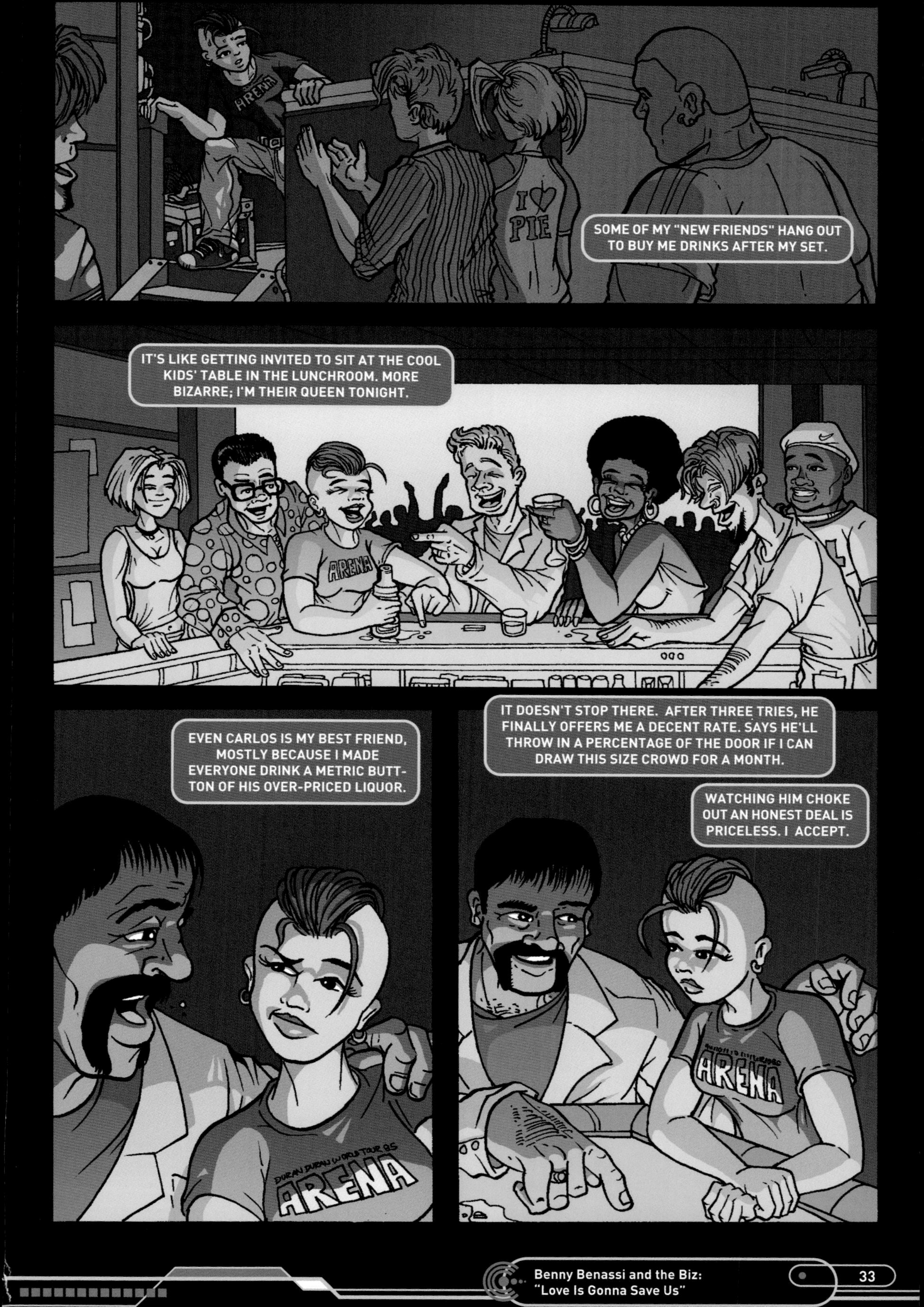
SOME OF MY "NEW FRIENDS" HANG OUT TO BUY ME DRINKS AFTER MY SET.
IT'S LIKE GETTING INVITED TO SIT AT THE COOL KIDS' TABLE IN THE LUNCHROOM. MORE BIZARRE; I'M THEIR QUEEN TONIGHT.
EVEN CARLOS IS MY BEST FRIEND, MOSTLY BECAUSE I MADE EVERYONE DRINK A METRIC BUTT-TON OF HIS OVER-PRICED LIQUOR.
IT DOESN'T STOP THERE. AFTER THREE TRIES, HE FINALLY OFFERS ME A DECENT RATE. SAYS HE'LL THROW IN A PERCENTAGE OF THE DOOR IF I CAN DRAW THIS SIZE CROWD FOR A MONTH.
WATCHING HIM CHOKE OUT AN HONEST DEAL IS PRICELESS. I ACCEPT.

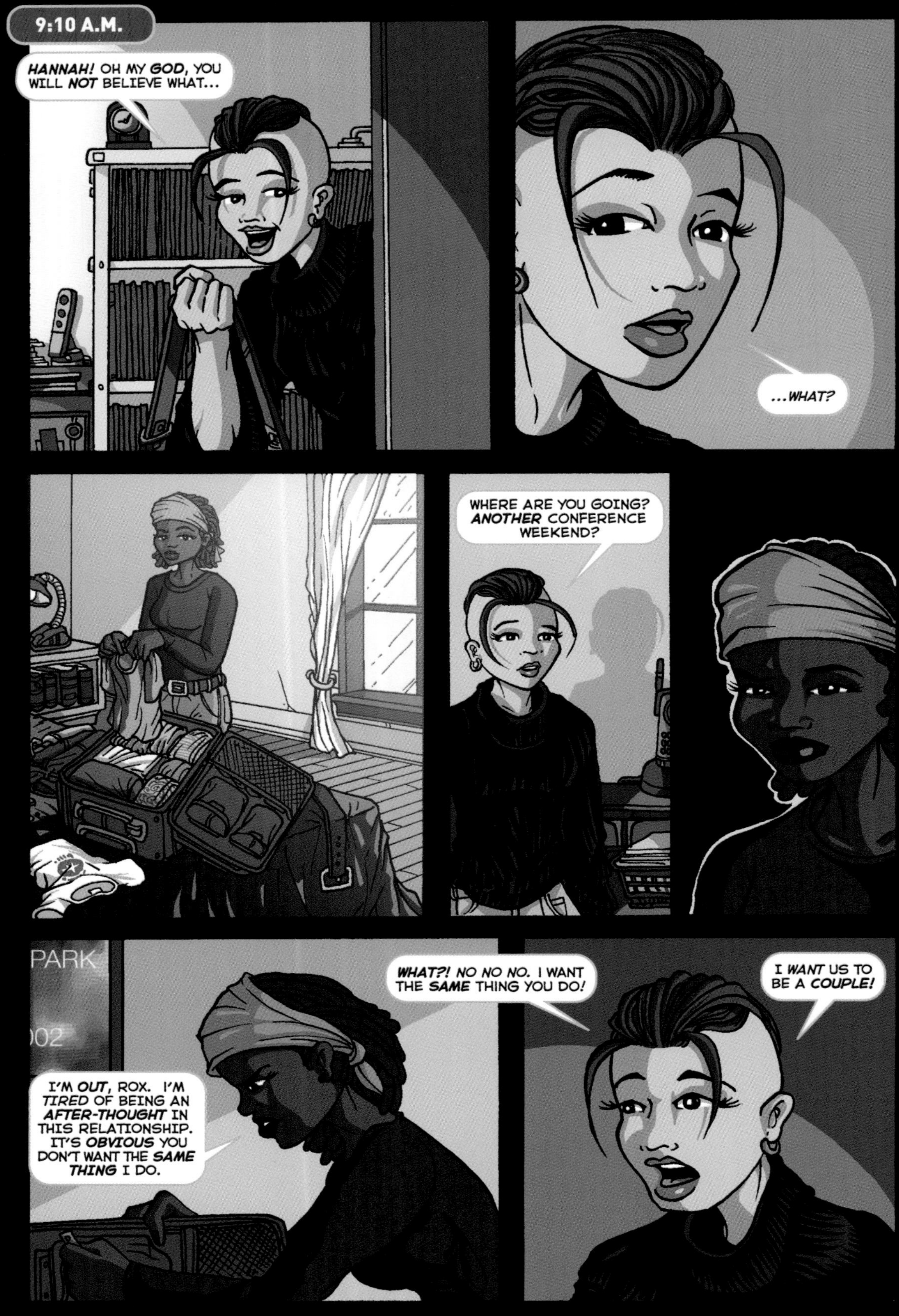
9:10 A.M.
HANNAH! OH MY GOD, YOU WILL NOT BELIEVE WHAT...
...WHAT?
WHERE ARE YOU GOING? ANOTHER CONFERENCE WEEKEND?
PARK
I'M OUT, ROX. I'M TIRED OF BEING AN AFTER-THOUGHT IN THIS RELATIONSHIP. IT'S OBVIOUS YOU DON'T WANT THE SAME THING I DO.
WHAT?! NO NO NO. I WANT THE SAME THING YOU DO!
I WANT US TO BE A COUPLE!

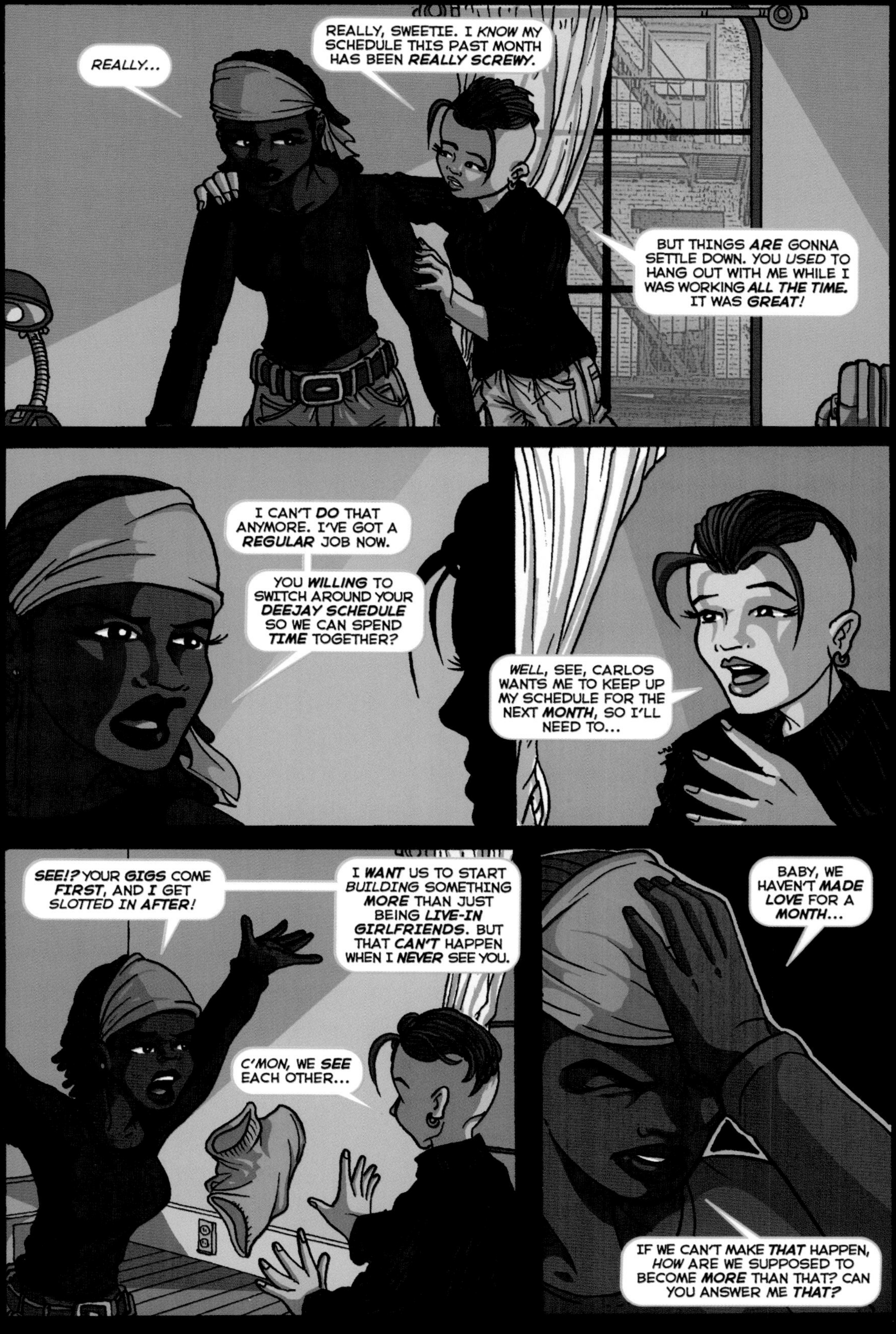
REALLY...
REALLY, SWEETIE. I KNOW MY SCHEDULE THIS PAST MONTH HAS BEEN REALLY SCREWY.
BUT THINGS ARE GONNA SETTLE DOWN. YOU USED TO HANG OUT WITH ME WHILE I WAS WORKING ALL THE TIME. IT WAS GREAT!
I CAN'T DO THAT ANYMORE. I'VE GOT A REGULAR JOB NOW.
YOU WILLING TO SWITCH AROUND YOUR DEEJAY SCHEDULE SO WE CAN SPEND TIME TOGETHER?
WELL, SEE, CARLOS WANTS ME TO KEEP UP MY SCHEDULE FOR THE NEXT MONTH, SO I'LL NEED TO...
SEE!? YOUR GIGS COME FIRST, AND I GET SLOTTED IN AFTER!
I WANT US TO START BUILDING SOMETHING MORE THAN JUST BEING LIVE-IN GIRLFRIENDS. BUT THAT CAN'T HAPPEN WHEN I NEVER SEE YOU.
C'MON, WE SEE EACH OTHER...
BABY, WE HAVEN'T MADE LOVE FOR A MONTH...
IF WE CAN'T MAKE THAT HAPPEN, HOW ARE WE SUPPOSED TO BECOME MORE THAN THAT? CAN YOU ANSWER ME THAT?

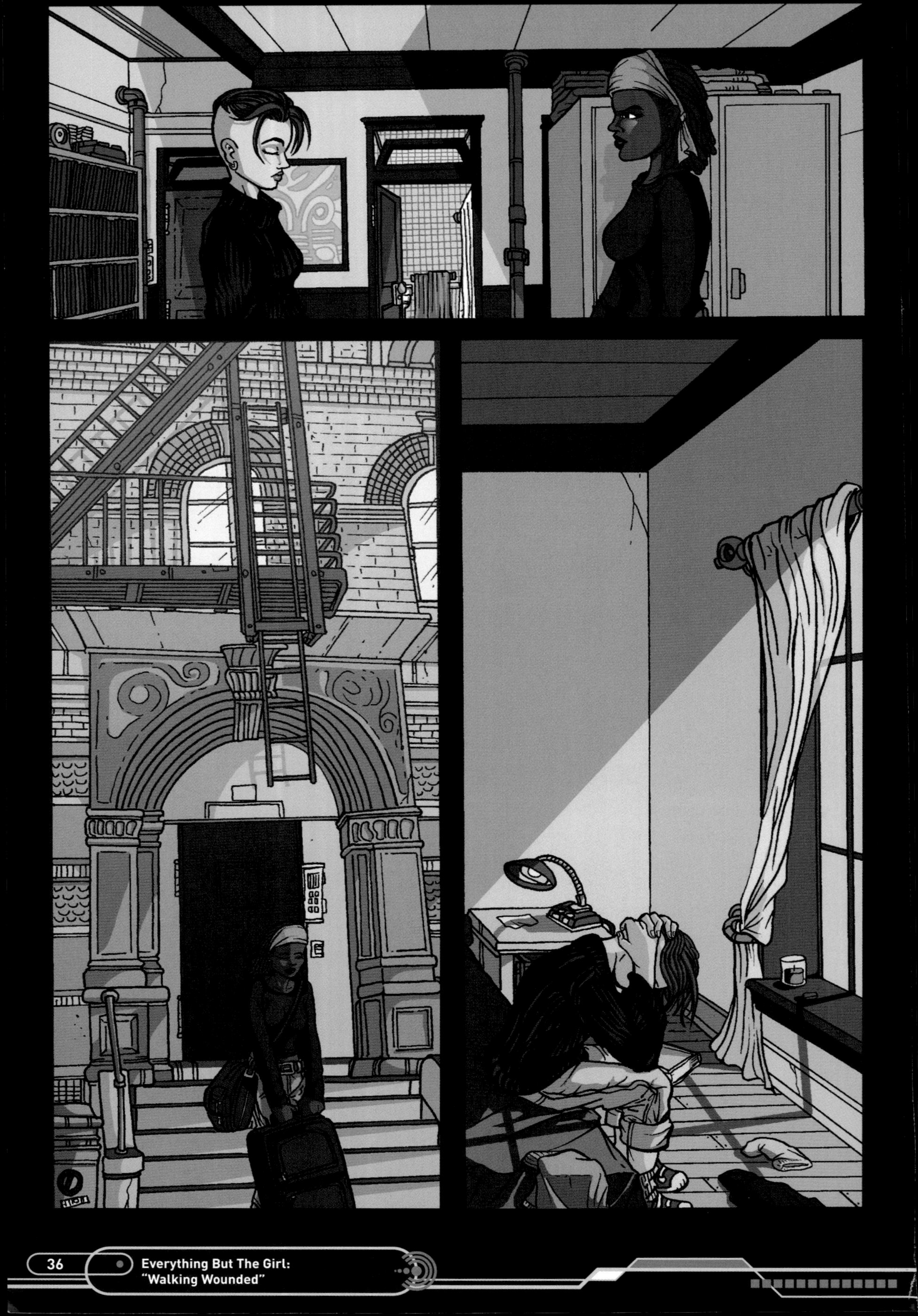

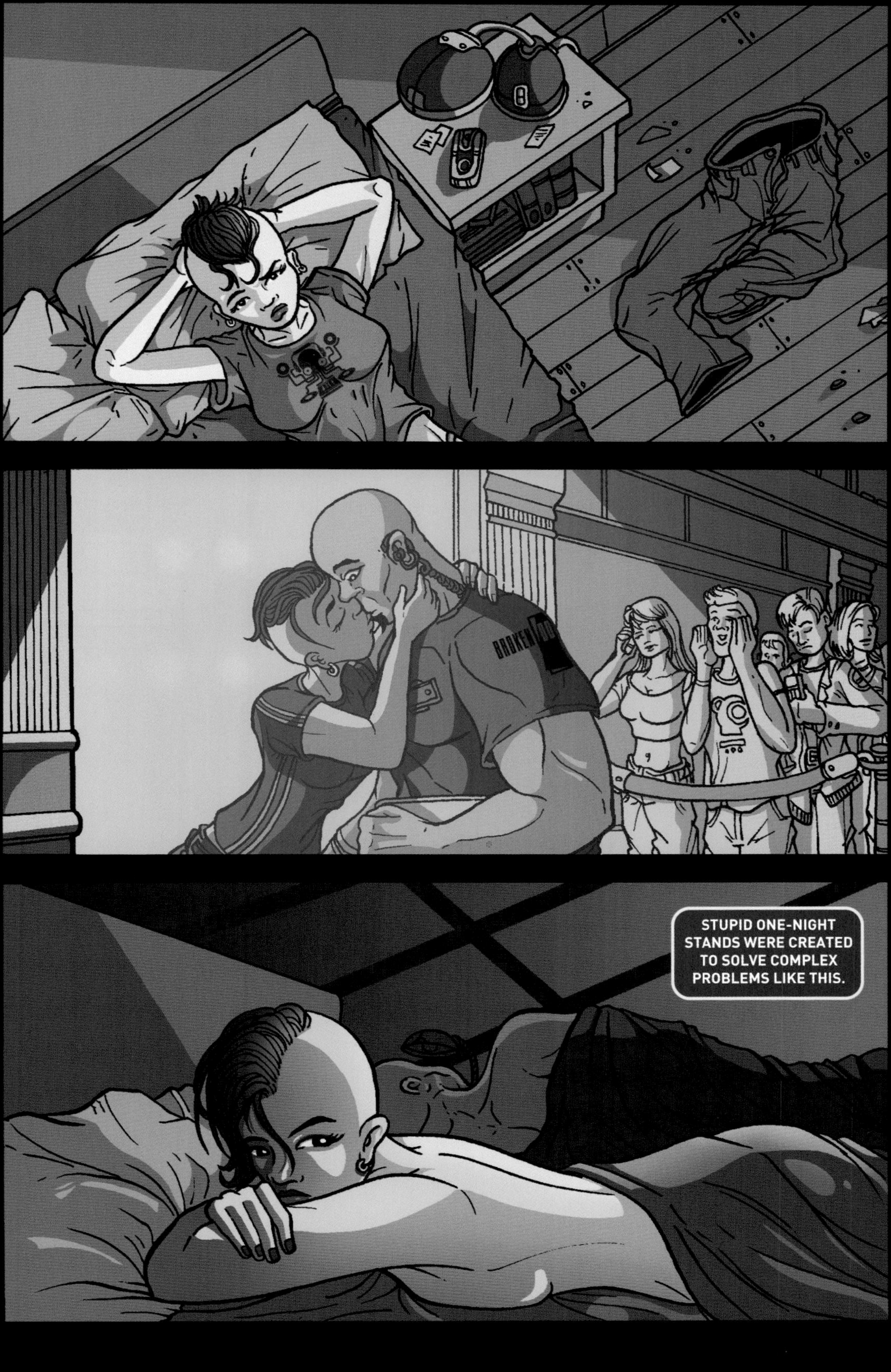
BROKEN
STUPID ONE-NIGHT STANDS WERE CREATED TO SOLVE COMPLEX PROBLEMS LIKE THIS.

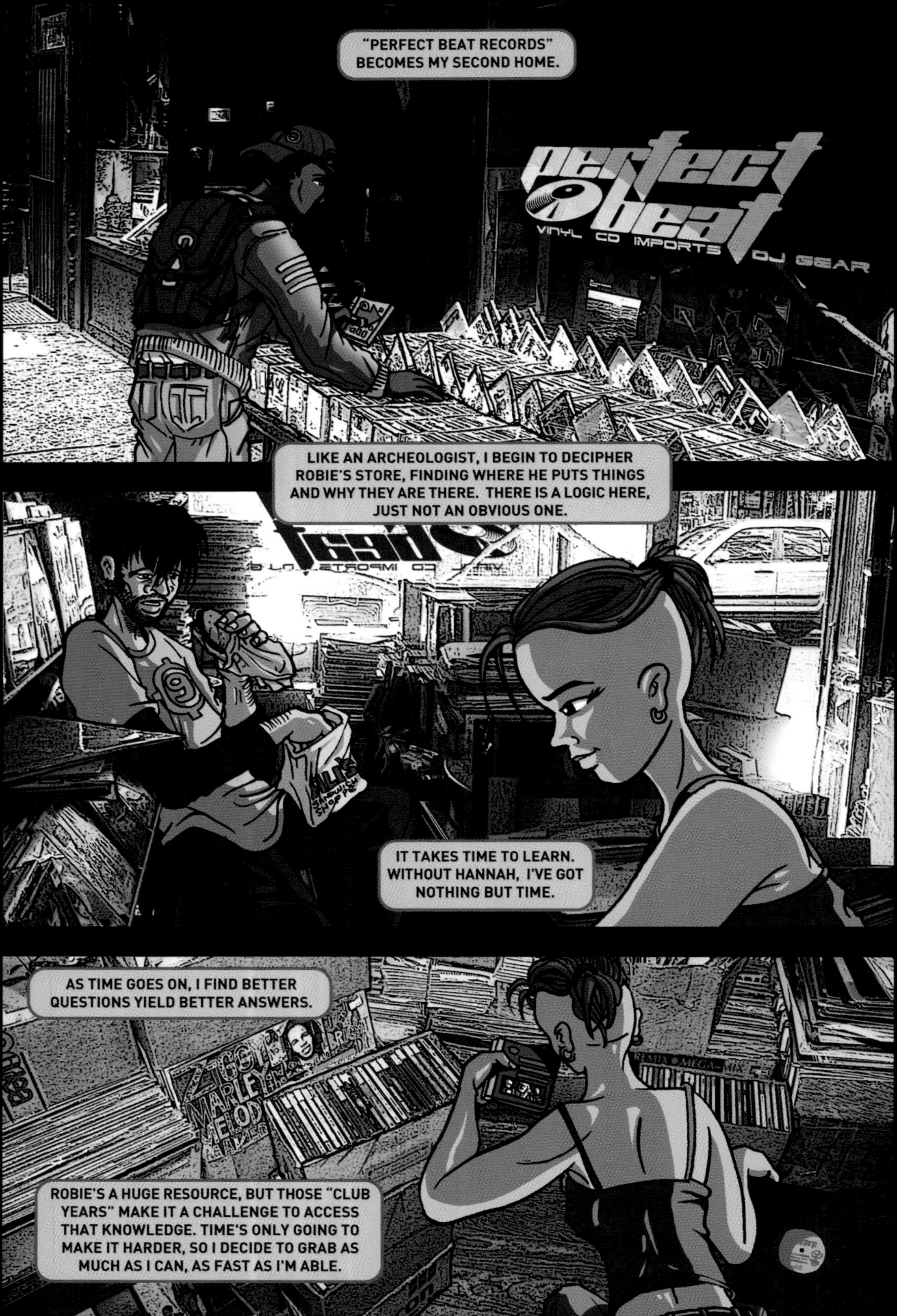
"PERFECT BEAT RECORDS" BECOMES MY SECOND HOME.
perfect beat
VINYL CD IMPORTS DJ GEAR
LIKE AN ARCHEOLOGIST, I BEGIN TO DECIPHER ROBIE'S STORE, FINDING WHERE HE PUTS THINGS AND WHY THEY ARE THERE. THERE IS A LOGIC HERE, JUST NOT AN OBVIOUS ONE.
IT TAKES TIME TO LEARN. WITHOUT HANNAH, I'VE GOT NOTHING BUT TIME.
AS TIME GOES ON, I FIND BETTER QUESTIONS YIELD BETTER ANSWERS.
ROBIE'S A HUGE RESOURCE, BUT THOSE "CLUB YEARS" MAKE IT A CHALLENGE TO ACCESS THAT KNOWLEDGE. TIME'S ONLY GOING TO MAKE IT HARDER, SO I DECIDE TO GRAB AS MUCH AS I CAN, AS FAST AS I'M ABLE.

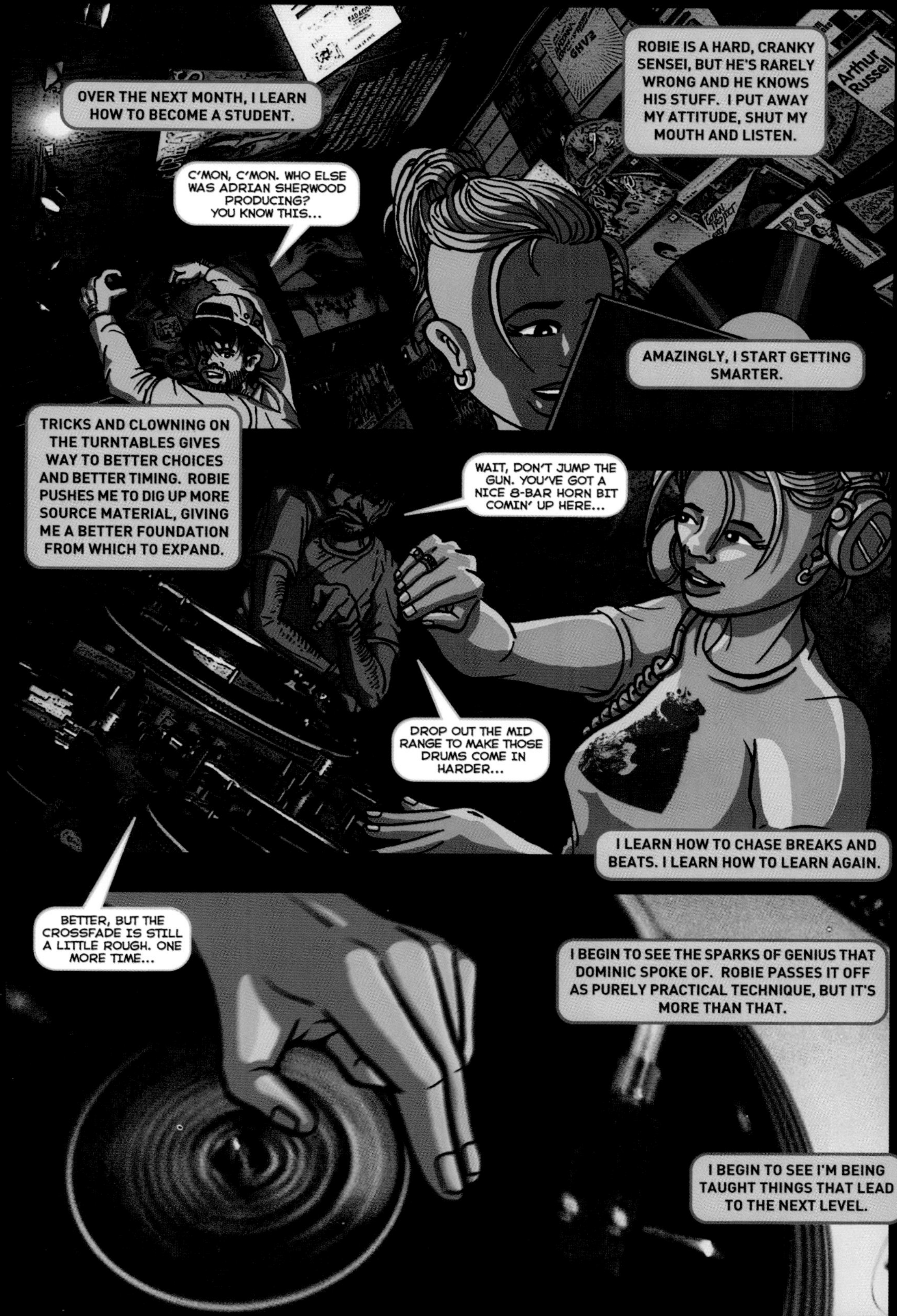
OVER THE NEXT MONTH, I LEARN HOW TO BECOME A STUDENT.
C'MON, C'MON. WHO ELSE WAS ADRIAN SHERWOOD PRODUCING? YOU KNOW THIS...
ROBIE IS A HARD, CRANKY SENSEI, BUT HE'S RARELY WRONG AND HE KNOWS HIS STUFF. I PUT AWAY MY ATTITUDE, SHUT MY MOUTH AND LISTEN.
Arthur Russell
AMAZINGLY, I START GETTING SMARTER.
TRICKS AND CLOWNING ON THE TURNTABLES GIVES WAY TO BETTER CHOICES AND BETTER TIMING. ROBIE PUSHES ME TO DIG UP MORE SOURCE MATERIAL, GIVING ME A BETTER FOUNDATION FROM WHICH TO EXPAND.
WAIT, DON'T JUMP THE GUN. YOU'VE GOT A NICE 8-BAR HORN BIT COMIN' UP HERE...
DROP OUT THE MID RANGE TO MAKE THOSE DRUMS COME IN HARDER...
I LEARN HOW TO CHASE BREAKS AND BEATS. I LEARN HOW TO LEARN AGAIN.
BETTER, BUT THE CROSSFADE IS STILL A LITTLE ROUGH. ONE MORE TIME...
I BEGIN TO SEE THE SPARKS OF GENIUS THAT DOMINIC SPOKE OF. ROBIE PASSES IT OFF AS PURELY PRACTICAL TECHNIQUE, BUT IT'S MORE THAN THAT.
I BEGIN TO SEE I'M BEING TAUGHT THINGS THAT LEAD TO THE NEXT LEVEL.

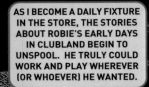

AS I BECOME A DAILY FIXTURE IN THE STORE, THE STORIES ABOUT ROBIE'S EARLY DAYS IN CLUBLAND BEGIN TO UNSPOOL. HE TRULY COULD WORK AND PLAY WHEREVER (OR WHOEVER) HE WANTED.

HIS STORIES, FILLED WITH SEXUAL BRAVADO AND COCKINESS, ALWAYS SEEM MIXED WITH REGRET.

AS SUCCESSFUL AS HE WAS, HE STILL HELD PLENTY OF ANGER FOR LETTING THE DISTRACTIONS TAKE HIM AWAY FROM WHAT HE LOVED.

FOR EACH STORY OF A DREAM BEING REALIZED, THERE'S ONE WHERE THOSE DREAMS GET SIDETRACKED OR LOST.

WAKING UP ALONE ON A COLD SUNDAY MORNING SIDEWALK SEEMED A STRANGE REWARD FOR A NIGHT OF GIVING UP HIS GIFT...

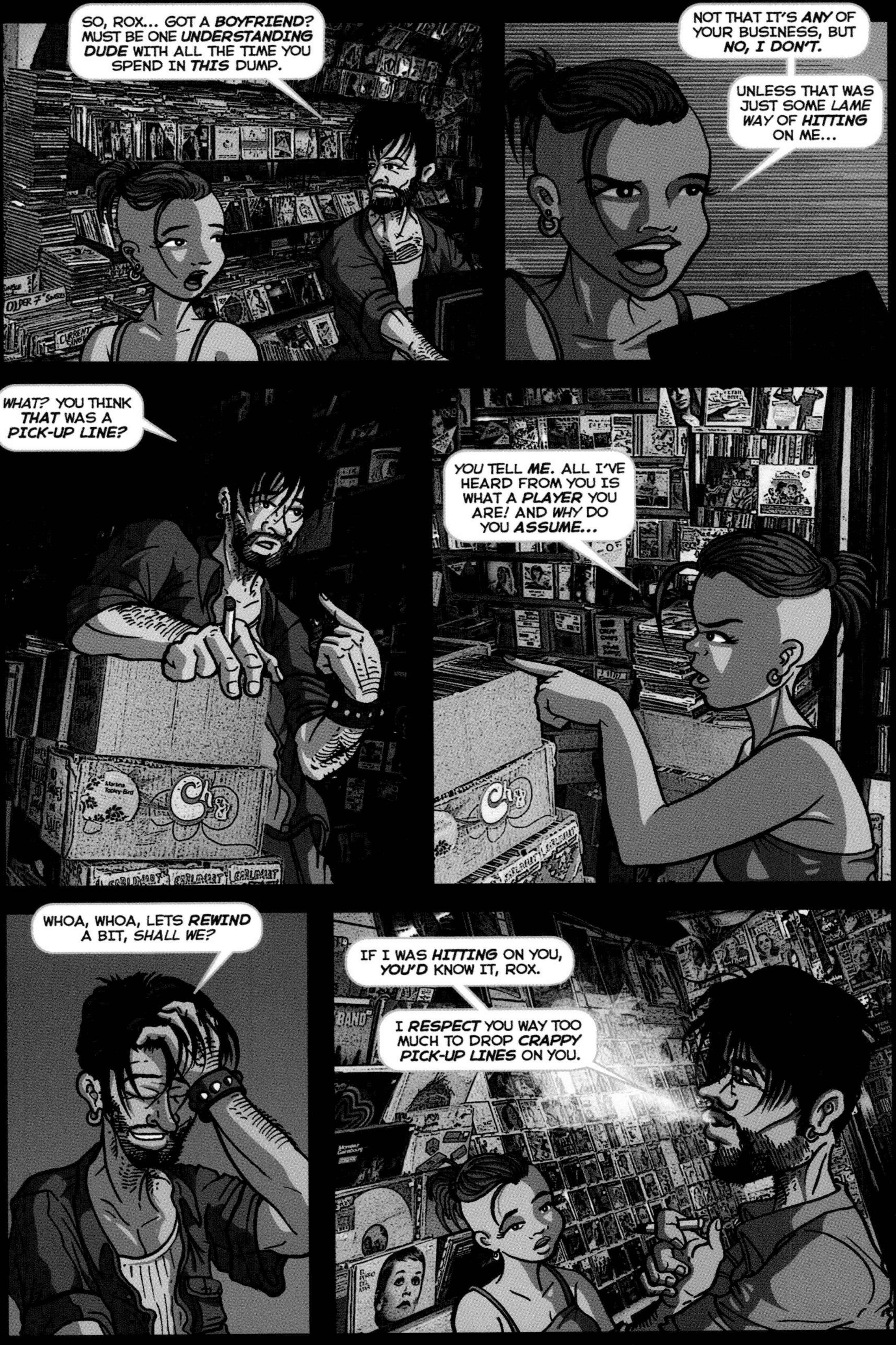
SO, ROX... GOT A BOYFRIEND? MUST BE ONE UNDERSTANDING DUDE WITH ALL THE TIME YOU SPEND IN THIS DUMP.
NOT THAT IT'S ANY OF YOUR BUSINESS, BUT NO, I DON'T.
UNLESS THAT WAS JUST SOME LAME WAY OF HITTING ON ME...
WHAT? YOU THINK THAT WAS A PICK-UP LINE?
YOU TELL ME. ALL I'VE HEARD FROM YOU IS WHAT A PLAYER YOU ARE! AND WHY DO YOU ASSUME...
WHOA, WHOA, LETS REWIND A BIT, SHALL WE?
IF I WAS HITTING ON YOU, YOU'D KNOW IT, ROX.
I RESPECT YOU WAY TOO MUCH TO DROP CRAPPY PICK-UP LINES ON YOU.

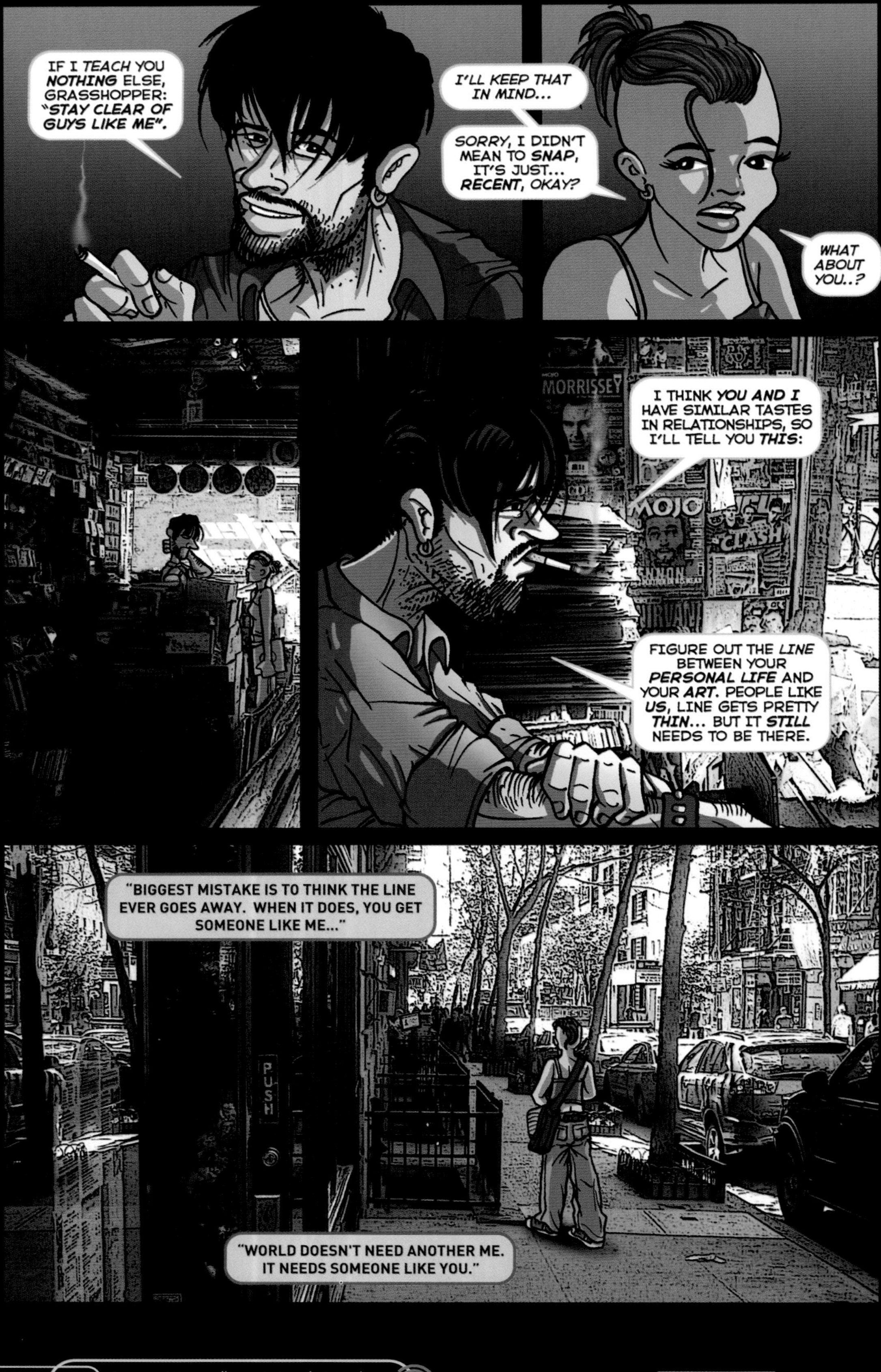
IF I *TEACH* YOU **NOTHING** ELSE, GRASSHOPPER: **"*STAY CLEAR OF GUYS LIKE ME*".**
I'LL KEEP THAT IN MIND...
*SORRY, I DIDN'T MEAN TO **SNAP**, IT'S JUST... **RECENT**, OKAY?*
WHAT ABOUT YOU..?
MORRISSEY
I THINK ***YOU AND I*** HAVE SIMILAR TASTES IN RELATIONSHIPS, SO I'LL TELL YOU ***THIS***:
MOJO
CLASH
FIGURE OUT THE *LINE* BETWEEN YOUR ***PERSONAL LIFE*** AND YOUR ***ART***. PEOPLE LIKE ***US***, LINE GETS PRETTY ***THIN...*** BUT IT ***STILL*** NEEDS TO BE THERE.
"BIGGEST MISTAKE IS TO THINK THE LINE EVER GOES AWAY. WHEN IT DOES, YOU GET SOMEONE LIKE ME..."
PUSH
"WORLD DOESN'T NEED ANOTHER ME. IT NEEDS SOMEONE LIKE YOU."

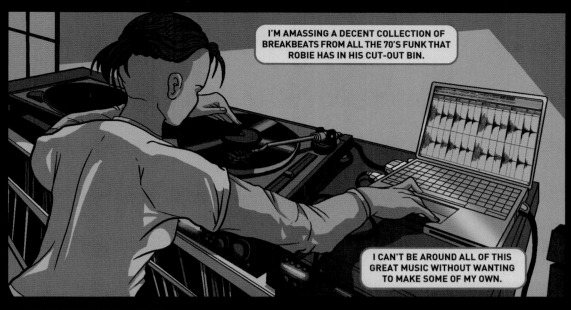

I'M AMASSING A DECENT COLLECTION OF BREAKBEATS FROM ALL THE 70'S FUNK THAT ROBIE HAS IN HIS CUT-OUT BIN.

I CAN'T BE AROUND ALL OF THIS GREAT MUSIC WITHOUT WANTING TO MAKE SOME OF MY OWN.

LAST MONTH, I DUSTED OFF MY MIDI KEYBOARD, SPRANG FOR SOME DECENT MUSIC SOFTWARE AND STARTED MESSING AROUND WITH SOME TRACKS.

SAMPLES GAVE WAY TO ME FIGURING OUT HOW TO CREATE THE BEATS MYSELF. SOFTWARE CORRECTED MY CLUMSY FINGERING.

SLOWLY, SOME OF THE NOODLING BEGAN TO SOUND HALFWAY DECENT. AND NOTHING SOUNDED LIKE WHAT I EXPECTED TO COME OUT OF ME.

WHETHER ANYONE OTHER THAN ME HEARS THIS STUFF IS ANOTHER MATTER ALTOGETHER...

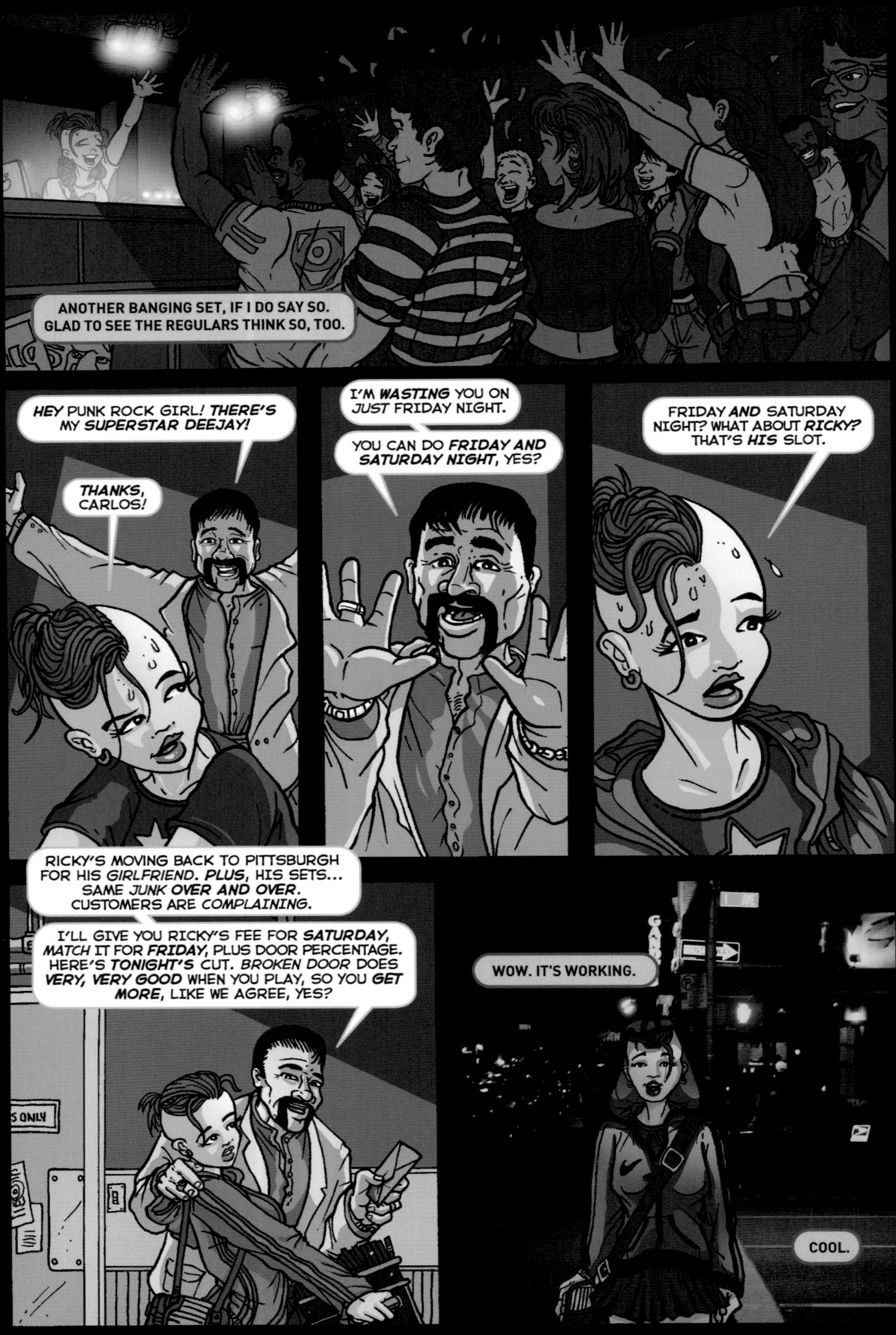
ANOTHER BANGING SET, IF I DO SAY SO. GLAD TO SEE THE REGULARS THINK SO, TOO.
HEY PUNK ROCK GIRL! THERE'S MY SUPERSTAR DEEJAY!
THANKS, CARLOS!
I'M WASTING YOU ON JUST FRIDAY NIGHT.
YOU CAN DO FRIDAY AND SATURDAY NIGHT, YES?
FRIDAY AND SATURDAY NIGHT? WHAT ABOUT RICKY? THAT'S HIS SLOT.
RICKY'S MOVING BACK TO PITTSBURGH FOR HIS GIRLFRIEND. PLUS, HIS SETS... SAME JUNK OVER AND OVER. CUSTOMERS ARE COMPLAINING.
I'LL GIVE YOU RICKY'S FEE FOR SATURDAY, MATCH IT FOR FRIDAY, PLUS DOOR PERCENTAGE. HERE'S TONIGHT'S CUT. BROKEN DOOR DOES VERY, VERY GOOD WHEN YOU PLAY, SO YOU GET MORE, LIKE WE AGREE, YES?
WOW. IT'S WORKING.
COOL.

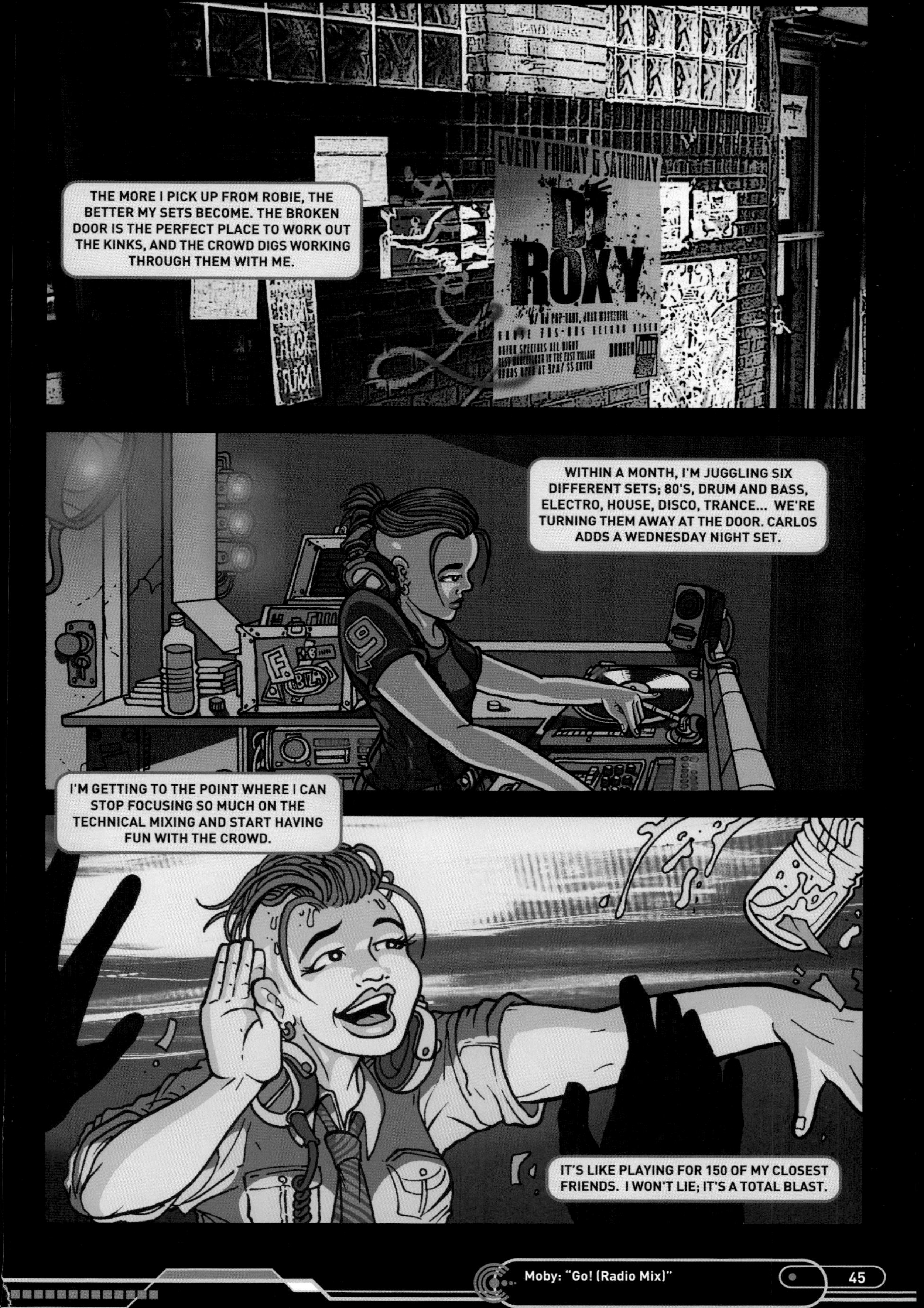
THE MORE I PICK UP FROM ROBIE, THE BETTER MY SETS BECOME. THE BROKEN DOOR IS THE PERFECT PLACE TO WORK OUT THE KINKS, AND THE CROWD DIGS WORKING THROUGH THEM WITH ME.
EVERY FRIDAY & SATURDAY
DJ ROXY
WITHIN A MONTH, I'M JUGGLING SIX DIFFERENT SETS; 80'S, DRUM AND BASS, ELECTRO, HOUSE, DISCO, TRANCE... WE'RE TURNING THEM AWAY AT THE DOOR. CARLOS ADDS A WEDNESDAY NIGHT SET.
I'M GETTING TO THE POINT WHERE I CAN STOP FOCUSING SO MUCH ON THE TECHNICAL MIXING AND START HAVING FUN WITH THE CROWD.
IT'S LIKE PLAYING FOR 150 OF MY CLOSEST FRIENDS. I WON'T LIE; IT'S A TOTAL BLAST.

LUNCH

OH MY GOD, COLIN. IT IS SO CRAZY RIGHT NOW!

THREE NIGHTS A WEEK. CAPACITY CROWDS. I'VE GOT PEOPLE WANTING SET LISTS, AUTOGRAPHS, DATES!...

TOTAL ROCK STAR LIFESTYLE. WELL, LESS THE MILLIONS OF DOLLARS...

INDEED.

AND MY SECRET WEAPON; ROBIE. MAN KNOWS HIS STUFF.

WE'VE GOT THIS COOL SENSEI/ STUDENT THING GOING ON, AND IT'S PAYING OFF BIG TIME!

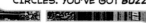

WELL MISS DIVA, YOUR GOOD WORK IS MOVING THROUGH THE CLUB KID CIRCLES. YOU'VE GOT BUZZ.

ENOUGH SO THAT MY CROWD IS SNEAKING OUT OF THE GAY CLUBS TO CHECK YOUR SET OUT. I'VE EVEN STARTED NAME-DROPPING YOU TO IMPRESS PEOPLE, FOR GOD'S SAKE.

WOW, I'M NAME-DROPPABLE? THANKS, THAT'S SWEET.

SO I RAN INTO *HANNAH* AT THE FLEA MARKETS LAST WEEKEND. SHE SAID SHE HASN'T *HEARD* FROM YOU..?

NO. I... *HAVEN'T* CALLED HER.

OH SWEETIE... *THAT'S* NOT GOOD...

I KNOW, I KNOW. I JUST DON'T THINK SHE'D *WANT* TO TALK WITH ME.

I WAS *KIND* OF AN *ASSHOLE* WHEN SHE LEFT.

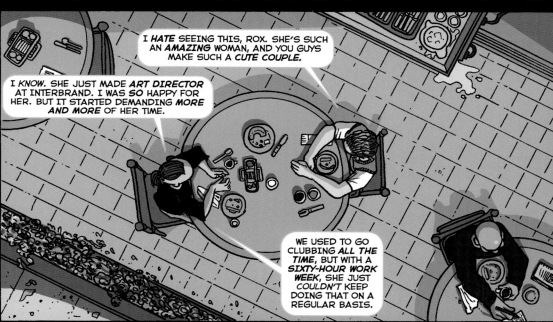

I *HATE* SEEING THIS, ROX. SHE'S SUCH AN *AMAZING* WOMAN, AND YOU GUYS MAKE SUCH A *CUTE COUPLE.*

I *KNOW.* SHE JUST MADE *ART DIRECTOR* AT INTERBRAND. I WAS *SO* HAPPY FOR HER. BUT IT STARTED DEMANDING *MORE AND MORE* OF HER TIME.

WE USED TO GO CLUBBING *ALL THE TIME,* BUT WITH A *SIXTY-HOUR WORK WEEK,* SHE JUST *COULDN'T* KEEP DOING THAT ON A REGULAR BASIS.

SHE TOLD ME YOU TWO BROKE UP BECAUSE YOU WOULDN'T GIVE UP YOUR SCHEDULE AT THE *"BROKEN DOOR"*...

SEE? IT MAKES ME LOOK LIKE AN *ASSHOLE,* BUT I WAS JUST STARTING TO GET *MORE WORK.* WAS I SUPPOSED TO JUST *THROW* ALL THAT OUT THE WINDOW?

WELL...

WHAT WOULD I SAY IF I *DID* CALL? I'M *BUSIER* NOW THAN WHEN WE BROKE UP.

HANNAH
212-
555-9884
CALL

MENU

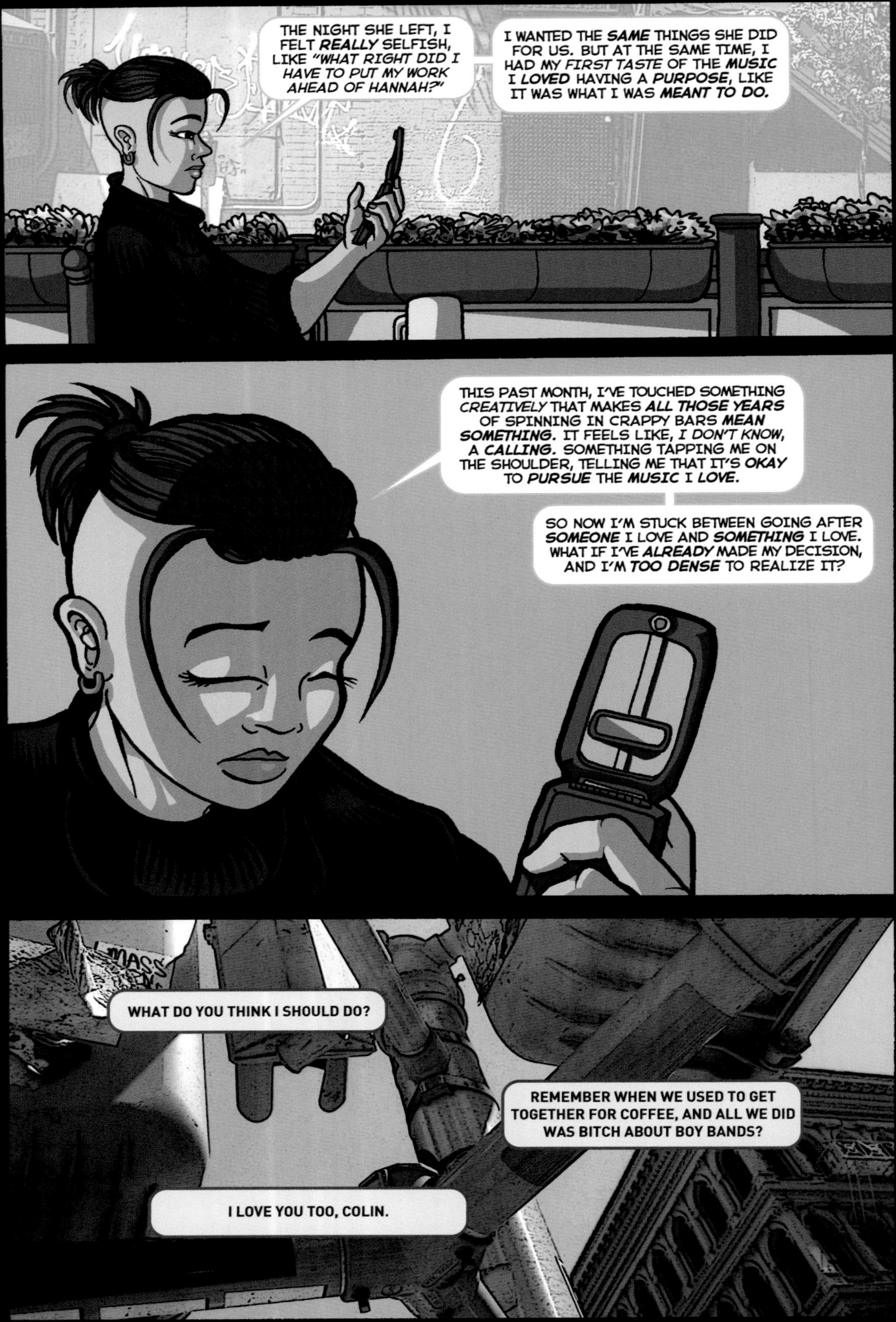
THE NIGHT SHE LEFT, I FELT REALLY SELFISH, LIKE "WHAT RIGHT DID I HAVE TO PUT MY WORK AHEAD OF HANNAH?"
I WANTED THE SAME THINGS SHE DID FOR US. BUT AT THE SAME TIME, I HAD MY FIRST TASTE OF THE MUSIC I LOVED HAVING A PURPOSE, LIKE IT WAS WHAT I WAS MEANT TO DO.
THIS PAST MONTH, I'VE TOUCHED SOMETHING CREATIVELY THAT MAKES ALL THOSE YEARS OF SPINNING IN CRAPPY BARS MEAN SOMETHING. IT FEELS LIKE, I DON'T KNOW, A CALLING. SOMETHING TAPPING ME ON THE SHOULDER, TELLING ME THAT IT'S OKAY TO PURSUE THE MUSIC I LOVE.
SO NOW I'M STUCK BETWEEN GOING AFTER SOMEONE I LOVE AND SOMETHING I LOVE. WHAT IF I'VE ALREADY MADE MY DECISION, AND I'M TOO DENSE TO REALIZE IT?
WHAT DO YOU THINK I SHOULD DO?
REMEMBER WHEN WE USED TO GET TOGETHER FOR COFFEE, AND ALL WE DID WAS BITCH ABOUT BOY BANDS?
I LOVE YOU TOO, COLIN.

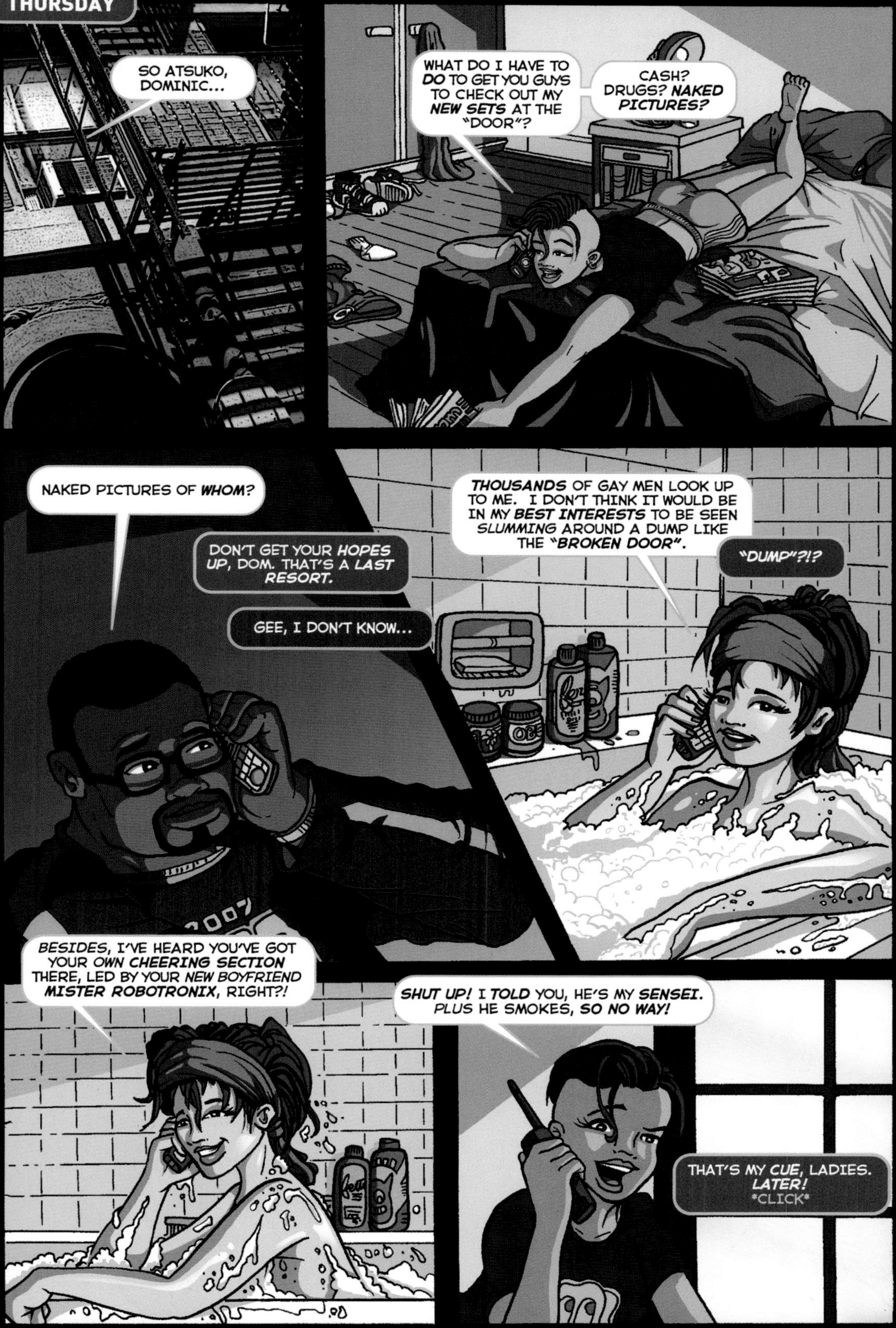
SO ATSUKO, DOMINIC...
WHAT DO I HAVE TO DO TO GET YOU GUYS TO CHECK OUT MY NEW SETS AT THE "DOOR"?
CASH? DRUGS? NAKED PICTURES?
NAKED PICTURES OF WHOM?
DON'T GET YOUR HOPES UP, DOM. THAT'S A LAST RESORT.
GEE, I DON'T KNOW...
THOUSANDS OF GAY MEN LOOK UP TO ME. I DON'T THINK IT WOULD BE IN MY BEST INTERESTS TO BE SEEN SLUMMING AROUND A DUMP LIKE THE "BROKEN DOOR".
"DUMP"?!?
BESIDES, I'VE HEARD YOU'VE GOT YOUR OWN CHEERING SECTION THERE, LED BY YOUR NEW BOYFRIEND MISTER ROBOTRONIX, RIGHT?!
SHUT UP! I TOLD YOU, HE'S MY SENSEI. PLUS HE SMOKES, SO NO WAY!
THAT'S MY CUE, LADIES. LATER! *CLICK*

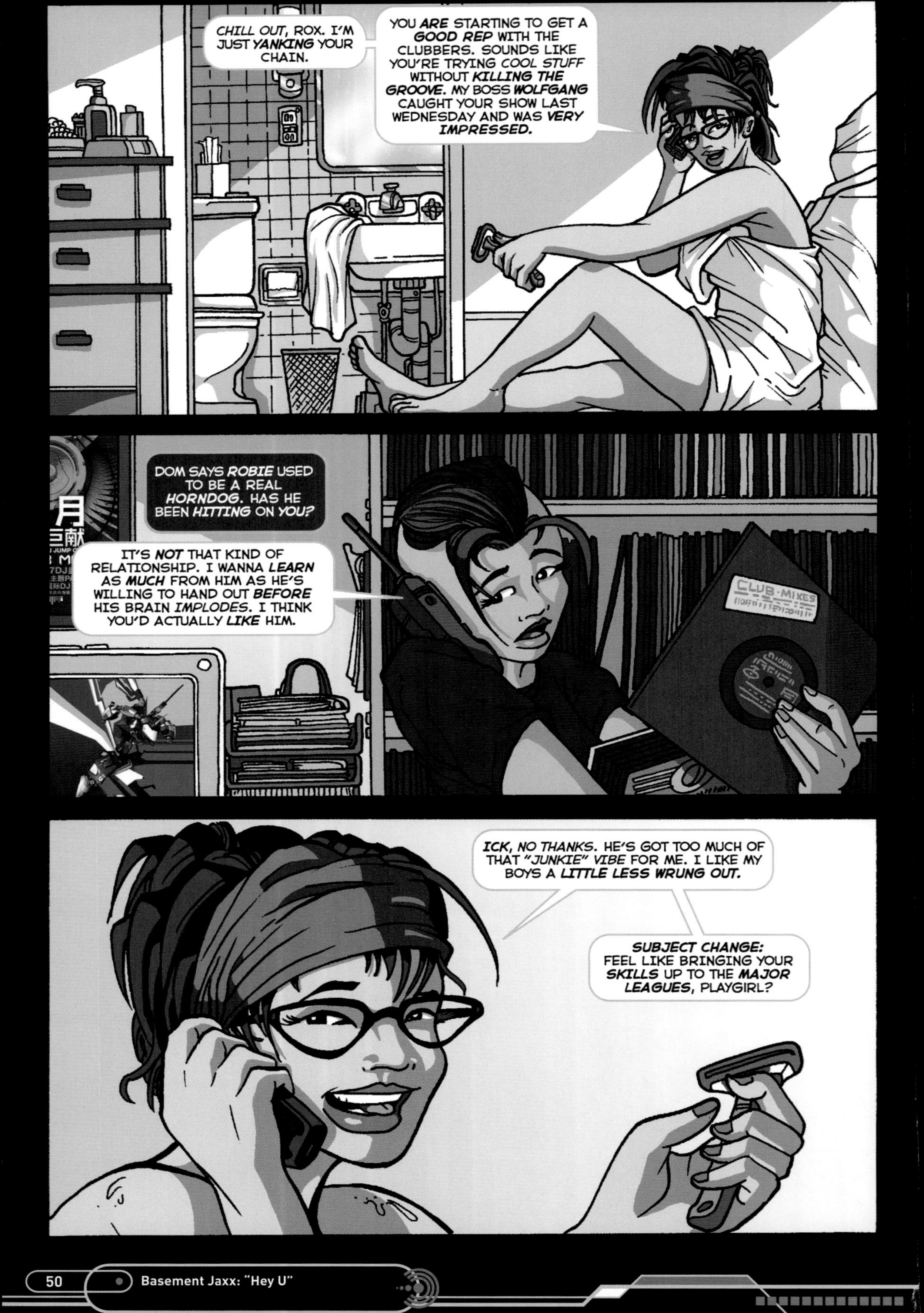

CHILL OUT, ROX. I'M JUST YANKING YOUR CHAIN.
YOU ARE STARTING TO GET A GOOD REP WITH THE CLUBBERS. SOUNDS LIKE YOU'RE TRYING COOL STUFF WITHOUT KILLING THE GROOVE. MY BOSS WOLFGANG CAUGHT YOUR SHOW LAST WEDNESDAY AND WAS VERY IMPRESSED.
DOM SAYS ROBIE USED TO BE A REAL HORNDOG. HAS HE BEEN HITTING ON YOU?
IT'S NOT THAT KIND OF RELATIONSHIP. I WANNA LEARN AS MUCH FROM HIM AS HE'S WILLING TO HAND OUT BEFORE HIS BRAIN IMPLODES. I THINK YOU'D ACTUALLY LIKE HIM.
CLUB MIXES
ICK, NO THANKS. HE'S GOT TOO MUCH OF THAT "JUNKIE" VIBE FOR ME. I LIKE MY BOYS A LITTLE LESS WRUNG OUT.
SUBJECT CHANGE: FEEL LIKE BRINGING YOUR SKILLS UP TO THE MAJOR LEAGUES, PLAYGIRL?

WOLFGANG *LIKED* WHAT HE SAW AND SAID WE SHOULD TRY AND *LURE YOU AWAY* FROM THE "BROKEN DOOR".

NO WAY!

YUP, WHICH LEADS VERY *NICELY* TO *MY SITUATION...*

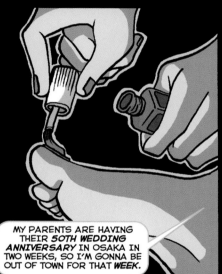

MY PARENTS ARE HAVING THEIR *50TH WEDDING ANNIVERSARY* IN OSAKA IN TWO WEEKS, SO I'M GONNA BE OUT OF TOWN FOR THAT *WEEK*.

DARIO IS GOING TO PICK UP MY *SATURDAY NIGHT* SLOT FOR THAT WEEK, BUT THAT STILL LEAVES HIS *FRIDAY NIGHT* SLOT *OPEN*.

YOU'RE ASKING IF I WANT TO DO A *FRIDAY NIGHT* FILL-IN SET AT *PLUSH?*

WOLFGANG *WANTS* TO GIVE YOU A TRYOUT, AND WE *NEED* THE SPOT FILLED. I'LL BE IN OSAKA UNTIL *MONDAY*, SO YOU'D BE *ON YOUR OWN. INTERESTED?*

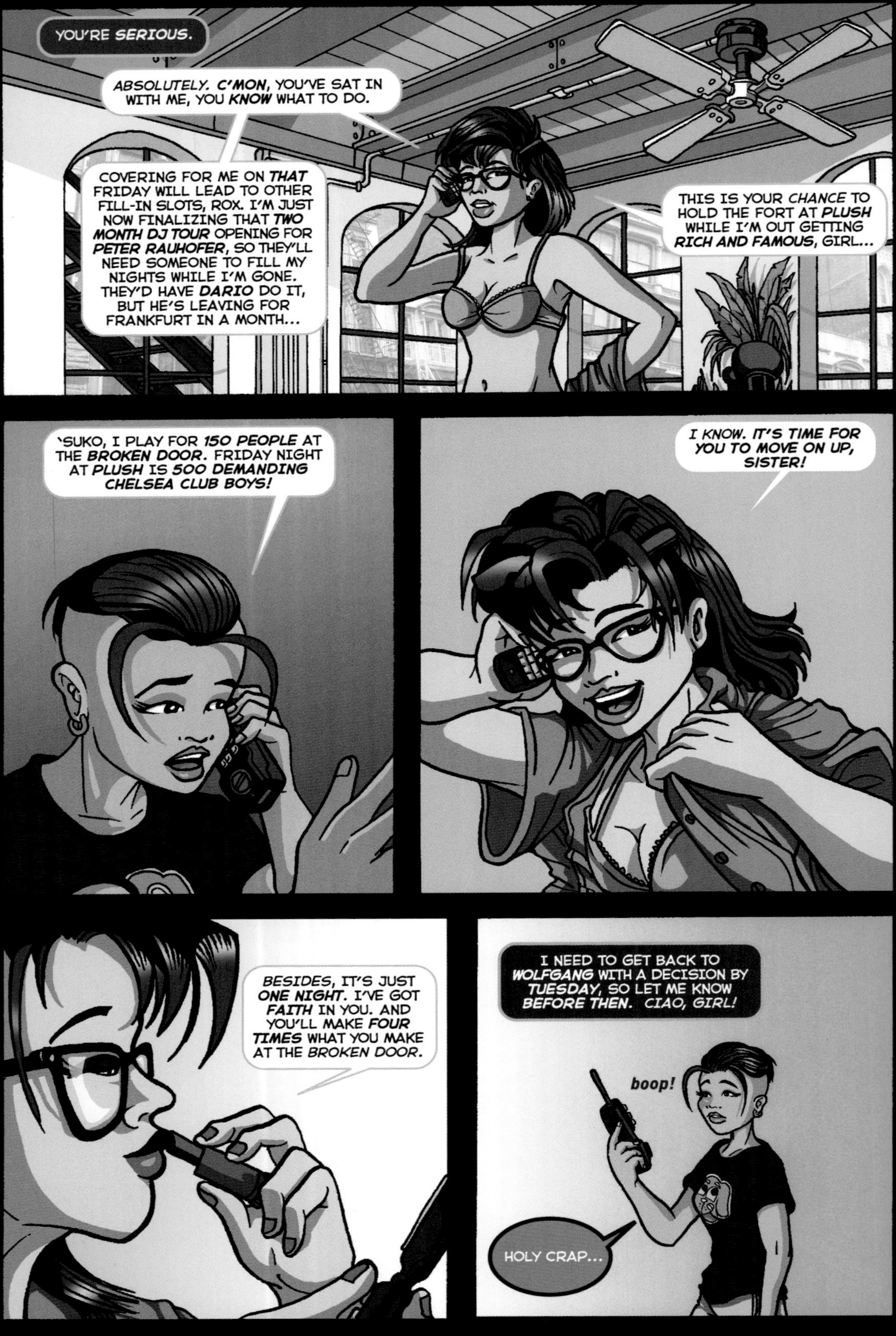
YOU'RE SERIOUS.
ABSOLUTELY. C'MON, YOU'VE SAT IN WITH ME, YOU KNOW WHAT TO DO.
COVERING FOR ME ON THAT FRIDAY WILL LEAD TO OTHER FILL-IN SLOTS, ROX. I'M JUST NOW FINALIZING THAT TWO MONTH DJ TOUR OPENING FOR PETER RAUHOFER, SO THEY'LL NEED SOMEONE TO FILL MY NIGHTS WHILE I'M GONE. THEY'D HAVE DARIO DO IT, BUT HE'S LEAVING FOR FRANKFURT IN A MONTH...
THIS IS YOUR CHANCE TO HOLD THE FORT AT PLUSH WHILE I'M OUT GETTING RICH AND FAMOUS, GIRL...
'SUKO, I PLAY FOR 150 PEOPLE AT THE BROKEN DOOR. FRIDAY NIGHT AT PLUSH IS 500 DEMANDING CHELSEA CLUB BOYS!
I KNOW. IT'S TIME FOR YOU TO MOVE ON UP, SISTER!
BESIDES, IT'S JUST ONE NIGHT. I'VE GOT FAITH IN YOU. AND YOU'LL MAKE FOUR TIMES WHAT YOU MAKE AT THE BROKEN DOOR.
I NEED TO GET BACK TO WOLFGANG WITH A DECISION BY TUESDAY, SO LET ME KNOW BEFORE THEN. CIAO, GIRL!
boop!
HOLY CRAP...

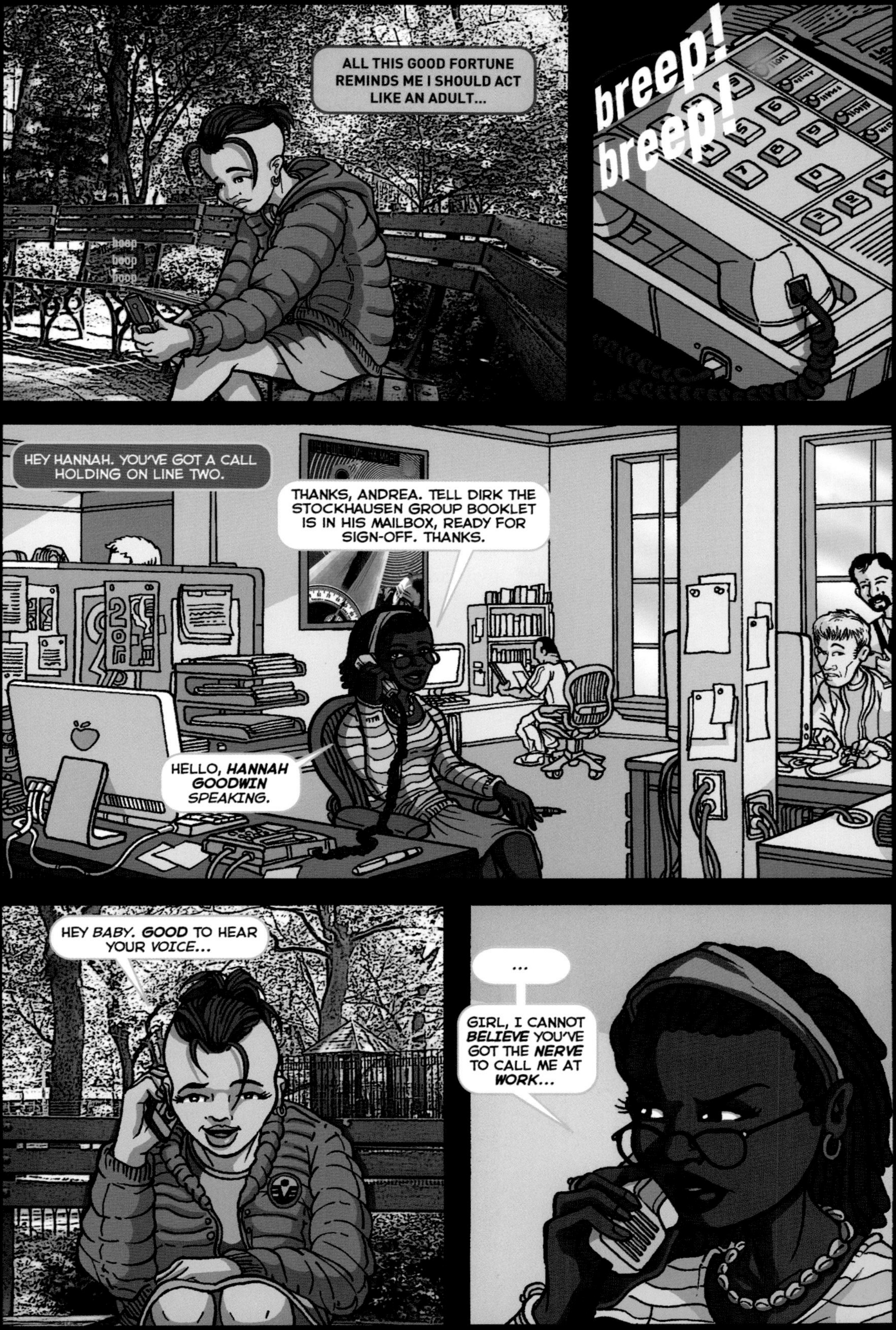
ALL THIS GOOD FORTUNE REMINDS ME I SHOULD ACT LIKE AN ADULT...
beep
beep
beep
breep! breep!
HEY HANNAH. YOU'VE GOT A CALL HOLDING ON LINE TWO.
THANKS, ANDREA. TELL DIRK THE STOCKHAUSEN GROUP BOOKLET IS IN HIS MAILBOX, READY FOR SIGN-OFF. THANKS.
HELLO, ***HANNAH GOODWIN*** *SPEAKING.*
HEY *BABY.* ***GOOD*** TO HEAR YOUR *VOICE...*
...
GIRL, I CANNOT ***BELIEVE*** YOU'VE GOT THE ***NERVE*** TO CALL ME AT ***WORK...***

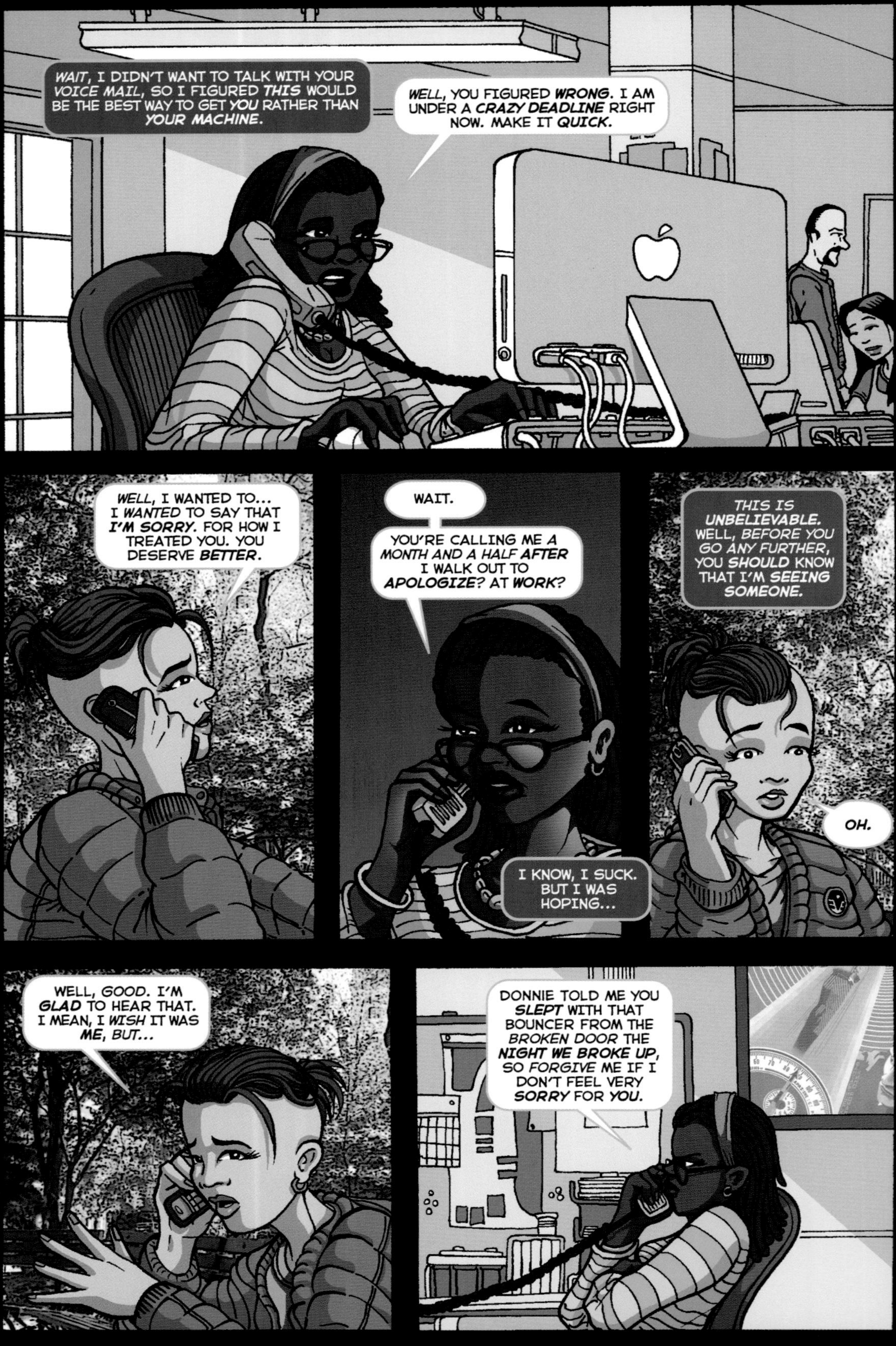
WAIT, I DIDN'T WANT TO TALK WITH YOUR VOICE MAIL, SO I FIGURED THIS WOULD BE THE BEST WAY TO GET YOU RATHER THAN YOUR MACHINE.
WELL, YOU FIGURED WRONG. I AM UNDER A CRAZY DEADLINE RIGHT NOW. MAKE IT QUICK.
WELL, I WANTED TO... I WANTED TO SAY THAT I'M SORRY. FOR HOW I TREATED YOU. YOU DESERVE BETTER.
WAIT.
YOU'RE CALLING ME A MONTH AND A HALF AFTER I WALK OUT TO APOLOGIZE? AT WORK?
I KNOW, I SUCK. BUT I WAS HOPING...
THIS IS UNBELIEVABLE. WELL, BEFORE YOU GO ANY FURTHER, YOU SHOULD KNOW THAT I'M SEEING SOMEONE.
OH.
WELL, GOOD. I'M GLAD TO HEAR THAT. I MEAN, I WISH IT WAS ME, BUT...
DONNIE TOLD ME YOU SLEPT WITH THAT BOUNCER FROM THE BROKEN DOOR THE NIGHT WE BROKE UP, SO FORGIVE ME IF I DON'T FEEL VERY SORRY FOR YOU.

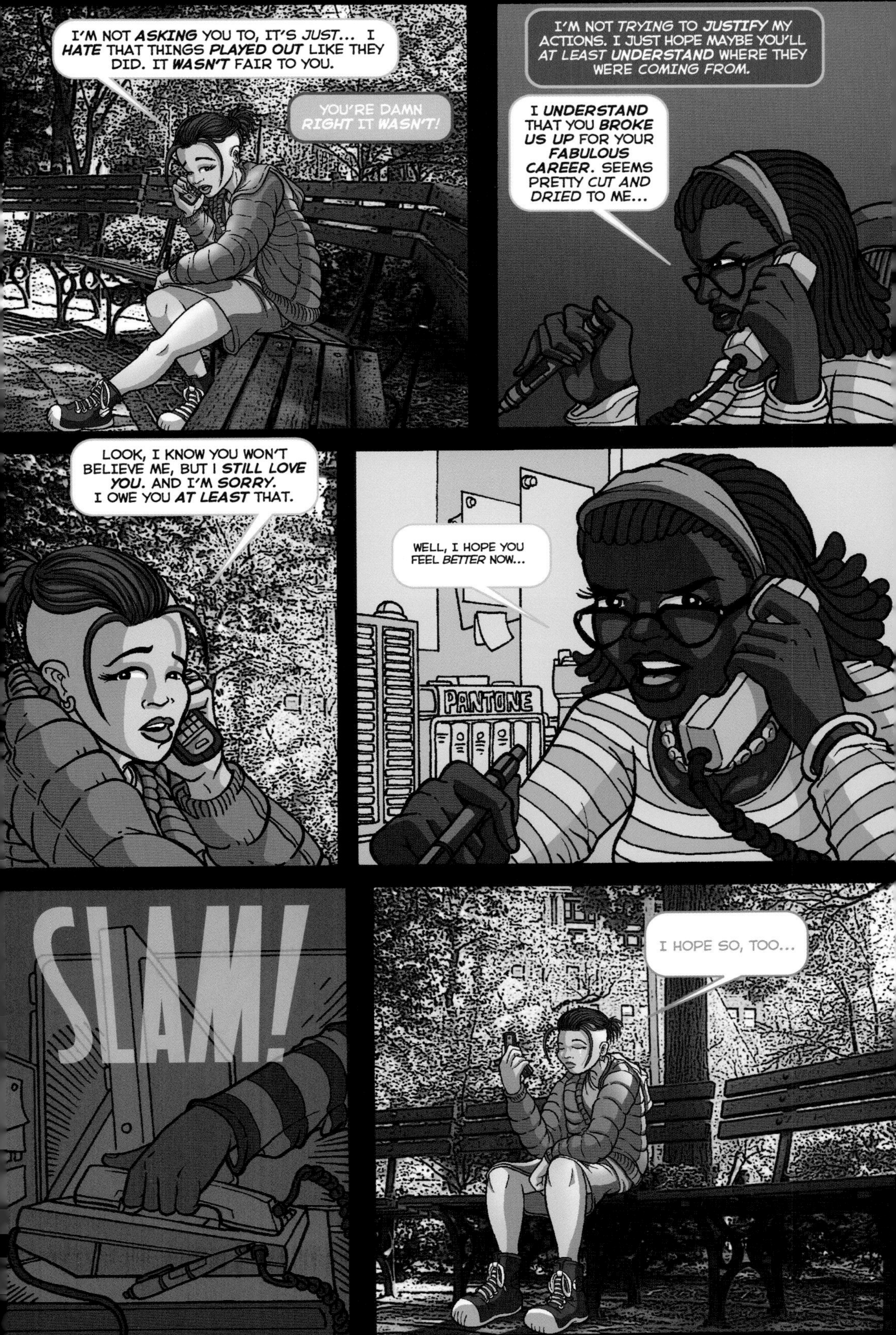
I'M NOT ASKING YOU TO, IT'S JUST... I HATE THAT THINGS PLAYED OUT LIKE THEY DID. IT WASN'T FAIR TO YOU.
YOU'RE DAMN RIGHT IT WASN'T!
I'M NOT TRYING TO JUSTIFY MY ACTIONS. I JUST HOPE MAYBE YOU'LL AT LEAST UNDERSTAND WHERE THEY WERE COMING FROM.
I UNDERSTAND THAT YOU BROKE US UP FOR YOUR FABULOUS CAREER. SEEMS PRETTY CUT AND DRIED TO ME...
LOOK, I KNOW YOU WON'T BELIEVE ME, BUT I STILL LOVE YOU. AND I'M SORRY. I OWE YOU AT LEAST THAT.
WELL, I HOPE YOU FEEL BETTER NOW...
PANTONE
SLAM!
I HOPE SO, TOO...

TRACK THREE

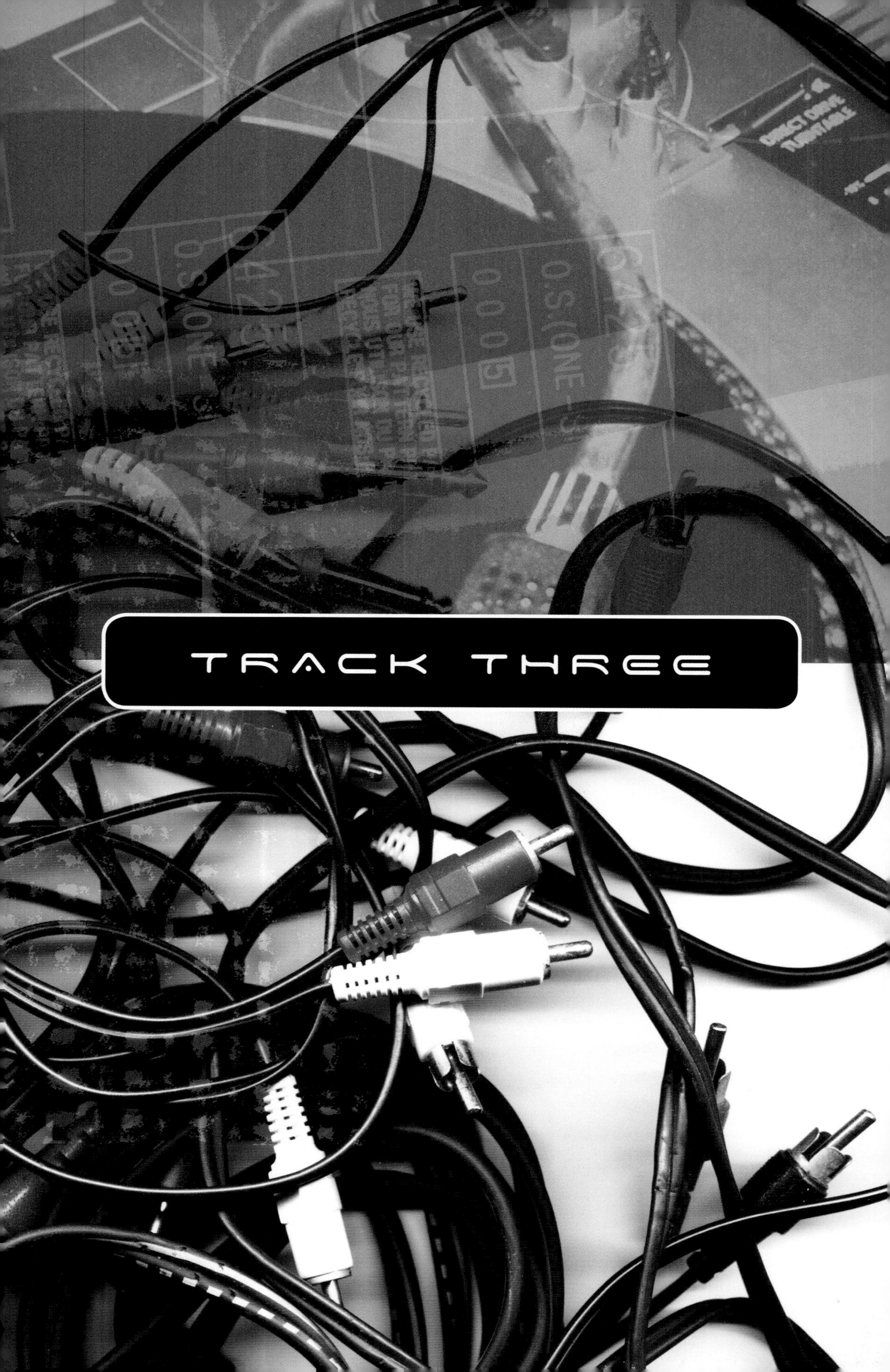

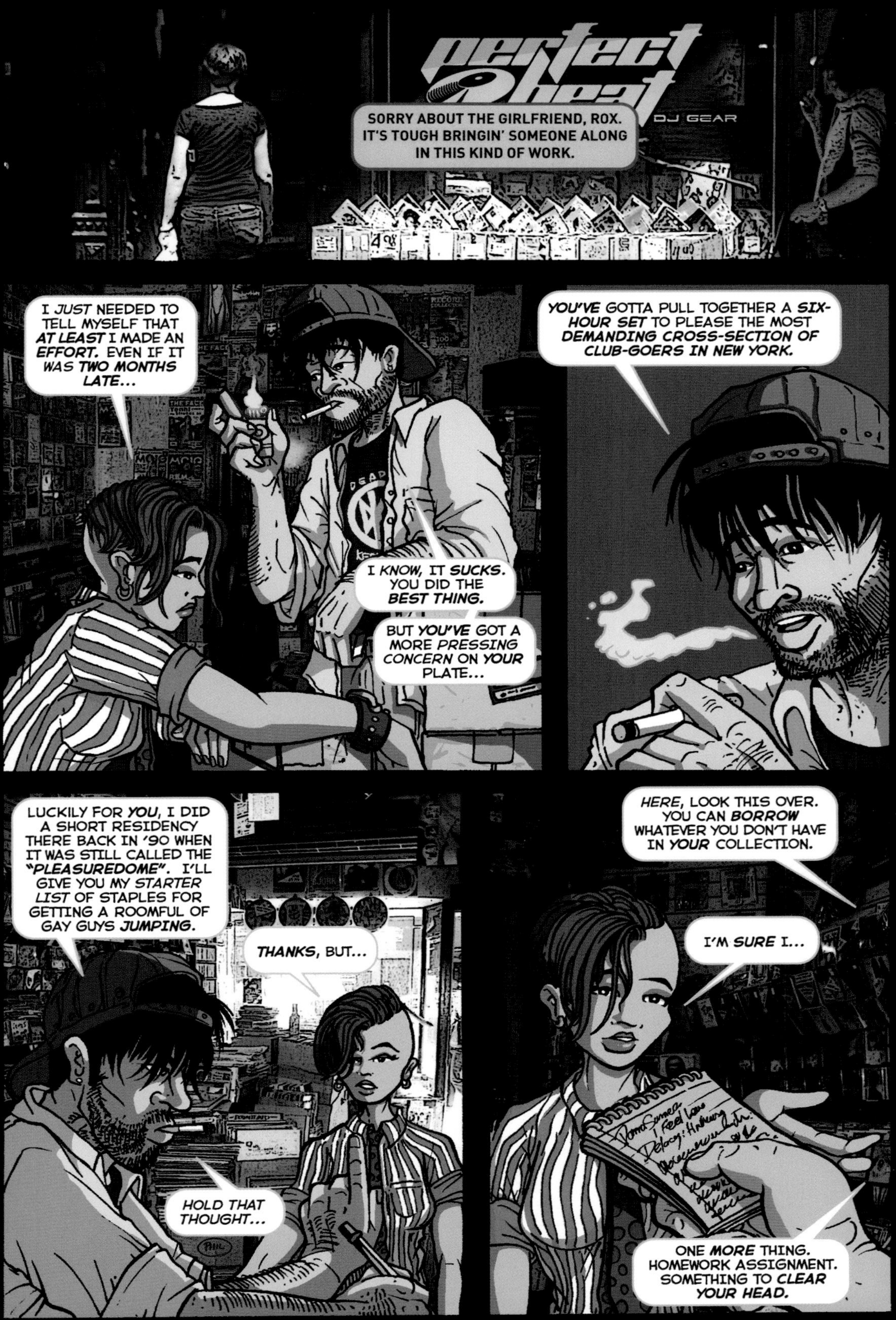
perfect beat
DJ GEAR
SORRY ABOUT THE GIRLFRIEND, ROX. IT'S TOUGH BRINGIN' SOMEONE ALONG IN THIS KIND OF WORK.
I JUST NEEDED TO TELL MYSELF THAT AT LEAST I MADE AN EFFORT. EVEN IF IT WAS TWO MONTHS LATE...
I KNOW, IT SUCKS. YOU DID THE BEST THING.
BUT YOU'VE GOT A MORE PRESSING CONCERN ON YOUR PLATE...
YOU'VE GOTTA PULL TOGETHER A SIX-HOUR SET TO PLEASE THE MOST DEMANDING CROSS-SECTION OF CLUB-GOERS IN NEW YORK.
LUCKILY FOR YOU, I DID A SHORT RESIDENCY THERE BACK IN '90 WHEN IT WAS STILL CALLED THE "PLEASUREDOME". I'LL GIVE YOU MY STARTER LIST OF STAPLES FOR GETTING A ROOMFUL OF GAY GUYS JUMPING.
THANKS, BUT...
HOLD THAT THOUGHT...
HERE, LOOK THIS OVER. YOU CAN BORROW WHATEVER YOU DON'T HAVE IN YOUR COLLECTION.
I'M SURE I...
ONE MORE THING. HOMEWORK ASSIGNMENT. SOMETHING TO CLEAR YOUR HEAD.

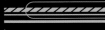

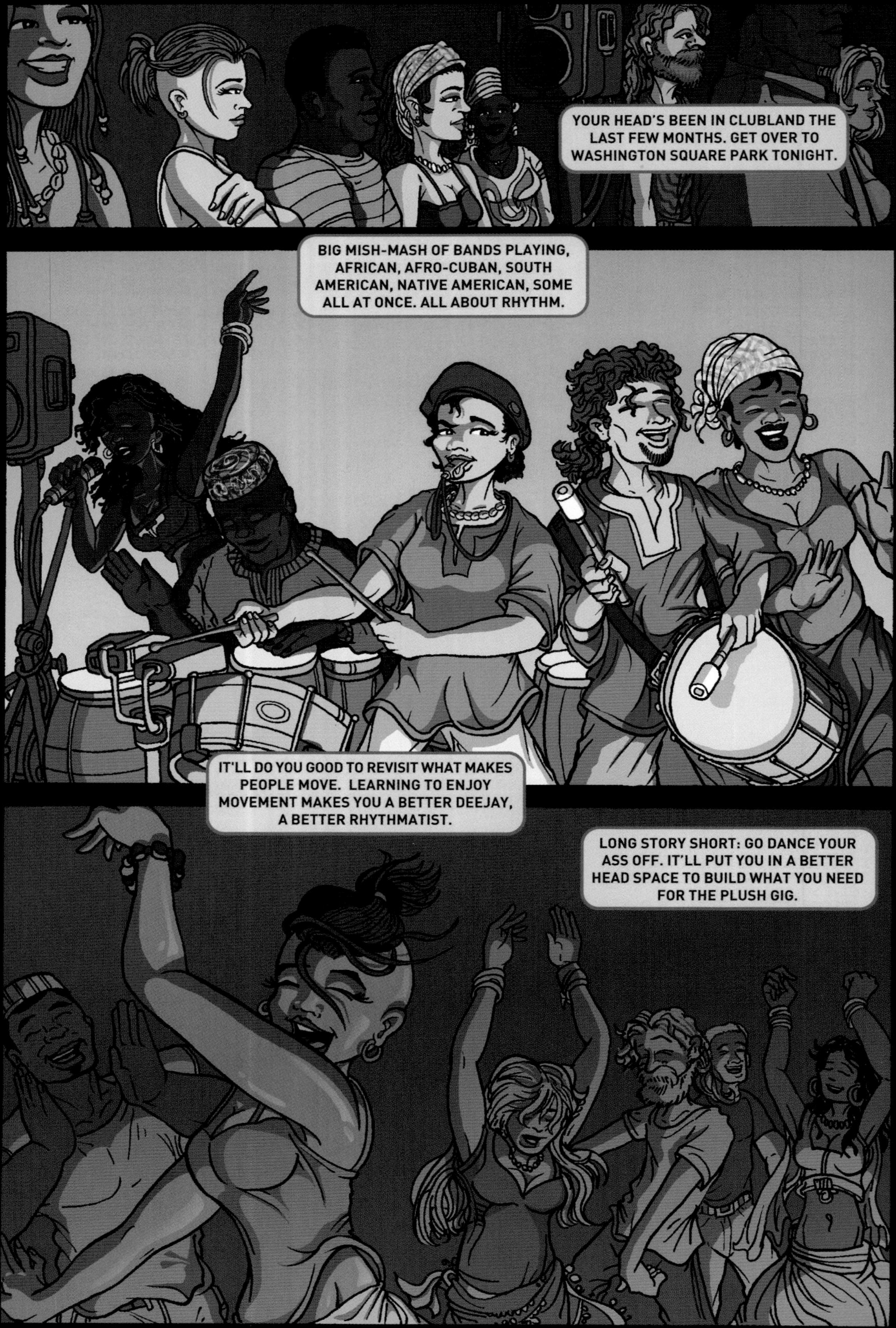
YOUR HEAD'S BEEN IN CLUBLAND THE LAST FEW MONTHS. GET OVER TO WASHINGTON SQUARE PARK TONIGHT.
BIG MISH-MASH OF BANDS PLAYING, AFRICAN, AFRO-CUBAN, SOUTH AMERICAN, NATIVE AMERICAN, SOME ALL AT ONCE. ALL ABOUT RHYTHM.
IT'LL DO YOU GOOD TO REVISIT WHAT MAKES PEOPLE MOVE. LEARNING TO ENJOY MOVEMENT MAKES YOU A BETTER DEEJAY, A BETTER RHYTHMATIST.
LONG STORY SHORT: GO DANCE YOUR ASS OFF. IT'LL PUT YOU IN A BETTER HEAD SPACE TO BUILD WHAT YOU NEED FOR THE PLUSH GIG.

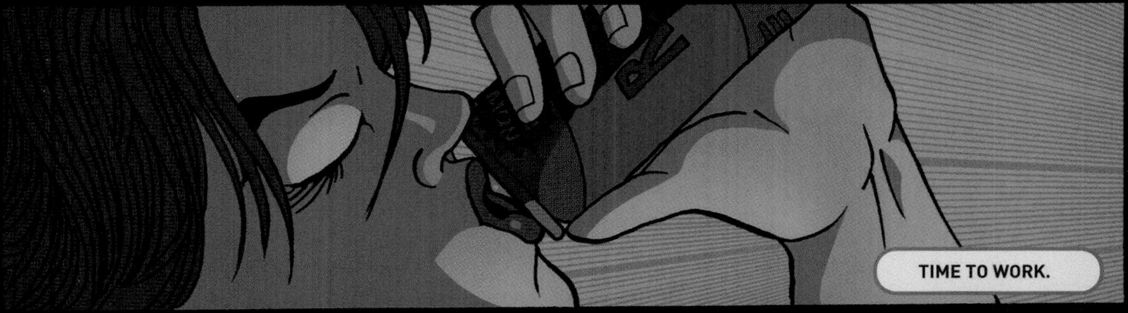
TIME TO WORK.

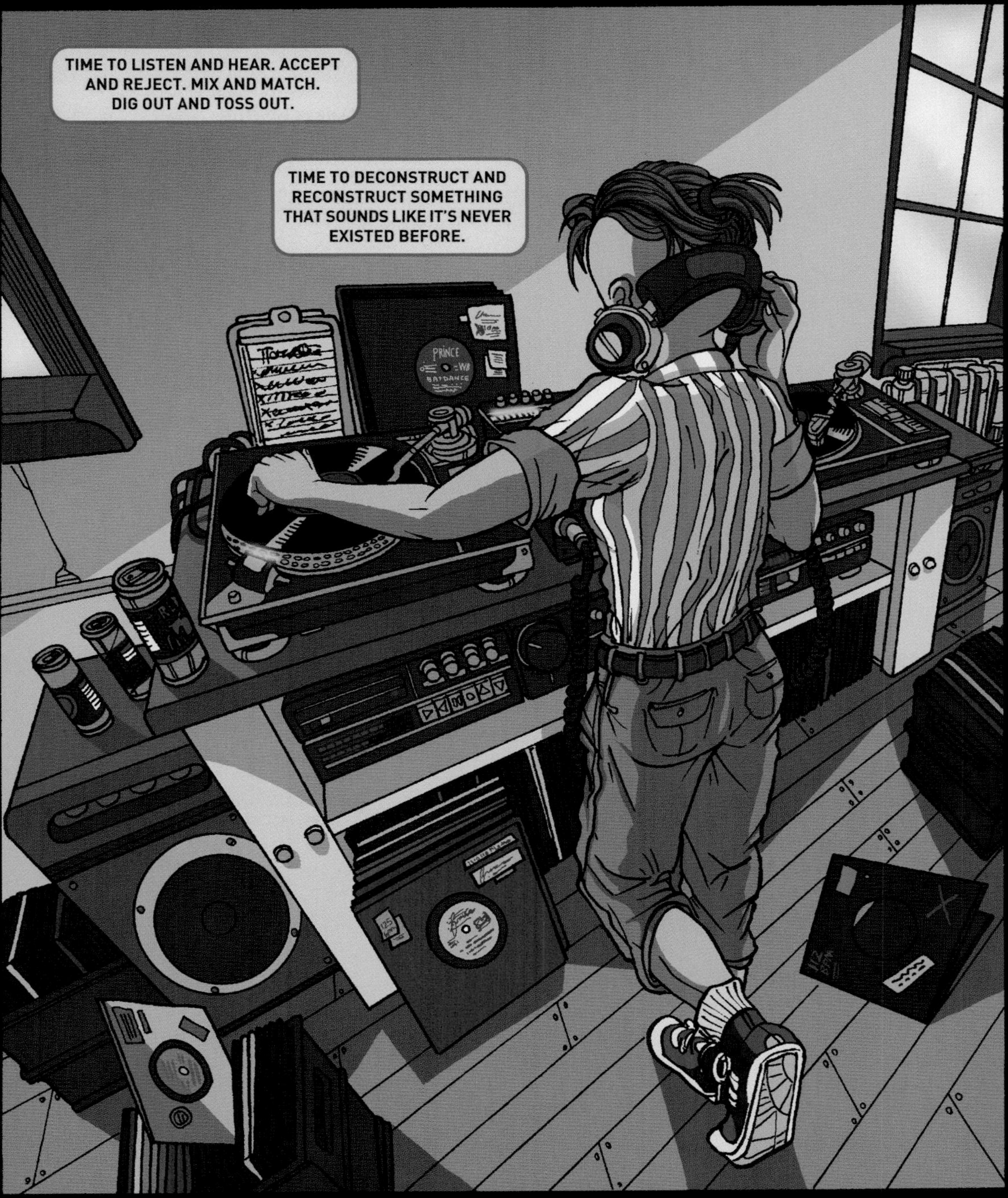
TIME TO LISTEN AND HEAR. ACCEPT AND REJECT. MIX AND MATCH. DIG OUT AND TOSS OUT.
TIME TO DECONSTRUCT AND RECONSTRUCT SOMETHING THAT SOUNDS LIKE IT'S NEVER EXISTED BEFORE.
PRINCE
BATDANCE

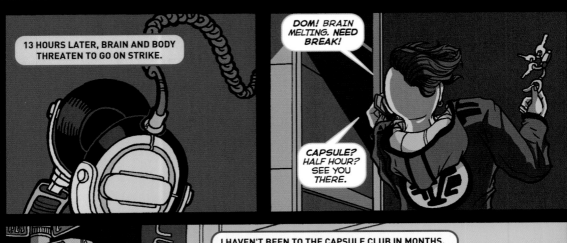

13 HOURS LATER, BRAIN AND BODY THREATEN TO GO ON STRIKE.

DOM! BRAIN MELTING. NEED BREAK!

CAPSULE? HALF HOUR? SEE YOU THERE.

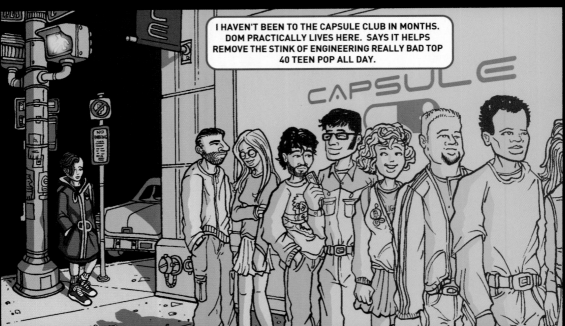

I HAVEN'T BEEN TO THE CAPSULE CLUB IN MONTHS. DOM PRACTICALLY LIVES HERE. SAYS IT HELPS REMOVE THE STINK OF ENGINEERING REALLY BAD TOP 40 TEEN POP ALL DAY.

CAPSULE

HOW YOU BEEN, HERMIT?

NEARLY THERE WITH THE SET. GONNA HAVE ROBIE GIVE IT A ONCE-OVER TOMORROW.

WHO'S ON THE DECKS TONIGHT?

DUDE FROM NEW ZEALAND, WINSTON SOMETHING.

ANY GOOD SO FAR?

ALIENS DROPPED THIS GUY OFF, ROX. CHECK HIM OUT...

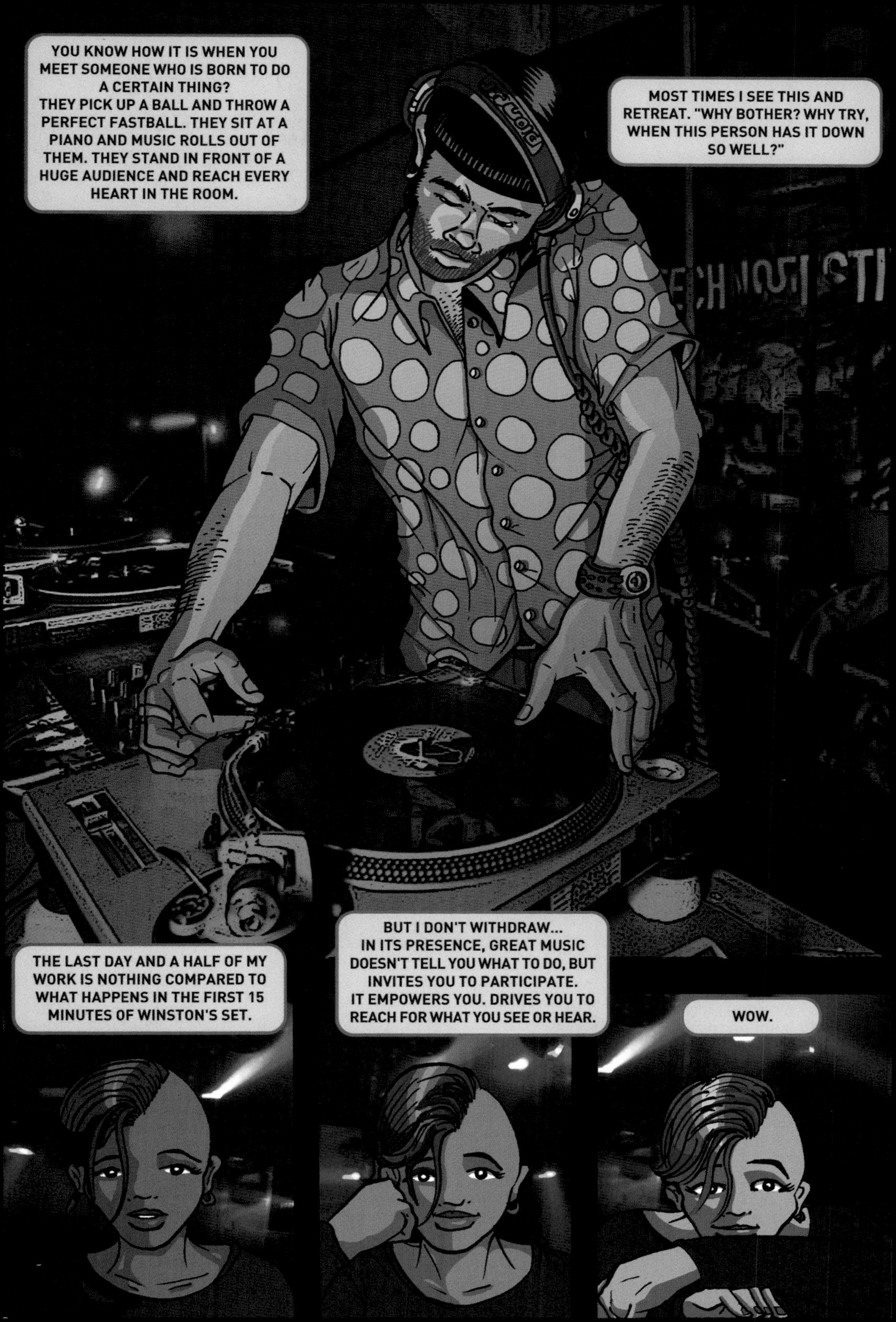

YOU KNOW HOW IT IS WHEN YOU MEET SOMEONE WHO IS BORN TO DO A CERTAIN THING?
THEY PICK UP A BALL AND THROW A PERFECT FASTBALL. THEY SIT AT A PIANO AND MUSIC ROLLS OUT OF THEM. THEY STAND IN FRONT OF A HUGE AUDIENCE AND REACH EVERY HEART IN THE ROOM.
MOST TIMES I SEE THIS AND RETREAT. "WHY BOTHER? WHY TRY, WHEN THIS PERSON HAS IT DOWN SO WELL?"
THE LAST DAY AND A HALF OF MY WORK IS NOTHING COMPARED TO WHAT HAPPENS IN THE FIRST 15 MINUTES OF WINSTON'S SET.
BUT I DON'T WITHDRAW... IN ITS PRESENCE, GREAT MUSIC DOESN'T TELL YOU WHAT TO DO, BUT INVITES YOU TO PARTICIPATE. IT EMPOWERS YOU. DRIVES YOU TO REACH FOR WHAT YOU SEE OR HEAR.
WOW.

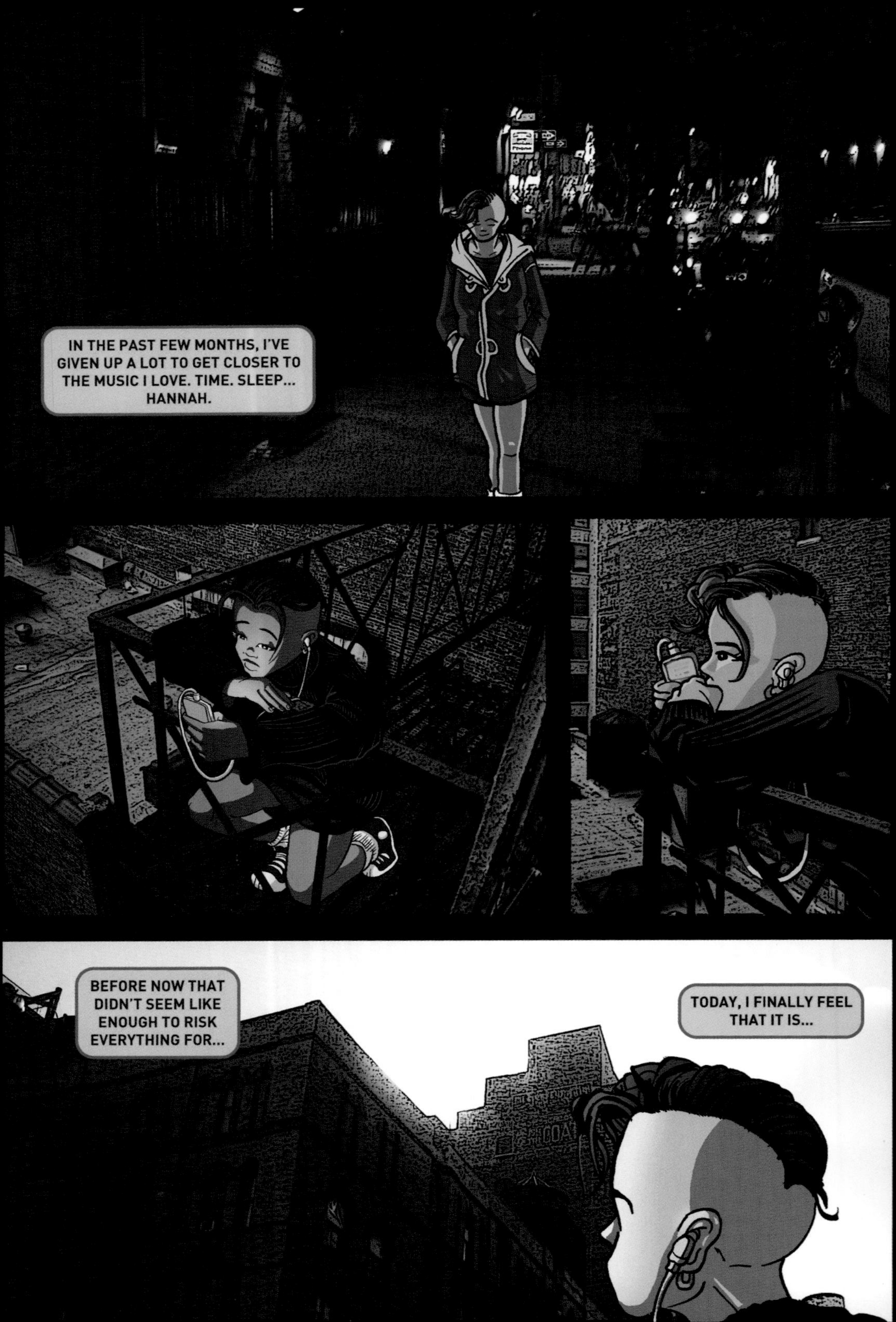
IN THE PAST FEW MONTHS, I'VE GIVEN UP A LOT TO GET CLOSER TO THE MUSIC I LOVE. TIME. SLEEP... HANNAH.
BEFORE NOW THAT DIDN'T SEEM LIKE ENOUGH TO RISK EVERYTHING FOR...
TODAY, I FINALLY FEEL THAT IT IS...

SHOW TIME.

JOHNNY Q IS COVERING MY SHIFT AT THE BROKEN DOOR, AND I'VE GOT A TIGHT 6-HOUR SET FOR THE BOYS AT PLUSH. NOT TOO PREDICTABLE, EDGY ENOUGH TO KEEP THINGS INTERESTING.

FINAL CHECK-OFF FROM ROBIE TO MAKE SURE MY SET IS READY...

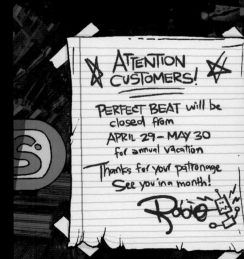

ATTENTION CUSTOMERS!

PERFECT BEAT will be closed from APRIL 29 - MAY 30 for annual vacation

Thanks for your patronage
See you in a month!

Robie

... AND SUDDENLY, I'M WORKING WITHOUT A SAFETY NET.

SON OF A BITCH...

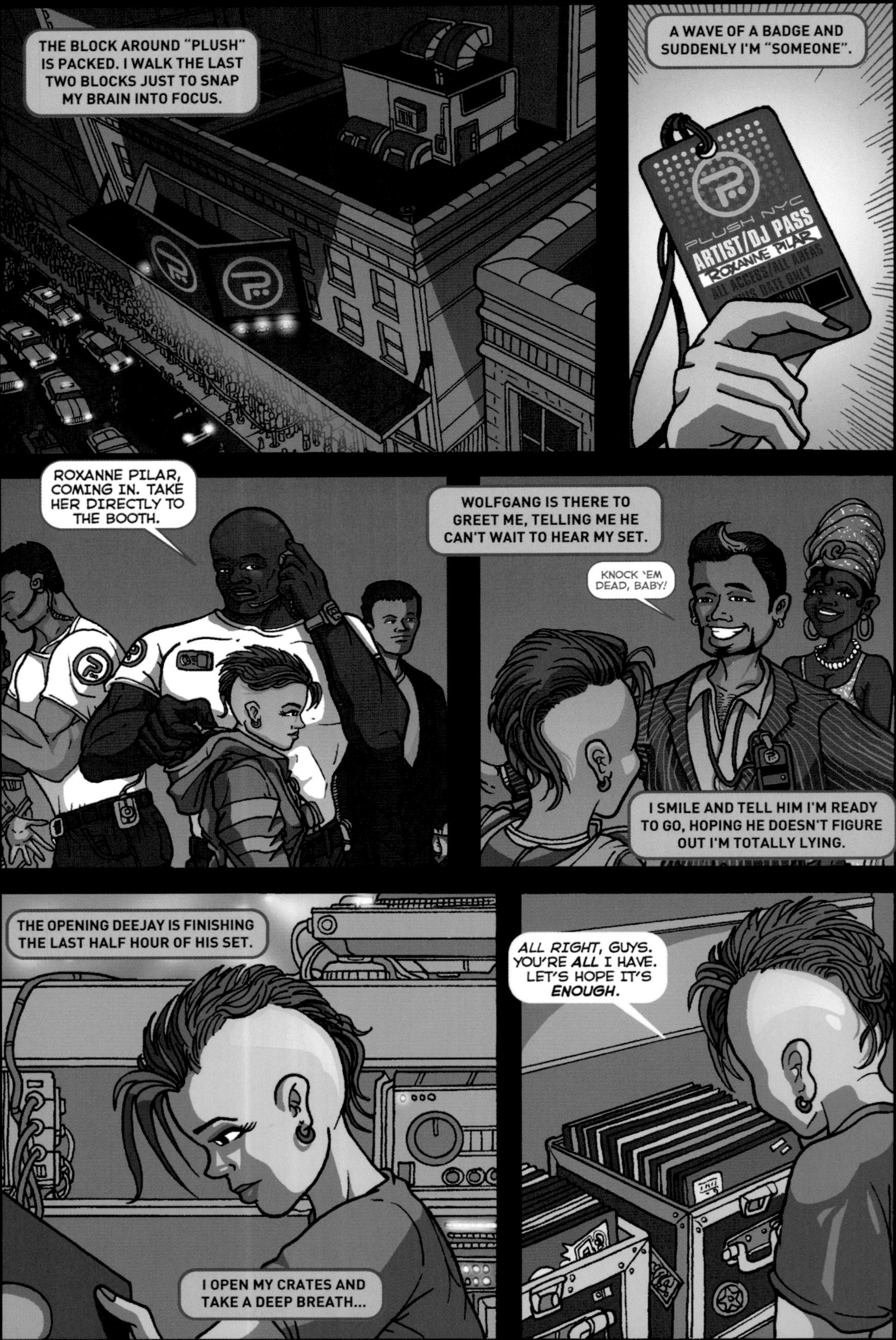
THE BLOCK AROUND "PLUSH" IS PACKED. I WALK THE LAST TWO BLOCKS JUST TO SNAP MY BRAIN INTO FOCUS.
A WAVE OF A BADGE AND SUDDENLY I'M "SOMEONE".
PLUSH NYC
ARTIST/DJ PASS
ROXANNE PILAR
ALL ACCESS/ALL AREAS
ROXANNE PILAR, COMING IN. TAKE HER DIRECTLY TO THE BOOTH.
WOLFGANG IS THERE TO GREET ME, TELLING ME HE CAN'T WAIT TO HEAR MY SET.
KNOCK 'EM DEAD, BABY!
I SMILE AND TELL HIM I'M READY TO GO, HOPING HE DOESN'T FIGURE OUT I'M TOTALLY LYING.
THE OPENING DEEJAY IS FINISHING THE LAST HALF HOUR OF HIS SET.
I OPEN MY CRATES AND TAKE A DEEP BREATH...
ALL RIGHT, GUYS. YOU'RE ALL I HAVE. LET'S HOPE IT'S ENOUGH.

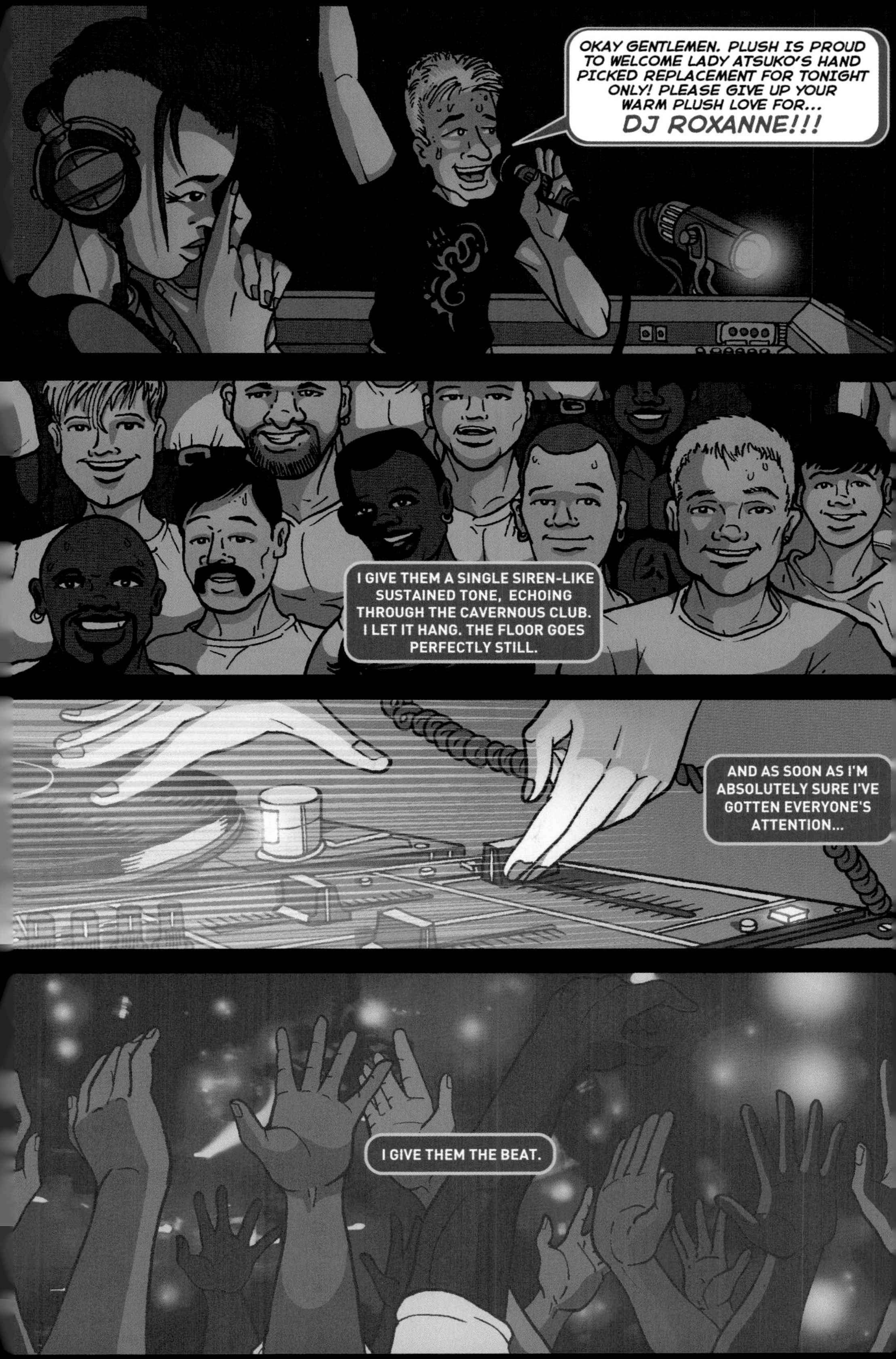
OKAY GENTLEMEN. PLUSH IS PROUD TO WELCOME LADY ATSUKO'S HAND PICKED REPLACEMENT FOR TONIGHT ONLY! PLEASE GIVE UP YOUR WARM PLUSH LOVE FOR... DJ ROXANNE!!!
I GIVE THEM A SINGLE SIREN-LIKE SUSTAINED TONE, ECHOING THROUGH THE CAVERNOUS CLUB. I LET IT HANG. THE FLOOR GOES PERFECTLY STILL.
AND AS SOON AS I'M ABSOLUTELY SURE I'VE GOTTEN EVERYONE'S ATTENTION...
I GIVE THEM THE BEAT.

Röyksopp: "49 Percent (Ewan Pearson Glass Half Full Remix)"

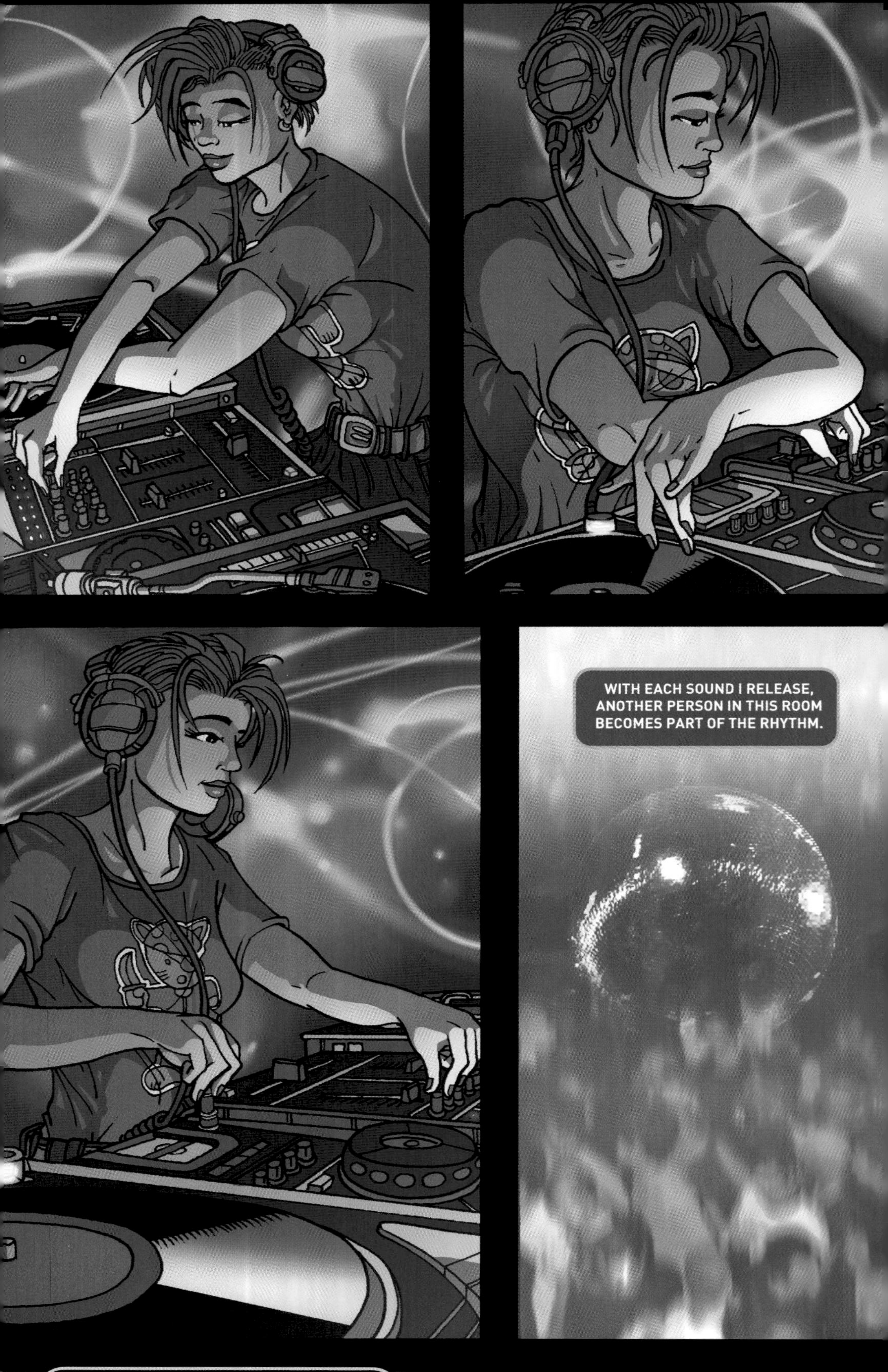
WITH EACH SOUND I RELEASE, ANOTHER PERSON IN THIS ROOM BECOMES PART OF THE RHYTHM.

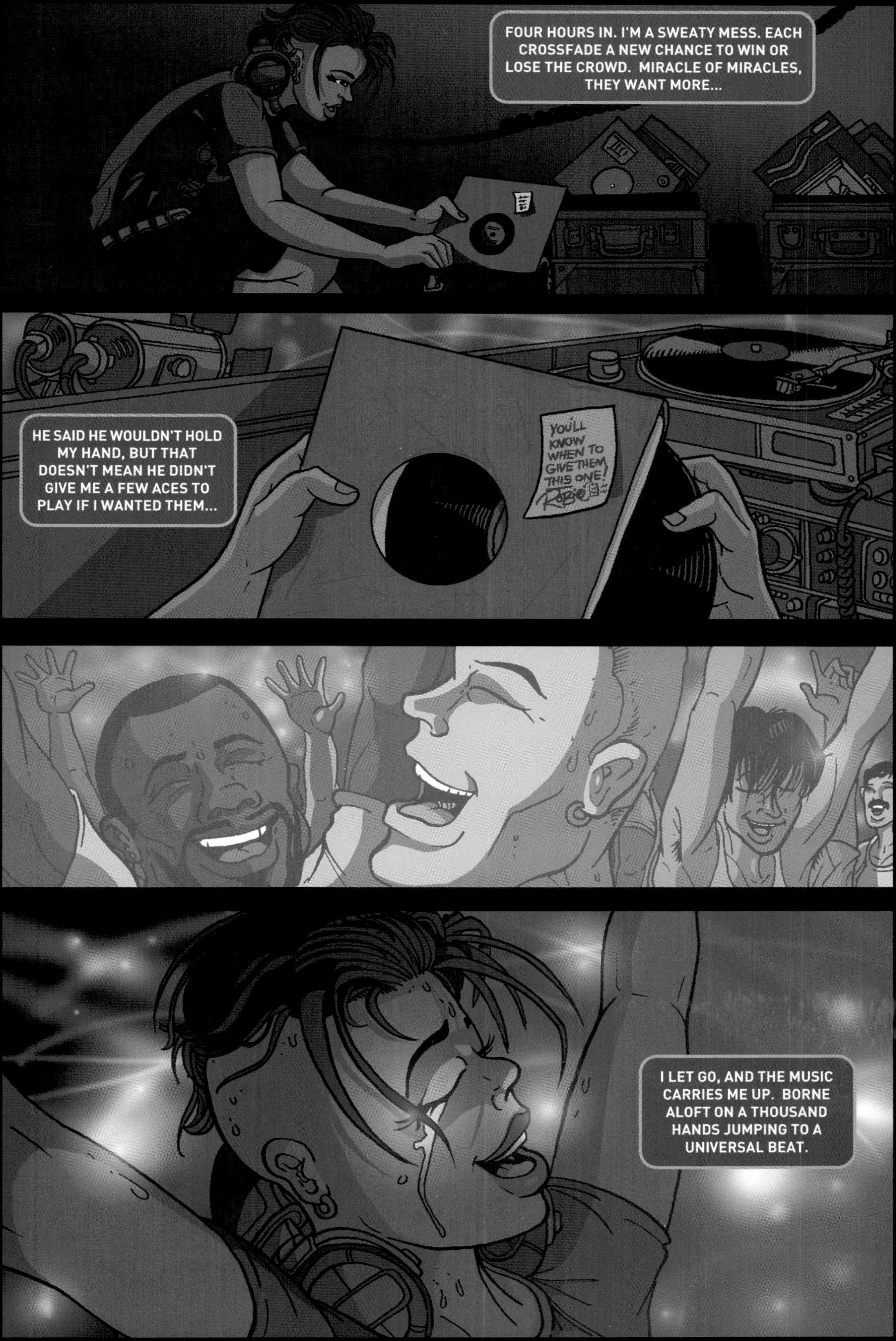
FOUR HOURS IN. I'M A SWEATY MESS. EACH CROSSFADE A NEW CHANCE TO WIN OR LOSE THE CROWD. MIRACLE OF MIRACLES, THEY WANT MORE...
HE SAID HE WOULDN'T HOLD MY HAND, BUT THAT DOESN'T MEAN HE DIDN'T GIVE ME A FEW ACES TO PLAY IF I WANTED THEM...
YOU'LL KNOW WHEN TO GIVE THEM THIS ONE!
I LET GO, AND THE MUSIC CARRIES ME UP. BORNE ALOFT ON A THOUSAND HANDS JUMPING TO A UNIVERSAL BEAT.

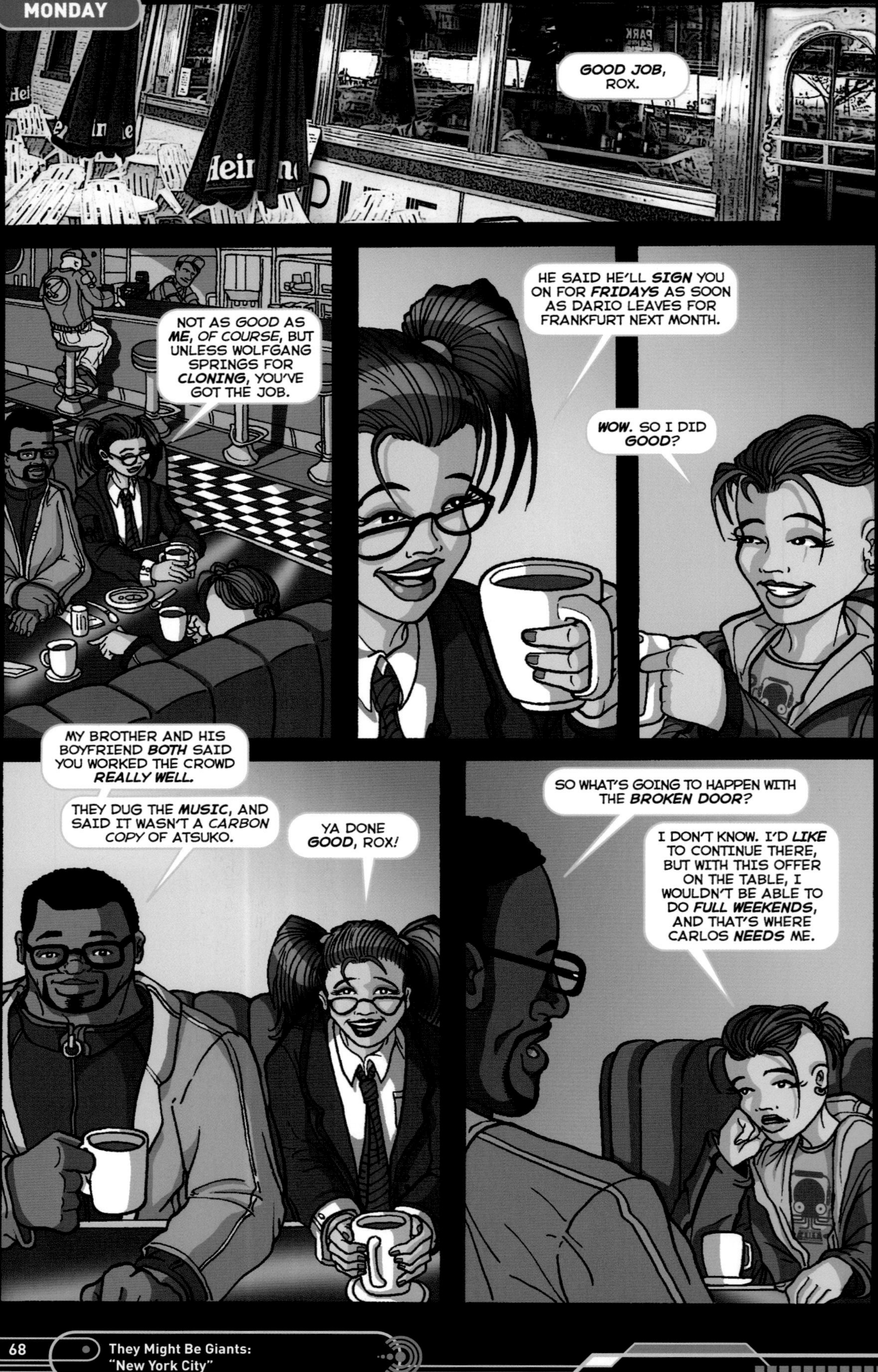
GOOD JOB, ROX.
NOT AS GOOD AS ME, OF COURSE, BUT UNLESS WOLFGANG SPRINGS FOR CLONING, YOU'VE GOT THE JOB.
HE SAID HE'LL SIGN YOU ON FOR FRIDAYS AS SOON AS DARIO LEAVES FOR FRANKFURT NEXT MONTH.
WOW. SO I DID GOOD?
MY BROTHER AND HIS BOYFRIEND BOTH SAID YOU WORKED THE CROWD REALLY WELL.
THEY DUG THE MUSIC, AND SAID IT WASN'T A CARBON COPY OF ATSUKO.
YA DONE GOOD, ROX!
SO WHAT'S GOING TO HAPPEN WITH THE BROKEN DOOR?
I DON'T KNOW. I'D LIKE TO CONTINUE THERE, BUT WITH THIS OFFER ON THE TABLE, I WOULDN'T BE ABLE TO DO FULL WEEKENDS, AND THAT'S WHERE CARLOS NEEDS ME.

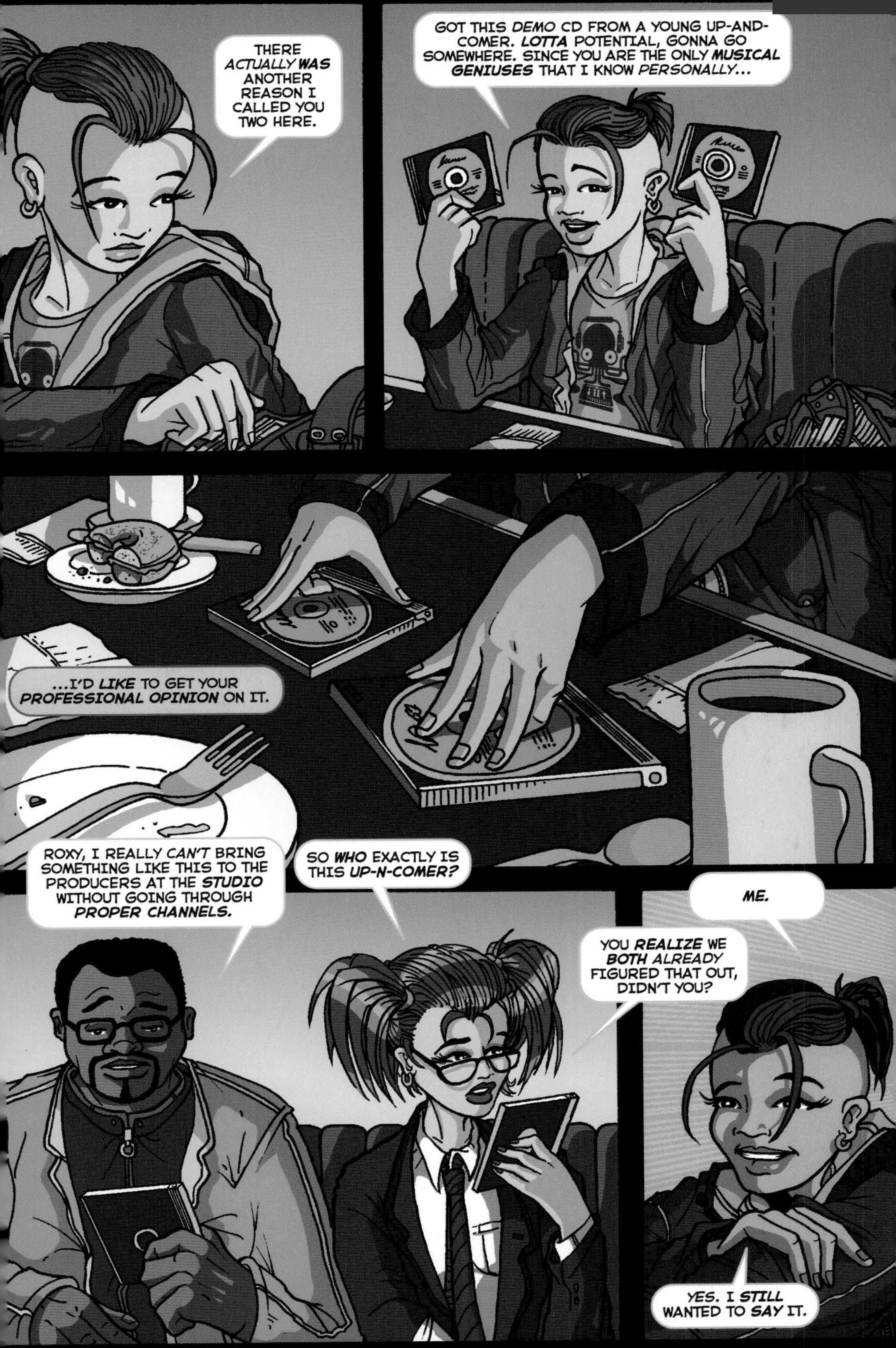
THERE ACTUALLY WAS ANOTHER REASON I CALLED YOU TWO HERE.
GOT THIS DEMO CD FROM A YOUNG UP-AND-COMER. LOTTA POTENTIAL, GONNA GO SOMEWHERE. SINCE YOU ARE THE ONLY MUSICAL GENIUSES THAT I KNOW PERSONALLY...
...I'D LIKE TO GET YOUR PROFESSIONAL OPINION ON IT.
ROXY, I REALLY CAN'T BRING SOMETHING LIKE THIS TO THE PRODUCERS AT THE STUDIO WITHOUT GOING THROUGH PROPER CHANNELS.
SO WHO EXACTLY IS THIS UP-N-COMER?
ME.
YOU REALIZE WE BOTH ALREADY FIGURED THAT OUT, DIDN'T YOU?
YES. I STILL WANTED TO SAY IT.

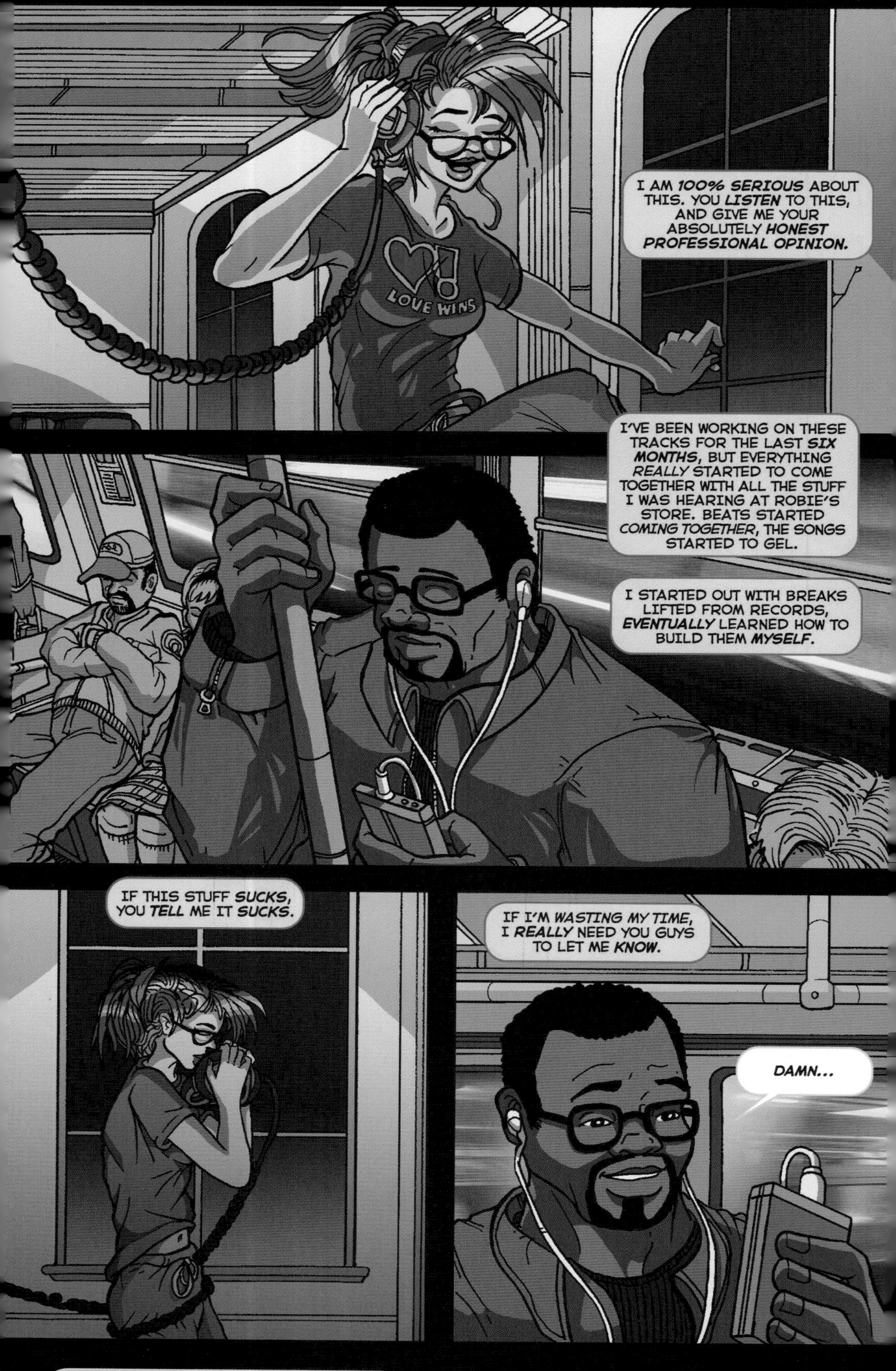
I AM 100% SERIOUS ABOUT THIS. YOU LISTEN TO THIS, AND GIVE ME YOUR ABSOLUTELY HONEST PROFESSIONAL OPINION.
LOVE WINS
I'VE BEEN WORKING ON THESE TRACKS FOR THE LAST SIX MONTHS, BUT EVERYTHING REALLY STARTED TO COME TOGETHER WITH ALL THE STUFF I WAS HEARING AT ROBIE'S STORE. BEATS STARTED COMING TOGETHER, THE SONGS STARTED TO GEL.
I STARTED OUT WITH BREAKS LIFTED FROM RECORDS, EVENTUALLY LEARNED HOW TO BUILD THEM MYSELF.
IF THIS STUFF SUCKS, YOU TELL ME IT SUCKS.
IF I'M WASTING MY TIME, I REALLY NEED YOU GUYS TO LET ME KNOW.
DAMN...

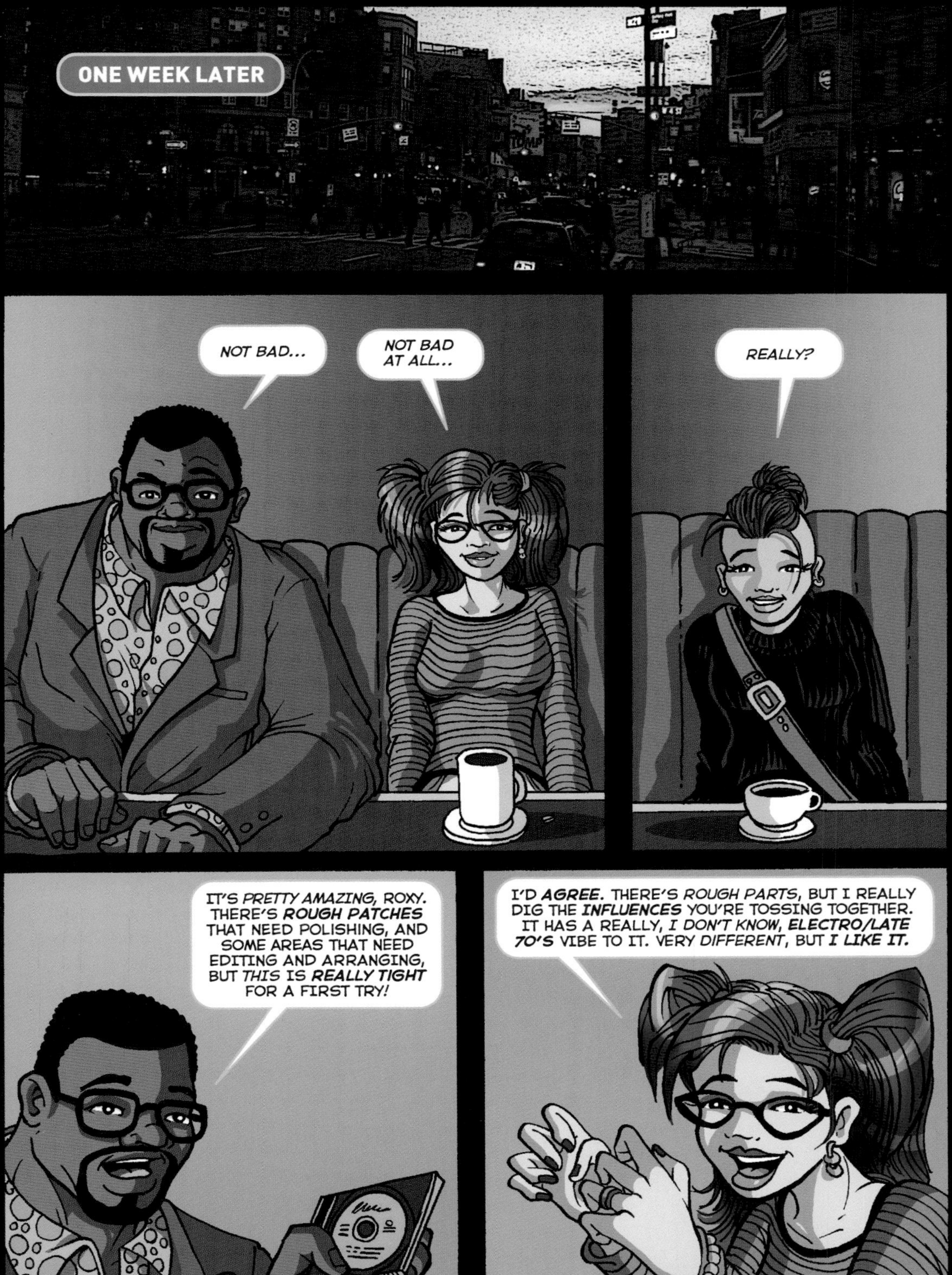
ONE WEEK LATER
NOT BAD...
NOT BAD AT ALL...
REALLY?
IT'S PRETTY AMAZING, ROXY. THERE'S ROUGH PATCHES THAT NEED POLISHING, AND SOME AREAS THAT NEED EDITING AND ARRANGING, BUT THIS IS REALLY TIGHT FOR A FIRST TRY!
I'D AGREE. THERE'S ROUGH PARTS, BUT I REALLY DIG THE INFLUENCES YOU'RE TOSSING TOGETHER. IT HAS A REALLY, I DON'T KNOW, ELECTRO/LATE 70'S VIBE TO IT. VERY DIFFERENT, BUT I LIKE IT.

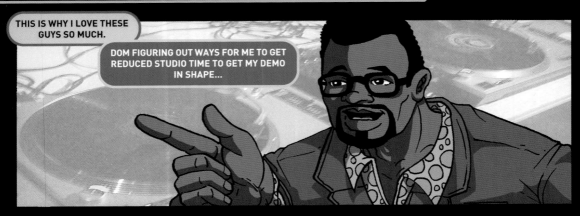

THIS IS WHY I LOVE THESE GUYS SO MUCH.

DOM FIGURING OUT WAYS FOR ME TO GET REDUCED STUDIO TIME TO GET MY DEMO IN SHAPE...

...WHILE ATSUKO FIGURES OUT HOW I CAN GET MORE BOOTH TIME WHILE SHE'S ON TOUR.

IN A WAY, THEY REPRESENT TWO OF THE POSSIBLE PATHS TO FOLLOW IN MY JOURNEY.

CREATIVITY OR CASHFLOW? ART OR COMMERCE? PURPOSE OR POPULARITY? EACH OPTION HAS A STRONG ARGUMENT. NOW I'M THROWING A THIRD, MORE UNCERTAIN PATH INTO THE MIX.

MAYBE MY MISTAKE HAS BEEN LOOKING AT THE DIFFERENCES IN THESE PATHS. I SHOULD LOOK AT WHAT THEIR COMMON GROUND IS...

DOMINIC FOLLOWS HIS ART, IMMERSING HIMSELF IN THE OUTER EDGES OF ELECTRONIC MUSIC. NEVER EXPECTING TO MAKE A DIME, YET EARNING THE UNQUESTIONED RESPECT OF HIS PEERS.

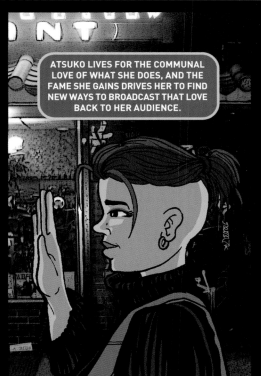

ATSUKO LIVES FOR THE COMMUNAL LOVE OF WHAT SHE DOES, AND THE FAME SHE GAINS DRIVES HER TO FIND NEW WAYS TO BROADCAST THAT LOVE BACK TO HER AUDIENCE.

ROBIE HAS GIVEN ME THE GIFT OF HISTORY, THE THRILL OF KNOWING YOUR ROOTS AND LEARNING HOW TO USE WHAT'S COME BEFORE TO DISCOVER WHAT CAN FOLLOW.

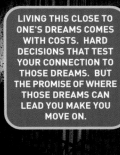

LIVING THIS CLOSE TO ONE'S DREAMS COMES WITH COSTS. HARD DECISIONS THAT TEST YOUR CONNECTION TO THOSE DREAMS. BUT THE PROMISE OF WHERE THOSE DREAMS CAN LEAD YOU MAKE YOU MOVE ON.

EVEN IF IT MEANS YOU TRAVEL SOLO FOR A WHILE...

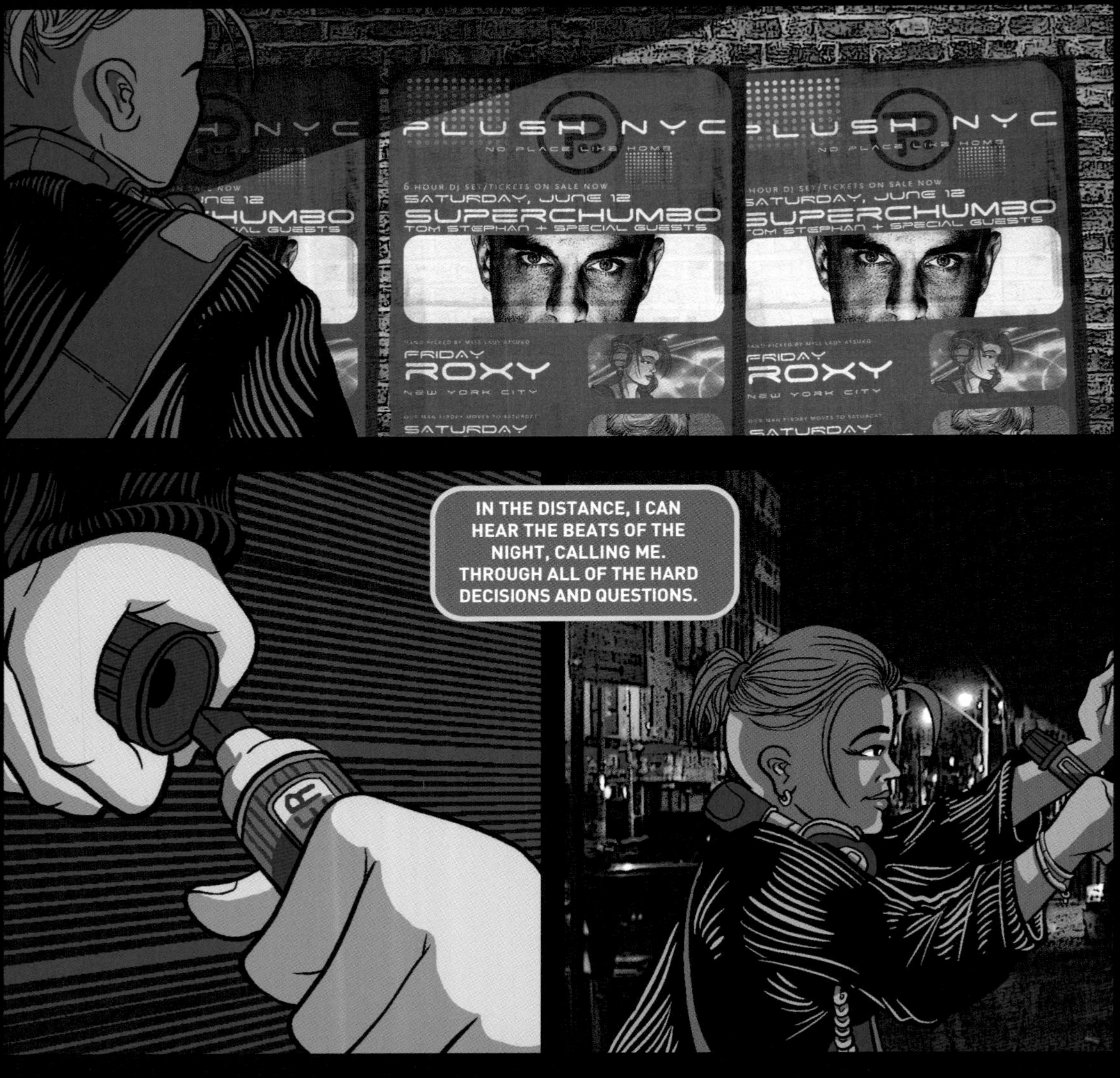
PLUSH NYC
NO PLACE LIKE HOME
6 HOUR DJ SET/TICKETS ON SALE NOW
SATURDAY, JUNE 12
SUPERCHUMBO
TOM STEPHAN + SPECIAL GUESTS
FRIDAY
ROXY
NEW YORK CITY
SATURDAY
IN THE DISTANCE, I CAN HEAR THE BEATS OF THE NIGHT, CALLING ME. THROUGH ALL OF THE HARD DECISIONS AND QUESTIONS.
I ♥ Music
Roxy
DARO
WWW.PLUSH-NYC.COM
I MAKE THE CHOICE TO FOLLOW THOSE BEATS.

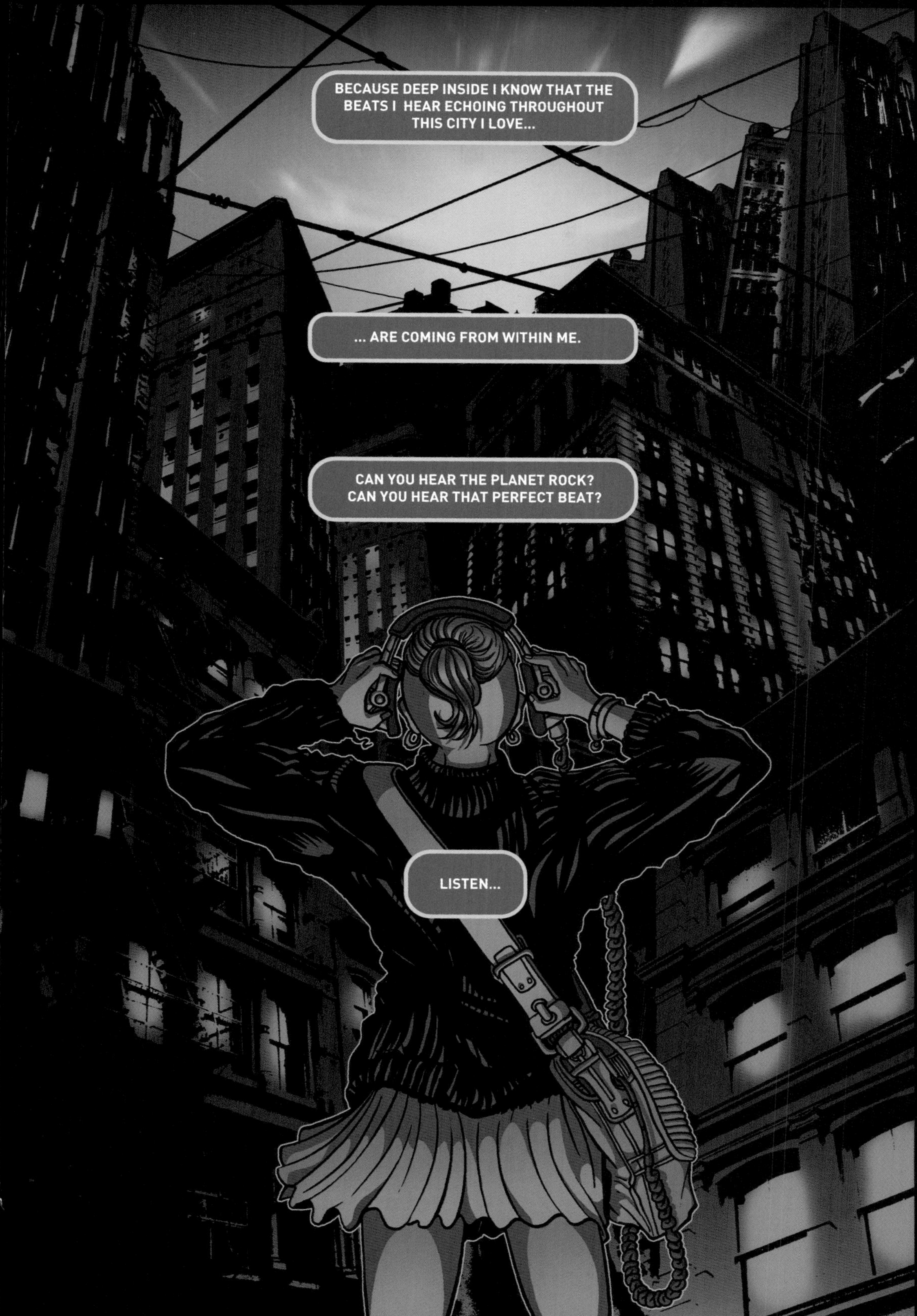
BECAUSE DEEP INSIDE I KNOW THAT THE BEATS I HEAR ECHOING THROUGHOUT THIS CITY I LOVE...
... ARE COMING FROM WITHIN ME.
CAN YOU HEAR THE PLANET ROCK? CAN YOU HEAR THAT PERFECT BEAT?
LISTEN...

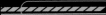

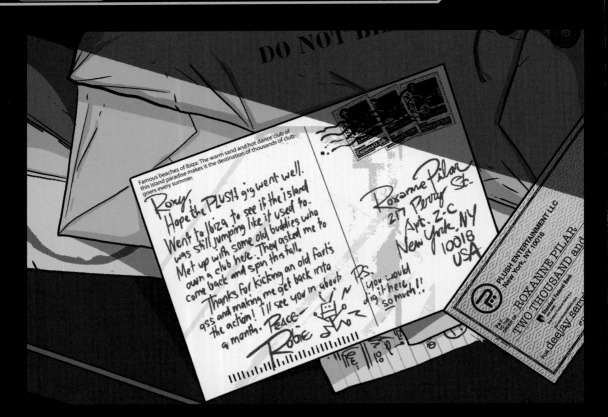

Famous beaches of Ibiza: The warm sand and hot dance club of this island paradise makes it the destination of thousands of club-goers every summer.
Roxy,
Hope the PLUSH gig went well.
Went to Ibiza to see if the island was still jumping like it used to. Met up with some old buddies who own a club here. They asked me to come back and spin this fall.
Thanks for kicking an old fart's ass and making me get back into the action! I'll see you in about a month. Peace-
Robie
P.S. You would dig it here so much!!
Roxanne Pilar
217 Perry St.
Apt. 2-C
New York, NY
10018
USA
España 0,58
PLUSH ENTERTAINMENT LLC
New York, NY 10016
PAY TO THE ORDER OF ROXANNE PILAR
Standard Federal Bank

For all those who stood up and were counted
For all those for whom money was no motive
For all those for whom music was a message
I want to thank you
For making me
A little more sure
A little more wise
And courageous

You told me to look much further
You told me to want much more
You told me that music matters
And to chase the dogs back from my door

I won't stop here
I won't be still until the sun sets
On us all...

Excerpt from "Music Matters" *by* Faithless

LINER NOTES & BAND PHOTOS

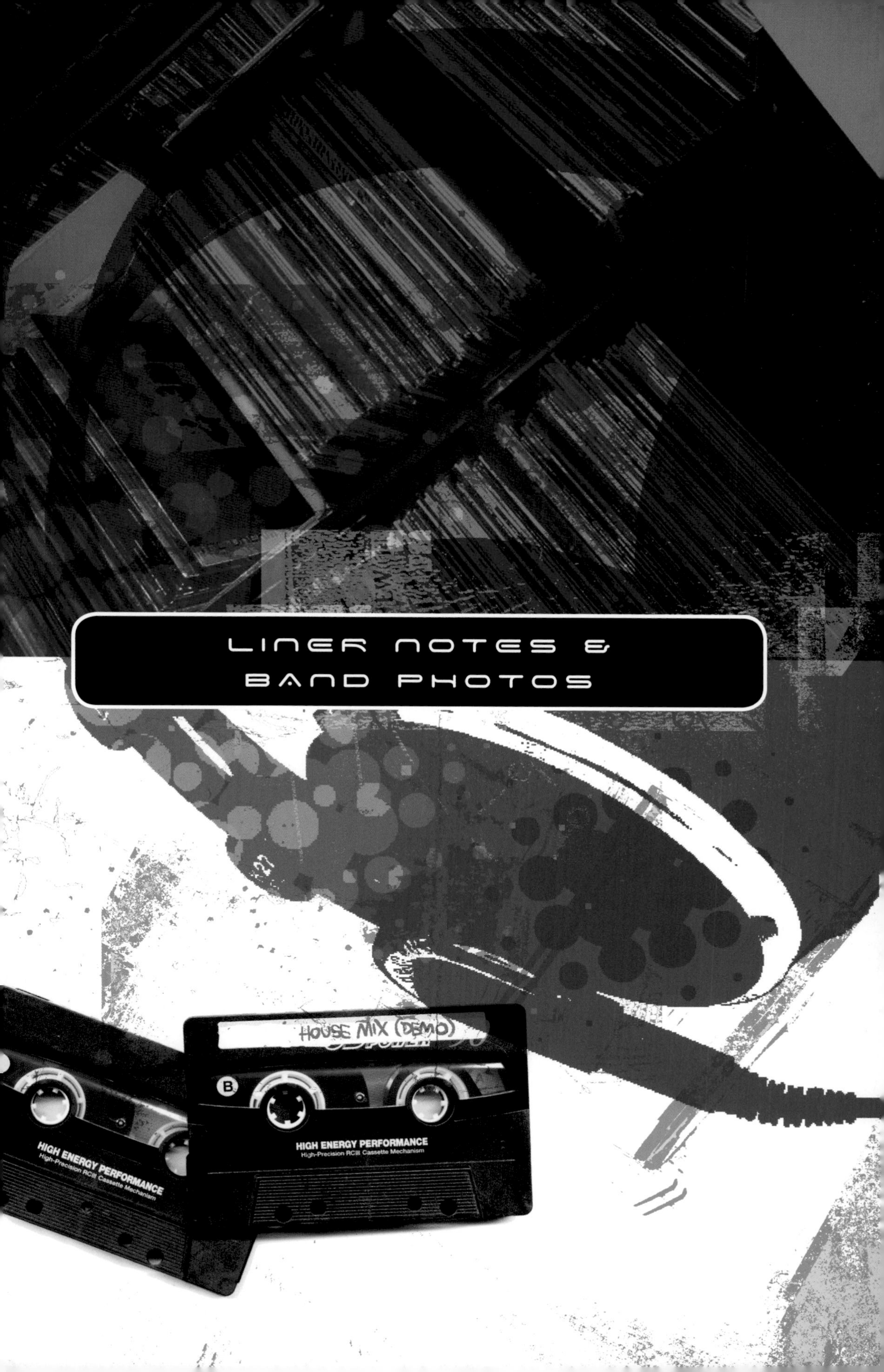
HOUSE MIX (DEMO)
B
HIGH ENERGY PERFORMANCE
High-Precision RCIII Cassette Mechanism
HIGH ENERGY PERFORMANCE
High-Precision RCIII Cassette Mechanism

With all the junk that I crammed into these pages, I thought it might be helpful to go through and point out some details that may not be apparent, but (hopefully) contribute to the story, conceptually and artistically.

PAGE 4
Amazing what you can capture with a really crappy old digital camera and a moving hand... Times Square.

PAGE 6
PLUSH, the fictional club at which Atsuko is the resident DJ, is modeled after the famous New York dance club "The Roxy NYC". A converted roller-rink/roller disco, it was THE gay dance club in the famous Chelsea district of New York City, and was host to some of the best DJs on Earth, including Junior Vasquez, Victor Calderone and Peter Rauhofer. Artists like Madonna would drop in to the club to debut new dance tracks for the eager clubbers. Every Saturday night was "Roxy Saturdays", where the dancefloor was a sea of shirtless gay men jumping to the beat and dancing all night long. The Roxy closed its doors for good in March of 2007 to be demolished for apartment buildings, the end of a true legend in the international dance world.

PAGE 7
Roxy and Atsuko are enjoying breakfast at the Empire Diner, a classic diner car style restaurant and favorite 24-hour stop for hungry (or drunk, or both) clubbers.

PAGE 8
To keep the environment of this story "realistic" for me, I had to mentally and photographically assign real addresses for all the locations. Roxy's apartment is located somewhere on Perry Street in Greenwich Village.

PAGE 10
Introduction of Dominic, who works by day as a recording engineer for a Manhattan recording studio. I can only imagine what it must be like to work on making sure the latest talentless pop-star's single sounds just right for 3 days straight. It pays the bills, I'm sure, but it would also drive me to seek out the good in music on my off hours.

PAGE 12
In keeping with my geographic positioning of the locations in the book, our first view of the Broken Door, the dance club that Roxy has been working at for the past few months, located in the lower East Village.

PAGE 13
Our first meeting with Philippe Robicheau, a.k.a. Robie. Robie's name is an homage to keyboard player and producer John Robie, who worked closely with producer Arthur Baker on the creation of such classic songs as "Planet Rock" by Afrika Bambaataa and "Confusion" by New Order. Robie was also a much sought-after remixer, whose staccato stutter editing was ground-breaking and defined a "New York electro" dance sound for electronic club music. He remixed songs by many artists on the New York based Tommy Boy label, as well as records by New Order, Cabaret Voltaire, Chaka Khan and others.

PAGE 17
Our first view of Perfect Beat Records (named after the Afrika Bambaataa song "Looking for the Perfect Beat"). This is the most specific "real world" reference to an actual place in the book; this is based on Rebel Rebel, an incredible music store in Greenwich Village that I visit every time I'm in the city. I have never been able to stump the owner when asking for a song or album. No matter what I ask for, as if by magic, he's been able to reach somewhere in the store and produce the LP or CD. It's amazing. This kind of a store is a dream come true for a record hunter, brimming with new releases and oldies, cut-outs and deleted singles, vinyl and CD. For an out-of-towner, it's also a chance to scour the best used CDs traded in or tossed out by the cream of the crop, kind of like going to garage sales in the richer neighborhoods; they toss out the best stuff.
I approached the owner and told them I was working on this book, asking if I could take pictures in the store for photo-reference. They let me have the run of the store and allowed me to shoot from behind the counters and from anywhere I needed a shot. It was perfect, and gave me a real place to put into my story.
Rebel Rebel, 319 Bleeker Street, New York City, NY, 10014 (212) 989-0770

PAGE 18
All of my beta readers wanted to know what record Robie gave to Roxy. I decided to leave that a mystery, as every DJ will have an idea of the set-saving single they would have in their crate. I have one in my head, and it will remain there.

PAGE 19
All of the clubs that are listed on Robie's profiles are real clubs around the world, and to the best of my ability, I've placed him in residency at those clubs while they were active. Part of the reality of most clubs is that they open and close as the years progress, either due to ownership changes, financial reasons or, in some cases, for legal and crime/drug-related problems.

PAGE 21
This story is a real life story that happened to a good friend of mine named Mia, who had this happen to her at a comic convention. Mia is a tall, leggy anime otaku girl and when this scumbag tried his ass-grab with her, she spun and embarrassed him in front of hundreds of convention goers; it was truly awesome. You can check out Mia's artwork on her Deviant Art site: http://rocketshoes.deviantart.com, and check out her killer pin-up in the gallery section!

PAGES 23-25
This section is taken from personal experience. The WORST deejaying for a wedding that I've ever been witness to was at a deejay's wedding, and it blew my mind how bad and predictable it was. For a while, I thought it was some kind of inside joke, one DJ friend playing for another DJ all the horrible stuff they were forced to play at most weddings; no such luck, it was all on purpose. I would like to say that there's nothing really wrong with any of the songs that I mention in this section, other than the fact that they get used in really predictable and boring ways at most weddings. Trust me, hearing "Oh Yeah" by Yello (one of my favorite groups of all time) played for the garter toss is a like a knife twisting in my side.
I deejayed my own wedding (thank you iTunes and iPod) and when I've done other friend's weddings, the list of what not to play is usually longer than the actual requested songs. A few years ago I was at a wedding where I amazed my table with pulling Roxy's stunt of naming all the songs that were going to be played before the DJ played them (I was much more courteous than Roxy) and it was in that moment that Wedding DJ Bingo was born. You can download your own set of Wedding DJ Bingo cards here: www.paulsizer.com/bpm/weddingdjbingo.htm

PAGE 26
To maintain a slight obscuring of reality in the story, I made up new names for a lot of the locations I used as photo-references and designed logos for each place. The "Dancing Egg Café" is where Roxy and Dominic discuss Robie's DJ career over lunch.

PAGE 27
The story of Robie's decadent behavior in the DJ booth is a compilation of truth, rumors and urban legends about famous DJs doing drugs and having sexual favors bestowed upon them during sets. While these are not improbable, they are such a mix of legend and popular rumor that it's hard to verify what's truth and what's industry gossip that fuels the mystique of certain individual's egos. I wanted to show these aspects of the profession not to glorify or endorse them, but to show all the distractions that exist in this and many other industries with the onset of fame and insane amounts of money. Drugs and sex are absolutely present in the club DJ world; it would be incredibly naïve to believe otherwise. My research and reading also found an equal number of DJ's who work to steer clear of these things and focus on their music.

PAGE 31
Notice that one of the posters in the entryway to The Broken Door is showing a guest DJ show featuring DJ Hamper Smell. "Hamper smell" is one of my favorite 8 year old level names to slam someone with.

PAGE 32
Roxy is holding one of my favorite records; "C'mon Every Beatbox" by Big Audio Dynamite, a group formed by ex-Clash guitarist Mick Jones and music writer/DJ Don Letts.

PAGE 36-37
Knowing when to shut up and let the images do the talking. I am finally learning THAT lesson, thank God...

PAGE 38-39
The dense, cluttered magic that is Rebel Rebel. Yes, it really is that packed full of stuff. It is awesome.

PAGE 47

Nerdy details: I'm sitting at the table next to Roxy and Colin in panel 3, working on the page layouts for "B.P.M." Roxy's cell phone background screen is Faye hugging Ein the data corgi from *Cowboy Bebop*.

PAGE 51

Roxy has a poster of *It's All Gone Pete Tong*, one of my favorite films about DJs and the club scene, and one of the films that got me thinking of doing B.P.M as a graphic novel and ways to talk about music in visual terms.

PAGE 52

Atsuko mentions signing up for touring with Peter Rauhofer, a very popular DJ and in-demand remixer, and a resident at the real Roxy NYC dance club during the late 90's/early 2000's. His remixes for Cher, Madonna, Britney Spears, the Pet Shop Boys, Christine Aguilera and dozens of other artists have assured his place in dance music history.

PAGE 53

Roxy is making her (attempted) reconciliation call from the north end of Washington Square Park, near where Meg Ryan dropped off Billy Crystal at the beginning of the film *When Harry Met Sally*. The best part of this photo shoot was knowing people were wondering why the hell I was taking pictures of empty park benches. I certainly was not the first time I've looked like an idiot in public, and it won't be the last, I'm sure.

PAGE 58

The band Roxy is watching is Dunuya Drum and Dance, a real life African/Cuban/Brazilian drum troupe from Kalamazoo, Michigan who are truly a wonder to see play live. Led by the amazing Carolyn Koebel (herself a percussive force of nature), this group was another point of reference for me to start examining how music can cross boundaries like no other medium and bring together incredibly diverse groups of people. And any group that can get me to dance for 4 hours straight is worth noting.
You can check out their music and schedule on their MySpace page: www.myspace.com/dunuyadrumanddance

PAGE 60, PANEL 3

Well, well, well, look who's on line to get into the Capsule Club. It's Jemaine and Bret of "Flight of the Conchords", along with their uber-fan Mel. If you love music and comedy, HBO's "Flight of the Conchords" is a near perfect synthesis of the two. Their skewering of popular music culture and their spot-on assimilation of styles into their own music made this show one of my all-time favorites. Check it out.

PAGE 63

I am assuming Robie has flown off to Ibiza for a rest in the sun. Ibiza is THE place for DJ culture and the European island of choice for club kids on vacation, home to Manumission, the largest club on the planet.

PAGE 64

I really had a blast designing the different logo systems for the various clubs and stores in this book. PLUSH was probably my favorite, and I wanted to make sure that it looked like they had their identity together with matching signage, passes and promotional posters.

PAGE 65

Roxy's intro to her set draws inspiration from a great set I was witness to a few years back. DJs Sasha and John Digweed were doing a guest set at the mega-club Twilo in New York City, and they opened their set with one long, sustained chord, shifting up and down a note, for nearly 15 minutes. It sounds like it would be grating, but in truth, it drove the crowd crazy in anticipation. Each chord change would elicit screams of excitement, anticipating that to be the introduction of the rhythm. When the beat finally did drop, the place exploded and stayed that way until 6 a.m. the next morning. Brilliant.

PAGE 67

Again, I wanted to keep the "set-saving" record ambiguous, for everyone to insert their own track that pushes the night into over-drive.

GLOSSARY

PAGE 74
Again, I wanted to show PLUSH as having their identity thing solid, so I designed this poster for an upcoming show featuring superstar DJ/remixer Superchumbo coming to PLUSH. You'll also notice the poster shows Roxy as a guest DJ, along with Dario (Atsuko's second-in-command) whose leaving opens up the spot for Roxy to spin at PLUSH.

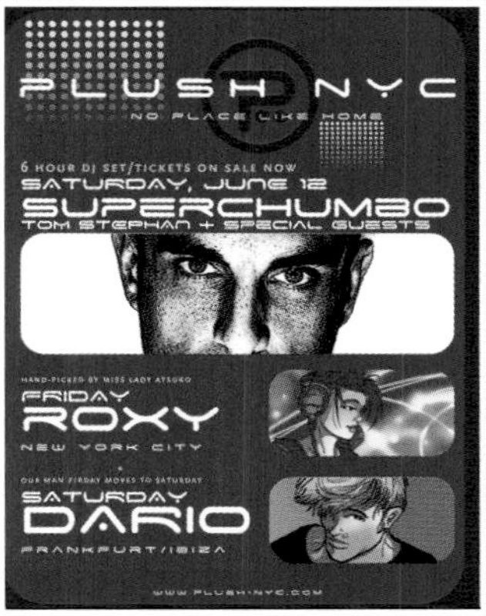
PLUSH NYC
NO PLACE LIKE HOME
6 HOUR DJ SET/TICKETS ON SALE NOW
SATURDAY, JUNE 12
SUPERCHUMBO
TOM STEPHAN + SPECIAL GUESTS
HAND-PICKED BY MISS LADY ATSUKO
FRIDAY
ROXY
NEW YORK CITY
OUR MAN FRIDAY MOVES TO SATURDAY
SATURDAY
DARIO
FRANKFURT/IBIZA
WWW.PLUSHNYC.COM

PAGE 75
After using this image for promotional pieces, I finally noticed that all the lit windows looked like VU meters on a mixing board, so I made them look more like that in this final version of the page.

A (VERY) BRIEF GLOSSARY OF MUSICAL GENRES AND TERMS REFERENCED IN "B.P.M."

Although genre labelling is incredibly subjective, these are some basic terms that may help to understand the various dominant styles of electronic/dance music out there today.

AMBIENT/CHILLOUT Environmental electronic music, usually without traditional song structures, using synthesizers, acoustic instruments and natural sound samples to make long, soothing/psychedelic soundscapes.

BEATMIXING The speeding up or slowing down of two records to make them play at the same tempo. DJs beatmix to blend different songs together to make a continuous flow of music in dance clubs.

BREAKBEAT Mostly instrumental drum-driven electronic music with heavily edited hip-hop/70's funk influenced rhythms and propulsive electronic basslines.

DISCO Mid to late 70's dance music, a mix of black R&B styles with lush, orchestral elements and funk inspired rhythms. As synthesizers and drum machines became more common, disco incorporated them as well.

DRUM AND BASS Originally termed "jungle", drum and bass refers to the UK music style which fuses speedy breakbeats with various instrumental styles, including ambient soundscapes, rap/hip-hop and vocal samples.

ELECTRO/ELECTRO-FUNK Style from the early 80's that married the funk/hip-hop styles of the New York music scene with mechanical European synthesizer music to create a hybrid that continues to influence dance music around the world.

HOUSE Originated in the mid-80's, house music was named from the updated disco and R&B records being played at the Warehouse, a popular Chicago dance club. Emulates "disco diva" style dance music.

INDUSTRIAL Electronic music (mostly dance-oriented) that incorporates metallic sounds, distorted samples and (sometimes) heavy metal musical elements to produce a hard, rhythmic aggressive musical style.

MICRO-HOUSE/INDIETRONIC Very minimal electronic music, made with older analog synthesizer sounds and sparse, filtered, funky beats, updated emulation of 80's electronic music with more current technology.

SYNTHPOP/TECHNOPOP Blanket term for early to mid 80's music made with newly affordable synthesizers, samplers and drum machines of the times. Used "pop" music song structures and lyrical forms.

TECHNO Predominantly instrumental electronic music that originated in Detroit, and spread around the world from there. "Techno" tends to be a blanket term for most dance-oriented electronic music.

TRANCE/PROGRESSIVE Lush, orchestral/symphonic techno dance music, sometimes with soaring vocals, geared for continuous beat-mixed club play. Dominant musical style in most international dance clubs.

ROXY (ROXANNE PILAR)

In my character designs, Roxy was always a small girl with some kind of cool hair; as you can see, she went through the gamut of hairstyles, from shaved to buzz-cut to Mohawk to faux-hawk to almost... normal? I was also working out how pierced and tattooed I wanted her to be. I worked hard to put Roxy through the paces visually, trying out a ton of different coloring and photo-compositing ideas to see what worked and what didn't. For some reason, the black oversized sweater was always a constant in my designs.

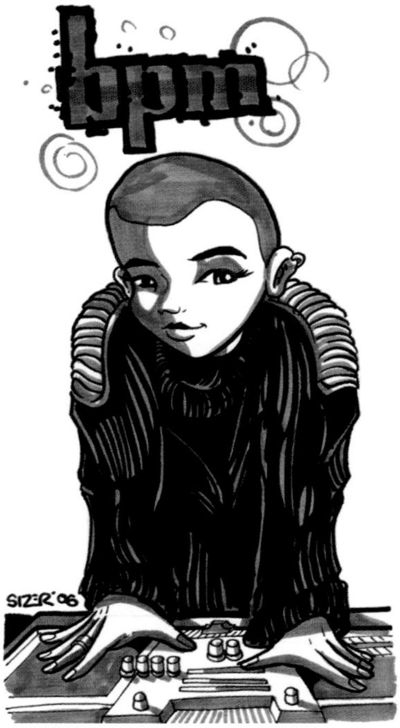
bpm
SIZER '06

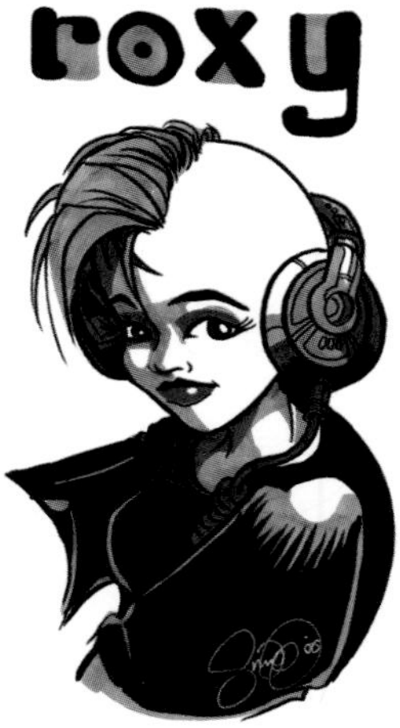
roxy

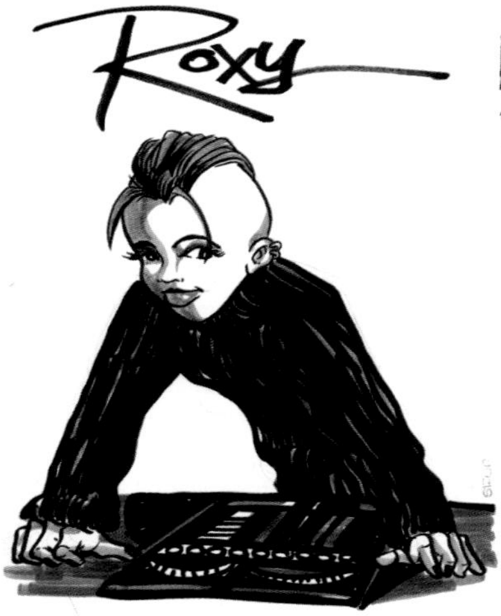
Roxy

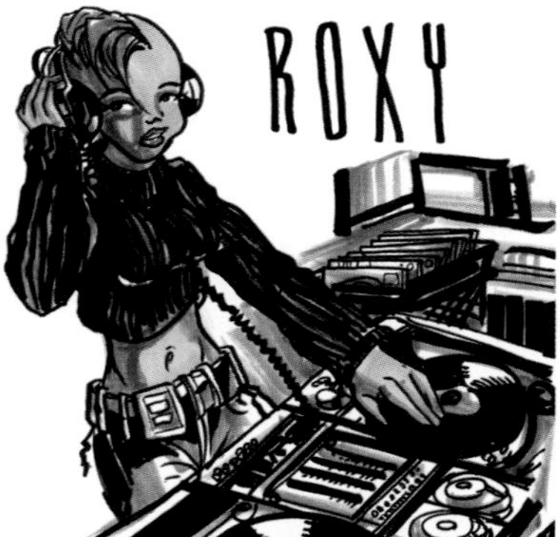
ROXY

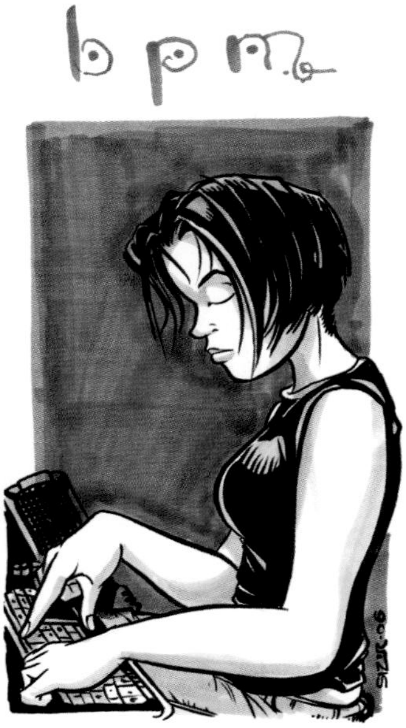
bpm

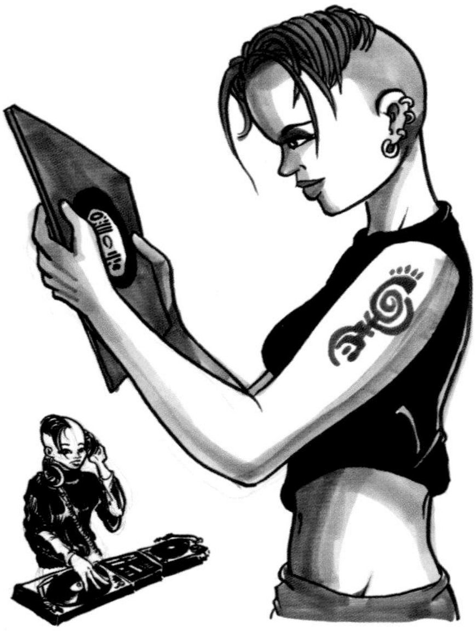

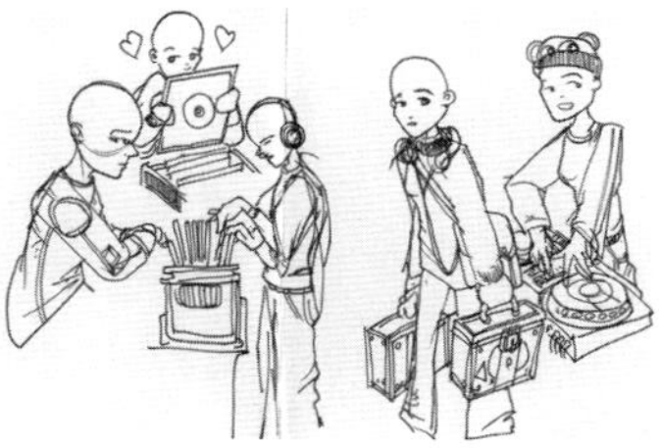

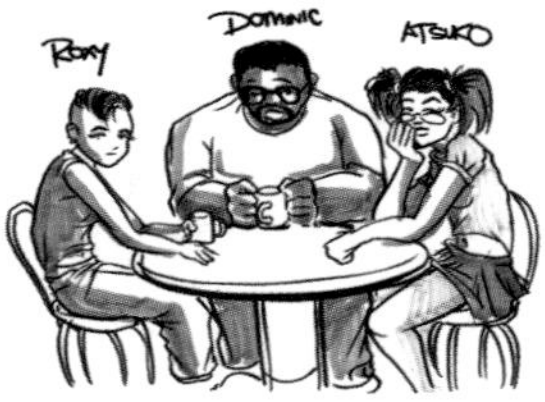
Roxy
Dominic
Atsuko

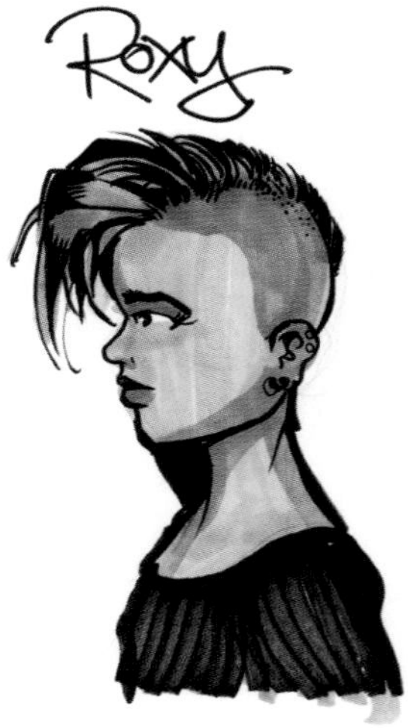
Roxy

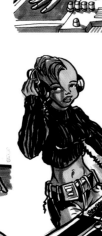

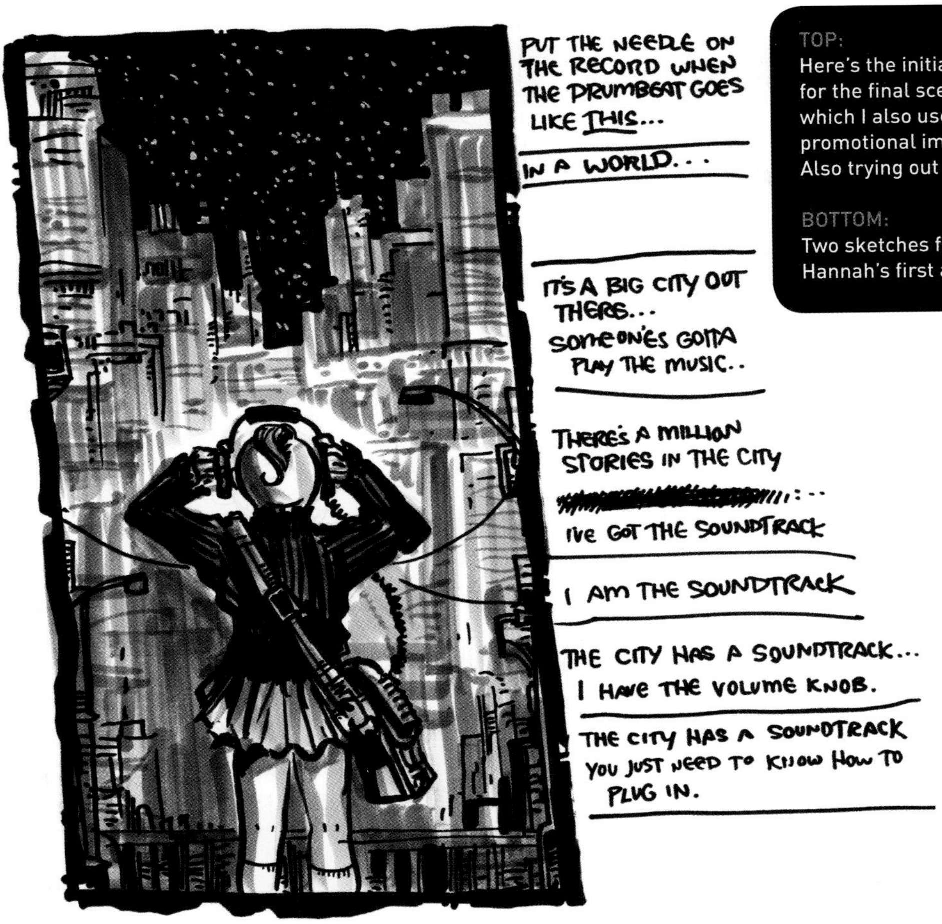
PUT THE NEEDLE ON
THE RECORD WHEN
THE DRUMBEAT GOES
LIKE THIS...
IN A WORLD...
IT'S A BIG CITY OUT
THERE...
SOMEONE'S GOTTA
PLAY THE MUSIC..
THERE'S A MILLION
STORIES IN THE CITY
I'VE GOT THE SOUNDTRACK
I AM THE SOUNDTRACK
THE CITY HAS A SOUNDTRACK...
I HAVE THE VOLUME KNOB.
THE CITY HAS A SOUNDTRACK
YOU JUST NEED TO KNOW HOW TO
PLUG IN.

TOP:
Here's the initial sketch I did for the final scene in the book, which I also used as the main promotional image for B.P.M. Also trying out various taglines.

BOTTOM:
Two sketches for Roxy and Hannah's first argument scene.

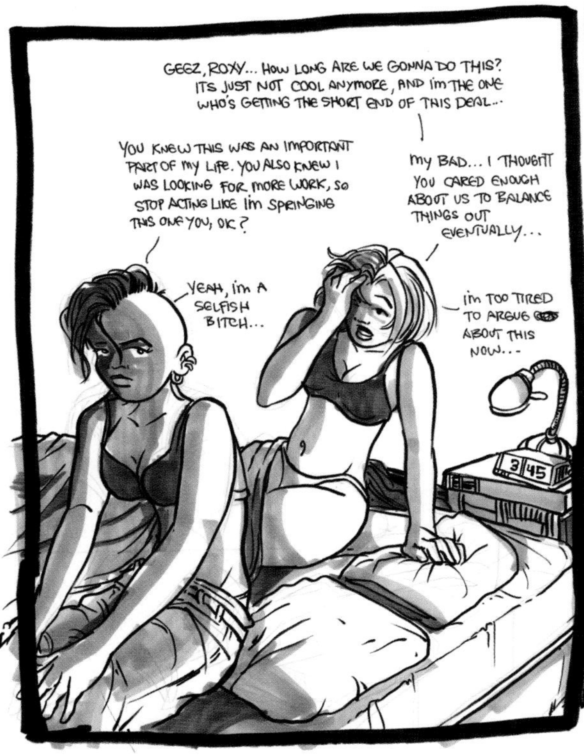
GEEZ, ROXY... HOW LONG ARE WE GONNA DO THIS? ITS JUST NOT COOL ANYMORE, AND I'M THE ONE WHO'S GETTING THE SHORT END OF THIS DEAL...
YOU KNEW THIS WAS AN IMPORTANT PART OF MY LIFE. YOU ALSO KNEW I WAS LOOKING FOR MORE WORK, SO STOP ACTING LIKE I'M SPRINGING THIS ONE YOU, OK?
MY BAD... I THOUGHT YOU CARED ENOUGH ABOUT US TO BALANCE THINGS OUT EVENTUALLY...
YEAH, I'M A SELFISH BITCH...
I'M TOO TIRED TO ARGUE ABOUT THIS NOW...
3:45

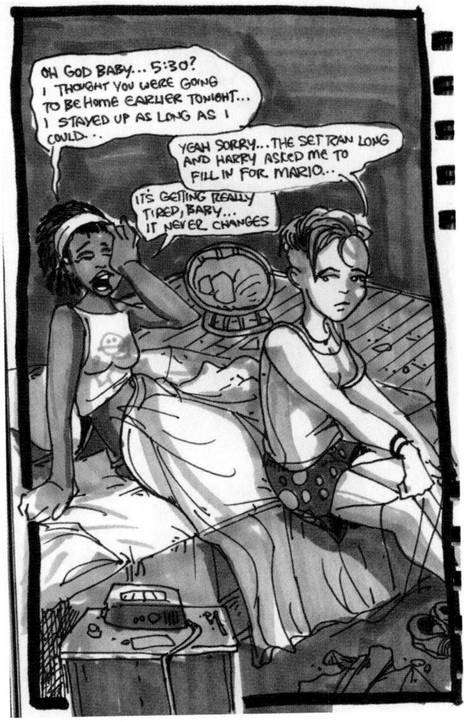
OH GOD BABY... 5:30? I THOUGHT YOU WERE GOING TO BE HOME EARLIER TONIGHT... I STAYED UP AS LONG AS I COULD...
YEAH SORRY... THE SET RAN LONG AND HARRY ASKED ME TO FILL IN FOR MARIO...
IT'S GETTING REALLY TIRED, BABY... IT NEVER CHANGES

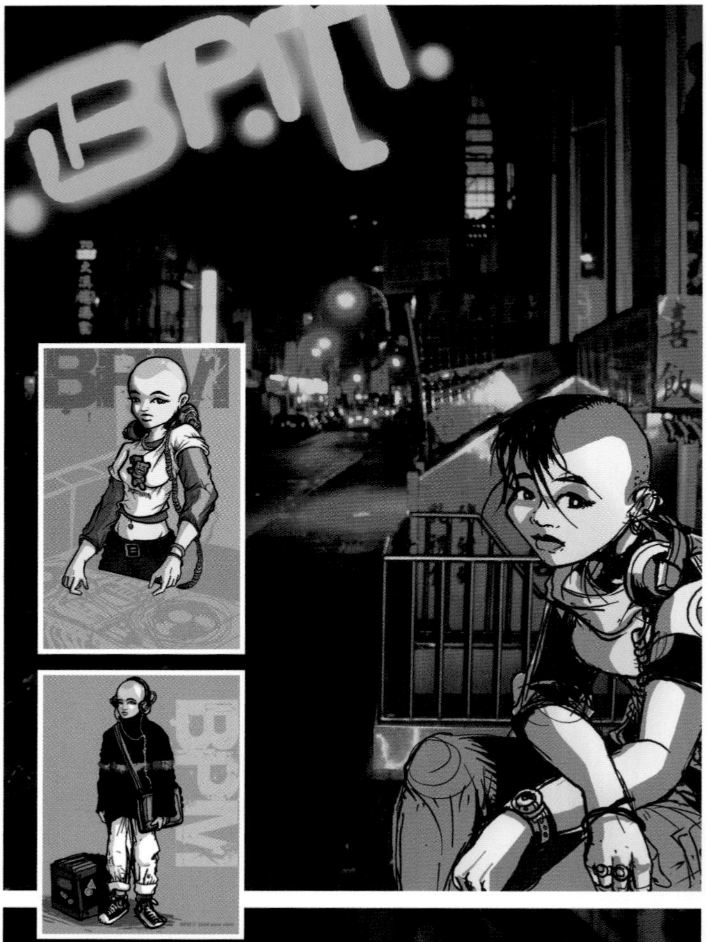
BPM

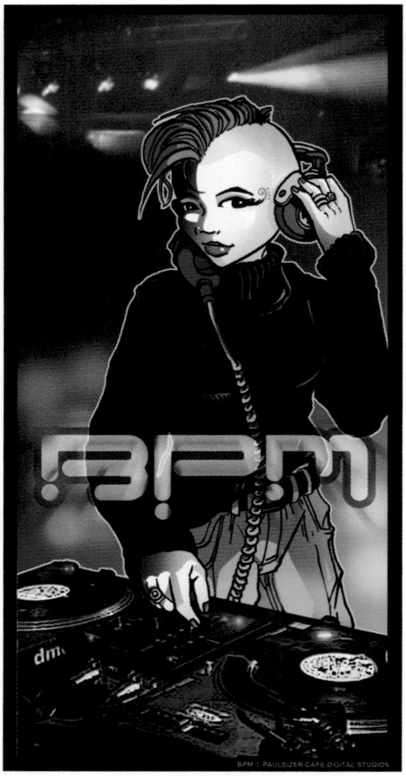
BPM
dm
BPM © PAULSIZER/CAFE DIGITAL STUDIOS

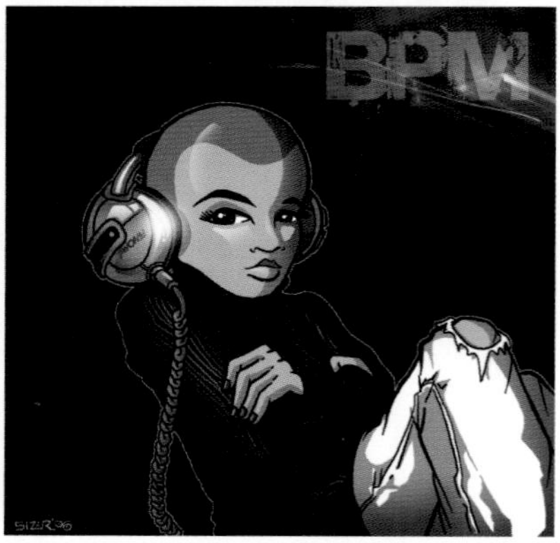
BPM
SIZER '06

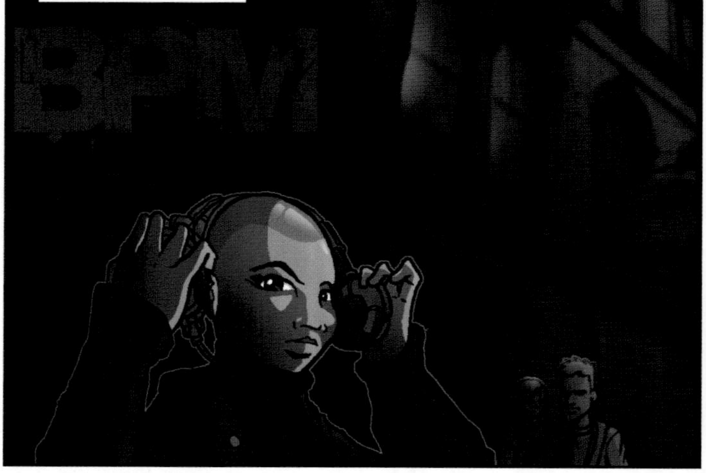
BPM

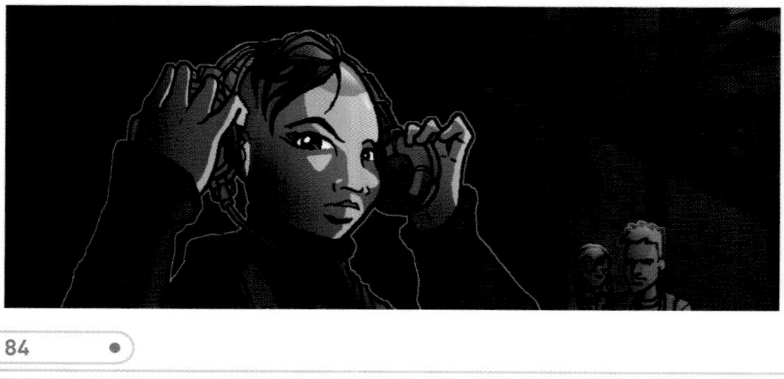

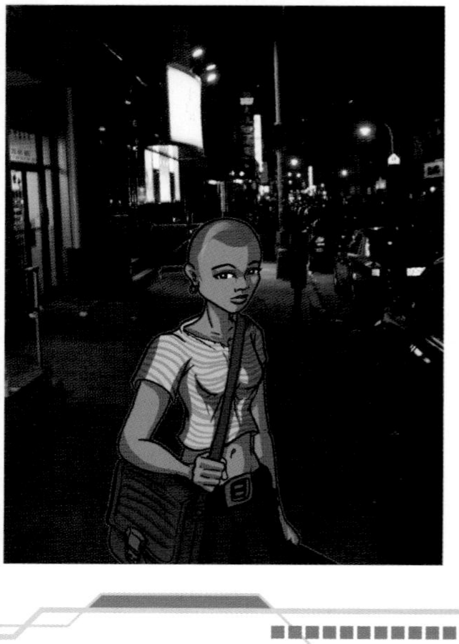

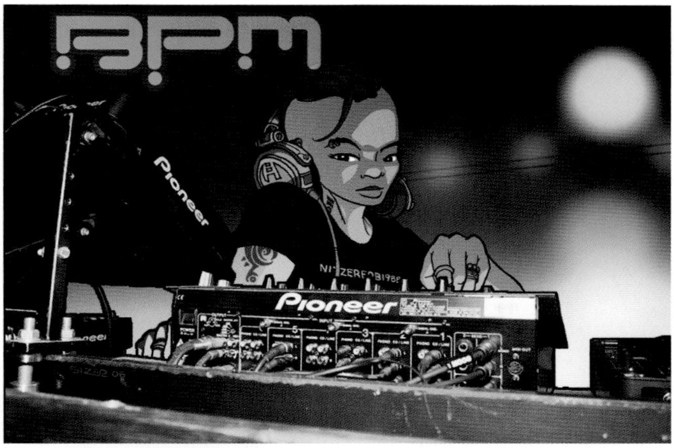
BPM
Pioneer

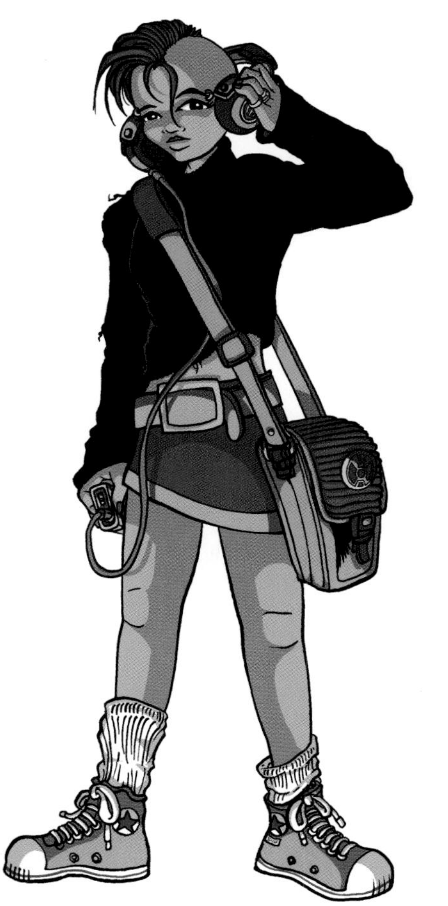

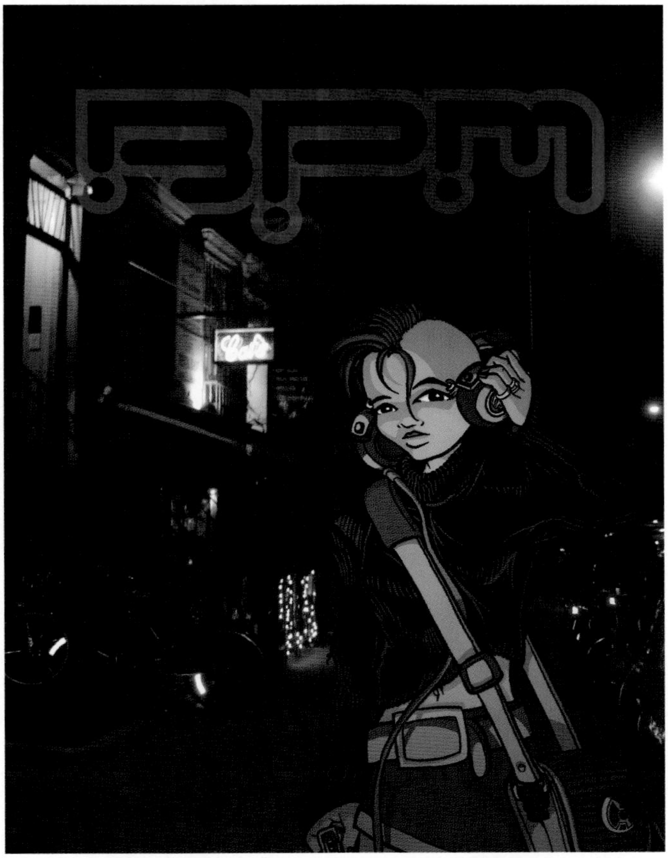
BPM

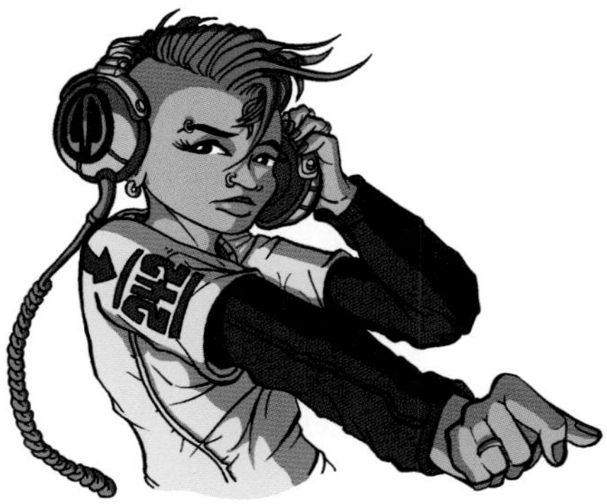

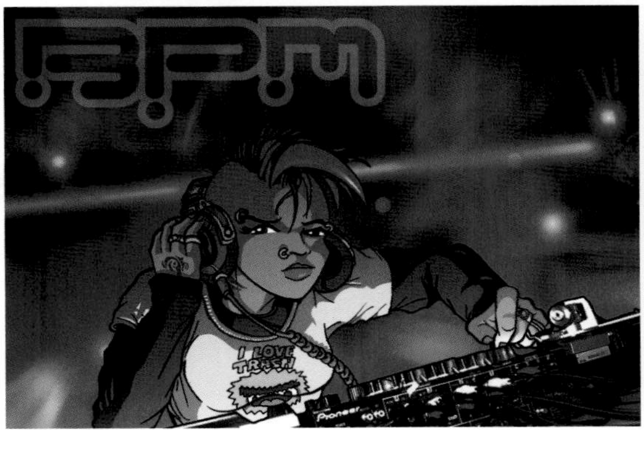
BPM

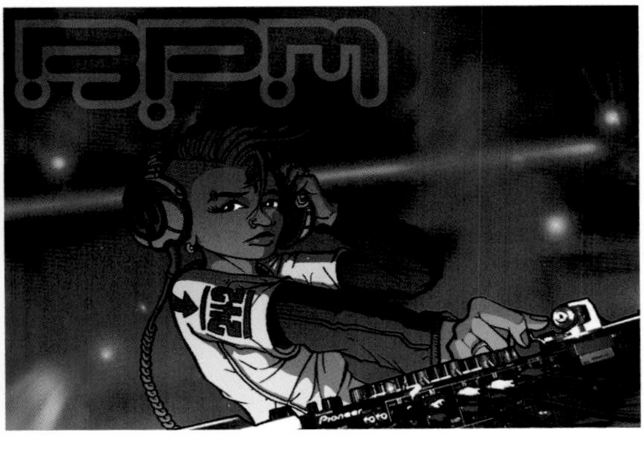
BPM

Dominic went through the most changes of any of the characters in B.P.M.; from skinny guy to skinny guy with dreads to hefty man with dreads to hefty man with close cut Afro, and nearly every other possible combination in between. I liked the visual contrast of a massive guy with huge hands spinning the most minimal of techno and micro-house beats.

CLOSE SHAVED AFRO

THICK EYEBROWS

SHORT DREADS? PULLED BACK IN A PONYTAIL BAND

↑ THE LOOK FOR DOMINIC

NO HEADGEAR CLOSE CROPPED AFRO, SHANTY LONGER SIDEBURNS THICK, CLUMSY STURDY BLACK NORTHERN (AFRO'S STYLE)
✻ 250 -275 lbs. DARK BLACK COMPLEXION THICK NECK NOT FAT, BUT THICK!

BREAKBEAT SCIENCE

DOMINIC 2

250-275 lbs.
6'5"
BIG HANDS BIG FEET BIG, NOT FALL THICK FRAME

MICRO HOUSE D.J. STYLE

100% FOCUS

TWEAKING EVERY SOUND, BREAKING IT INTO CAVERNOUS BASS OR EAR-SPLITTING HIGH END FREQUENCIES, THE NUCLEAR TECHNICIAN OF D.J's

TREVOR? DOMINIC?

LIKE A SURGEON, HE SPINS HIS MICROHOUSE RECORDS, PARING THE ~~PHASE~~ DOWN THE ~~████~~ MOST MINIMAL OF BEAT + BASS. THIS NO-FRILLS SET LEAVES NO ROOM FOR MIS-CALCULATION WITH MUSIC THIS MINIMAL EVERY BEAT IS AN EVENT, BUT ALSO A TRAGEDY WAITING TO HAPPEN

DOMINIC

DOMINIC

DOMINIC (FINAL VERSION)

7-30-06

DOMINIC

PLUS 8 RECORDS
+8

UNDERGROUND
RESISTANCE

ATSUKO (ATSUKO SAKAMOTO)

Atsuko (or DJ Neko-chan, as she was called until I found every anime girl on Earth was using that name) was originally just a party girl DJ, without any real aspirations. As the story developed, I liked the idea of Atsuko being the real "power player" of the group, making the big bucks and getting the recognition and fame. It worked out better to have the person who could offer Roxy the big deals be a woman, rather than falling to the cliché of the industry being dominated by males. Plus, I wanted her to be a real ass-kicker!

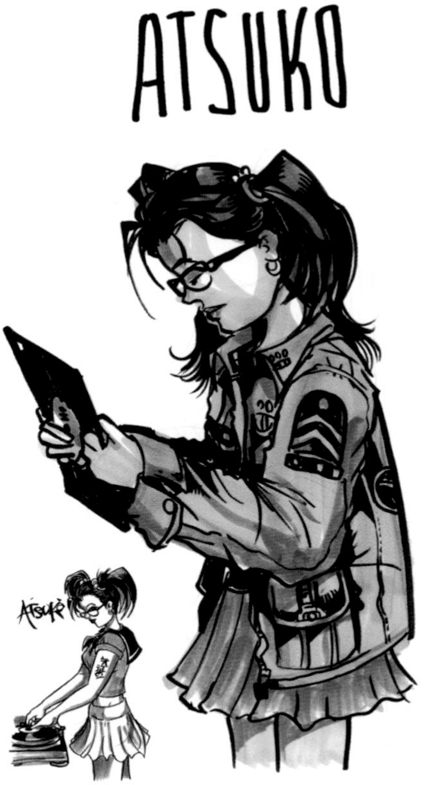
ATSUKO

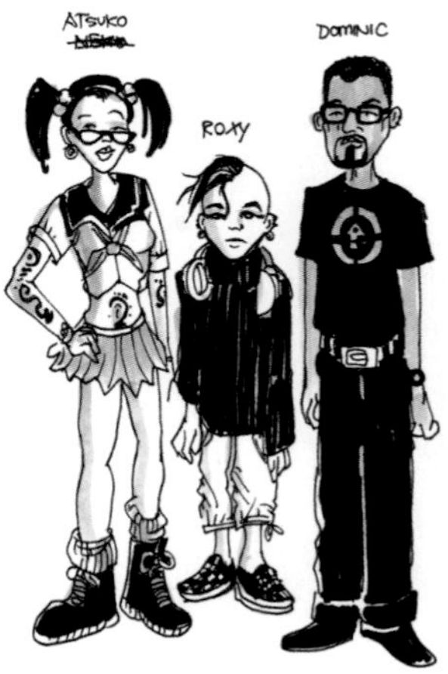
ATSUKO
ROXY
DOMINIC

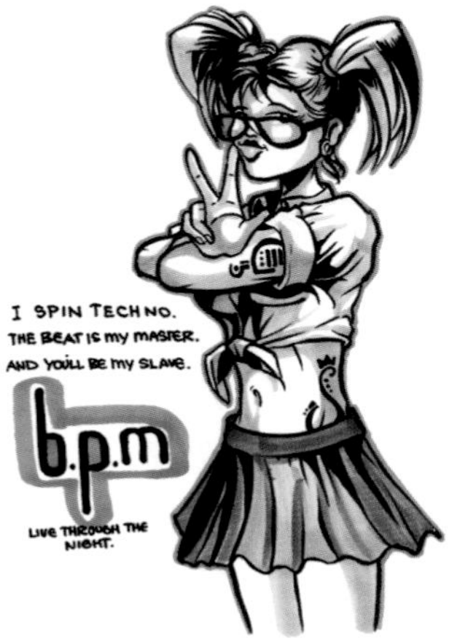
I SPIN TECHNO.
THE BEAT IS MY MASTER.
AND YOU'LL BE MY SLAVE.
b.p.m
LIVE THROUGH THE NIGHT.

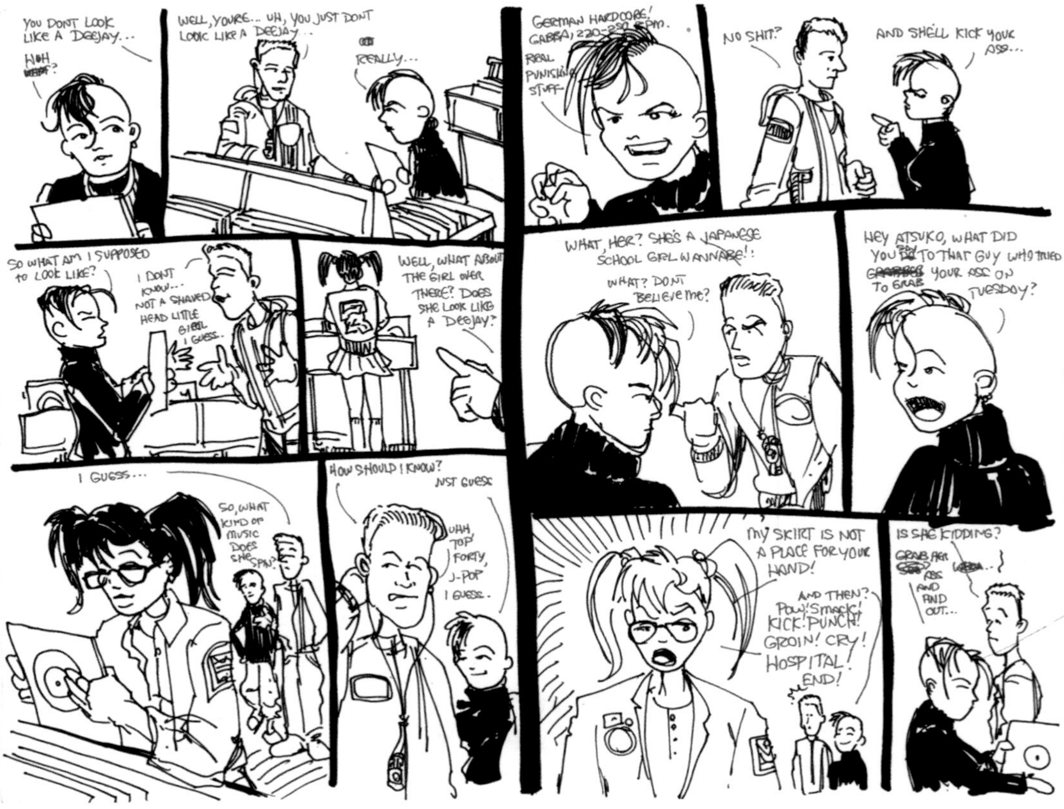
YOU DONT LOOK LIKE A DEEJAY...
HUH?
WELL, YOURE... UH, YOU JUST DONT LOOK LIKE A DEEJAY...
REALLY...
GERMAN HARDCORE! GABBA, 220-250 BPM.
REAL PUNISHING STUFF-
NO SHIT?
AND SHE'LL KICK YOUR ASS...
SO WHAT AM I SUPPOSED TO LOOK LIKE?
I DONT KNOW... NOT A SHAVED HEAD LITTLE GIRL I GUESS...
WELL, WHAT ABOUT THE GIRL OVER THERE? DOES SHE LOOK LIKE A DEEJAY?
WHAT, HER? SHE'S A JAPANESE SCHOOL GIRL WANNABE!
WHAT? DONT BELIEVE ME?
HEY ATSUKO, WHAT DID YOU SAY TO THAT GUY WHO TRIED TO GRAB YOUR ASS ON TUESDAY?
I GUESS...
SO, WHAT KIND OF MUSIC DOES SHE SPIN?
HOW SHOULD I KNOW? JUST GUESS
UHH, TOP FORTY, J-POP I GUESS.
MY SKIRT IS NOT A PLACE FOR YOUR HAND!
AND THEN? POW! SMACK! KICK! PUNCH! GROIN! CRY! HOSPITAL! END!
IS SHE KIDDING?
GRAB HER ASS AND FIND OUT...

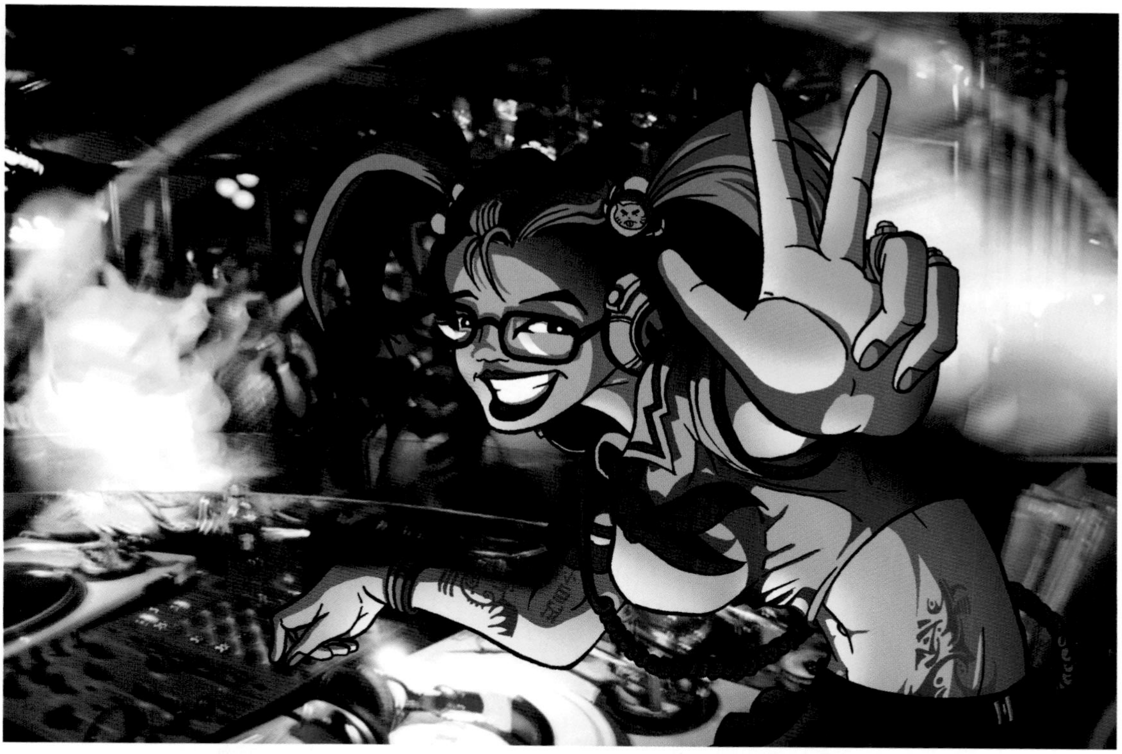

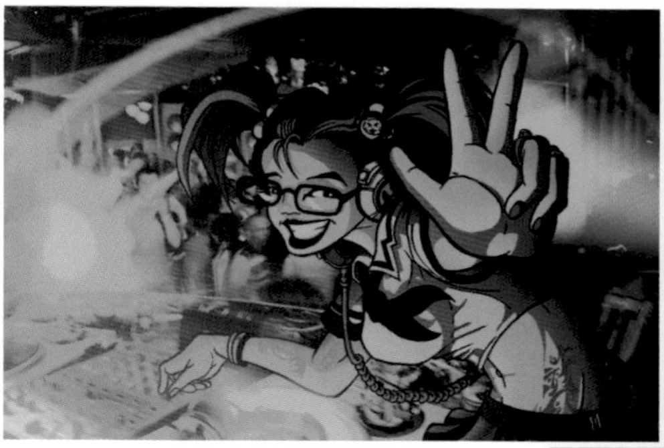

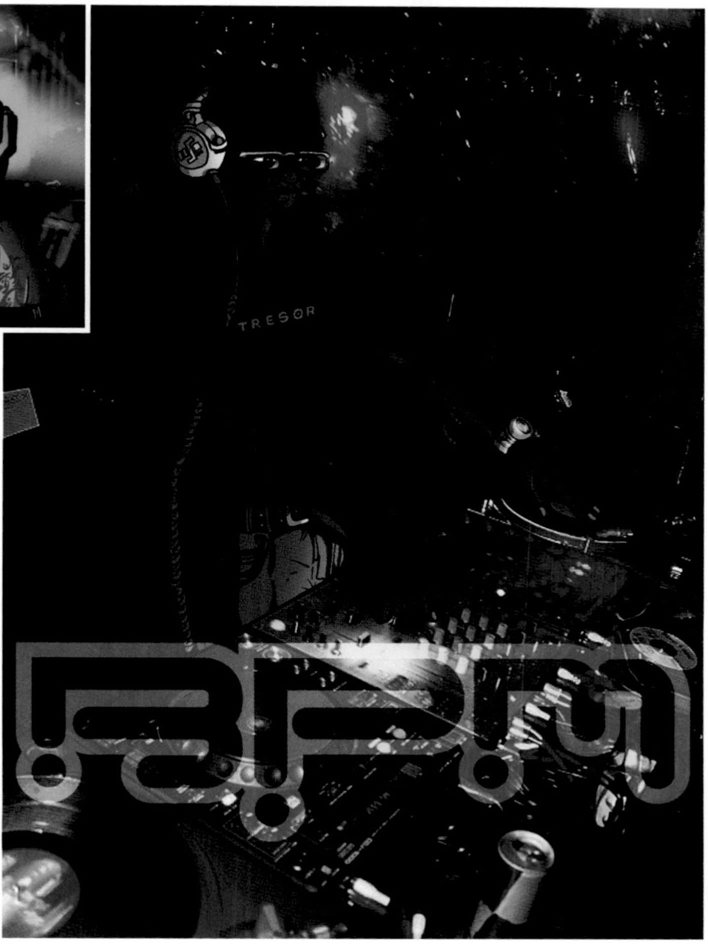
TRESOR

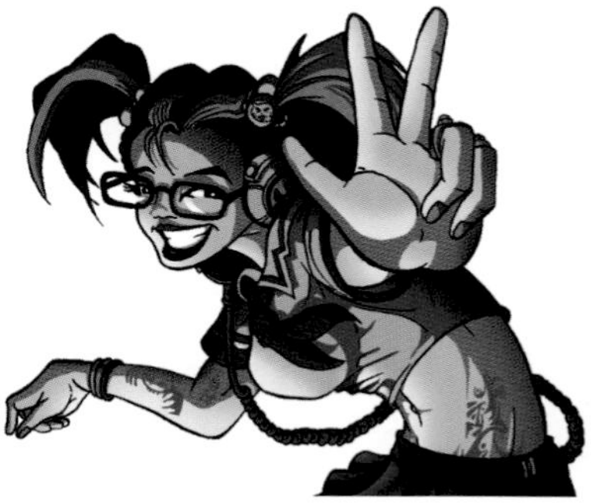

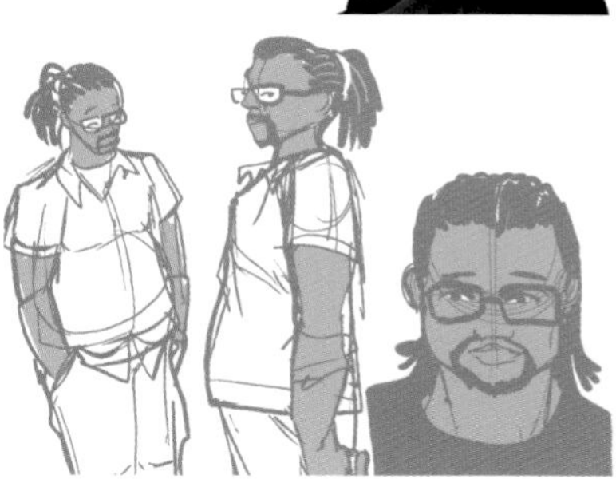

ROBIE (PHILIPPE GERARD ROBICHEAU)

The challenge with Robie was figuring out how "degraded" I wanted to make him. He had to have plenty of "mileage", but not be completely irredeemable. Although some have theorized Robie represents a particular DJ, he is in fact a true amalgam of personalities and egos.

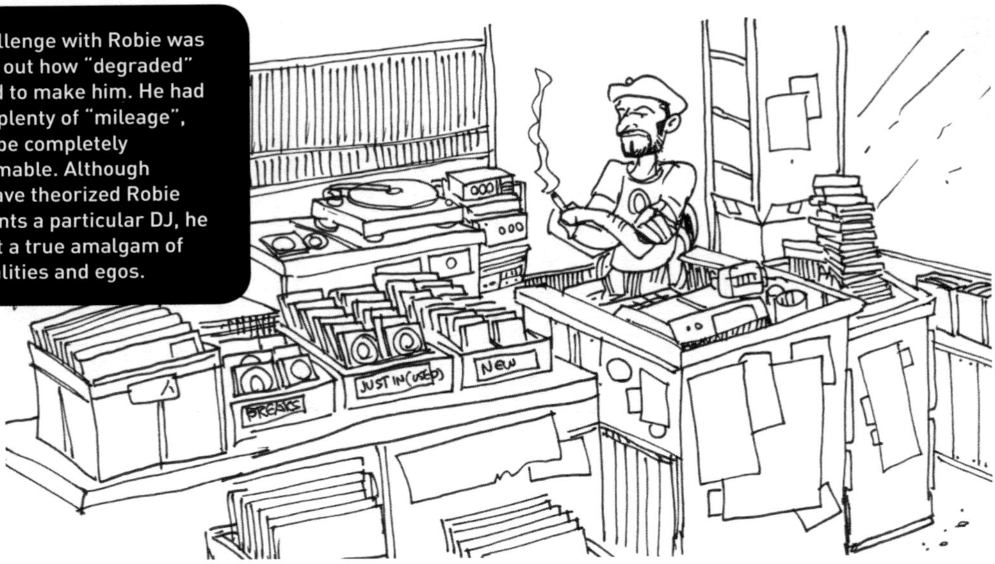
BREAKS
JUST IN (USED)
NEW

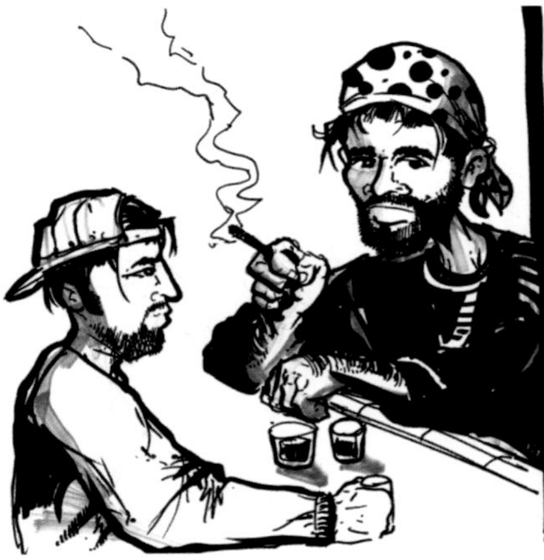

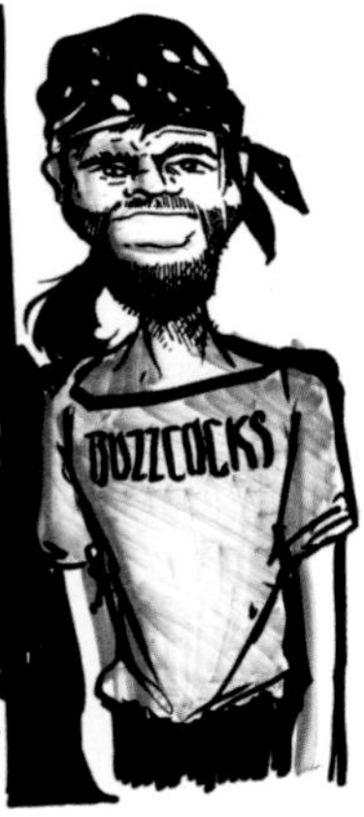
BUZZCOCKS

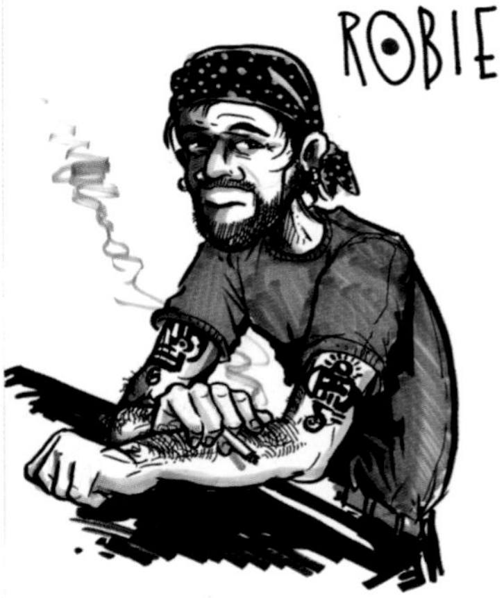
ROBIE

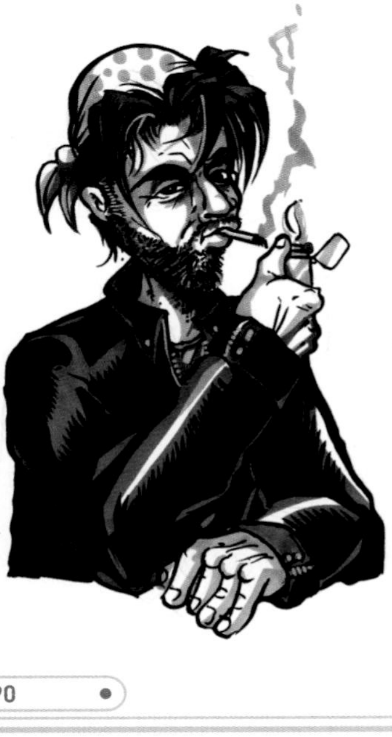

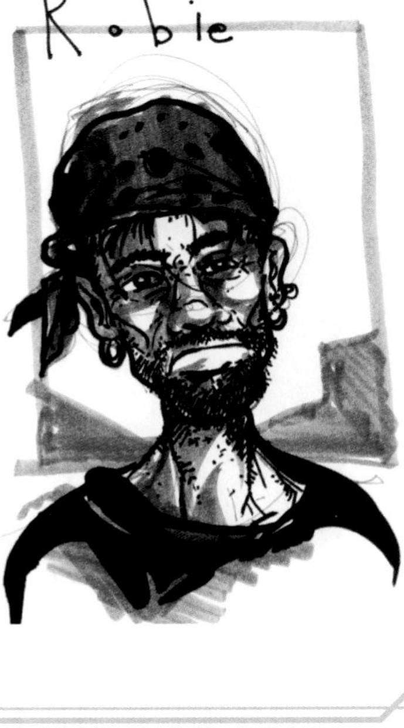
Robie

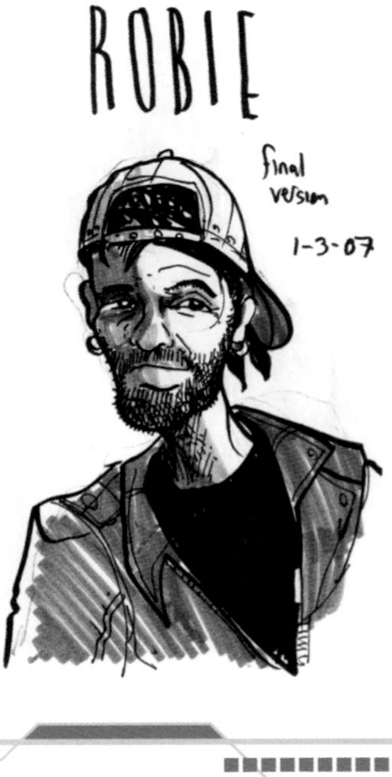
ROBIE
final version
1-3-07

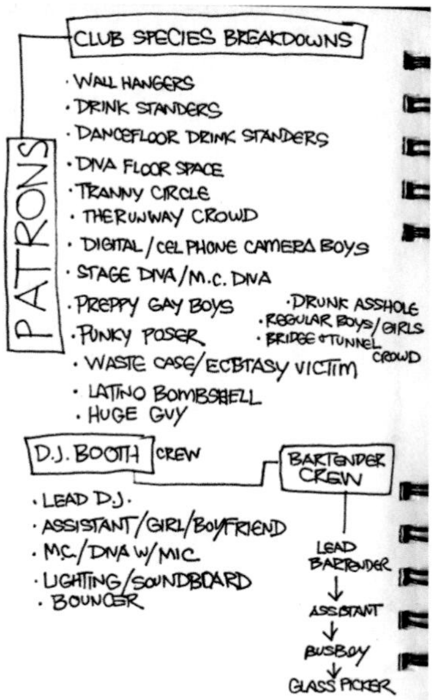
CLUB SPECIES BREAKDOWNS
PATRONS
· WALL HANGERS
· DRINK STANDERS
· DANCEFLOOR DRINK STANDERS
· DIVA FLOOR SPACE
· TRANNY CIRCLE
· THE RUNWAY CROWD
· DIGITAL/CEL PHONE CAMERA BOYS
· STAGE DIVA/M.C. DIVA
· PREPPY GAY BOYS
· DRUNK ASSHOLE
· PUNKY POSER
· REGULAR BOYS/GIRLS
· BRIDGE & TUNNEL CROWD
· WASTE CASE/ECSTASY VICTIM
· LATINO BOMBSHELL
· HUGE GUY
D.J. BOOTH CREW
· LEAD D.J.
· ASSISTANT/GIRL/BOYFRIEND
· MC/DIVA W/MIC
· LIGHTING/SOUNDBOARD
· BOUNCER
BARTENDER CREW
LEAD BARTENDER
ASSISTANT
BUSBOY
GLASS PICKER

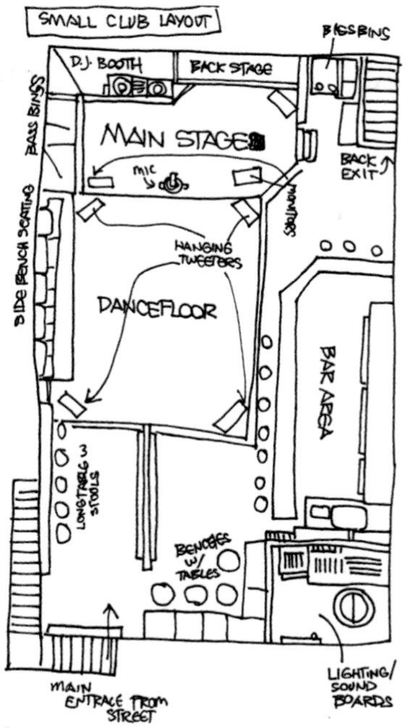
SMALL CLUB LAYOUT
D.J. BOOTH
BACK STAGE
BASS BINS
MAIN STAGE
MIC
BACK EXIT
MONITORS
SIDE BENCH SEATING
HANGING TWEETERS
DANCEFLOOR
BAR AREA
LONG TABLE 3 STOOLS
BENCHES W/ TABLES
MAIN ENTRACE FROM STREET
LIGHTING/SOUND BOARDS

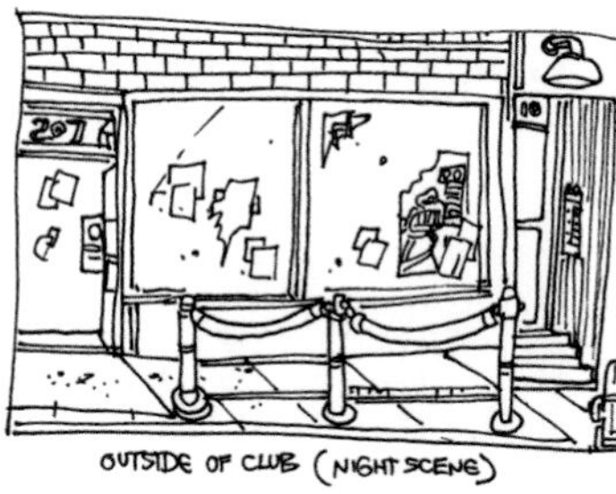
OUTSIDE OF CLUB (NIGHT SCENE)

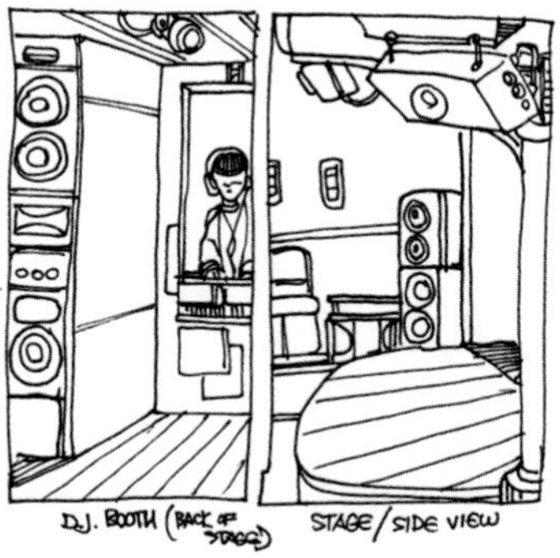
DJ. BOOTH (BACK OF STAGE)
STAGE/SIDE VIEW

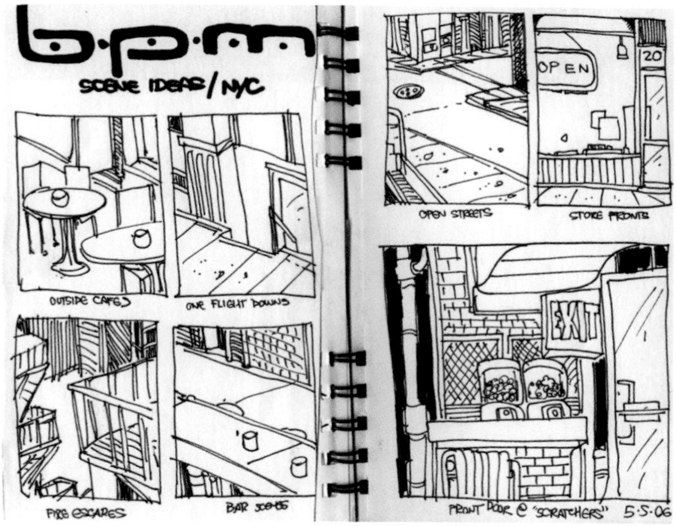
b.p.m
SCENE IDEAS/NYC
OUTSIDE CAFES
ONE FLIGHT DOWNS
FIRE ESCAPES
BAR SCENES
OPEN
OPEN STREETS
STORE FRONTS
EXIT
FRONT DOOR @ "SCRATCHERS" 5.5.06

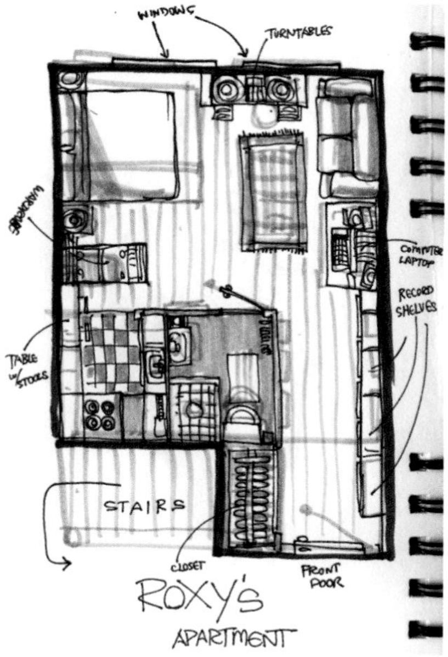
WINDOWS
TURNTABLES
COMPUTER LAPTOP
RECORD SHELVES
TABLE W/ STOOLS
STAIRS
CLOSET
FRONT DOOR
ROXY'S APARTMENT

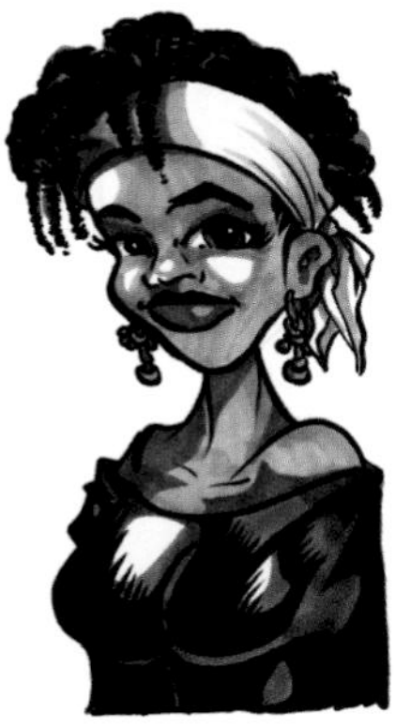

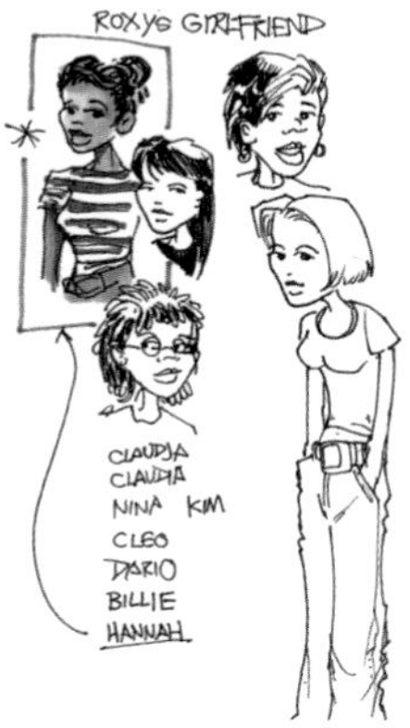
ROXY'S GIRLFRIEND
CLAUDIA
CLAUDIA
NINA KIM
CLEO
DARIO
BILLIE
HANNAH

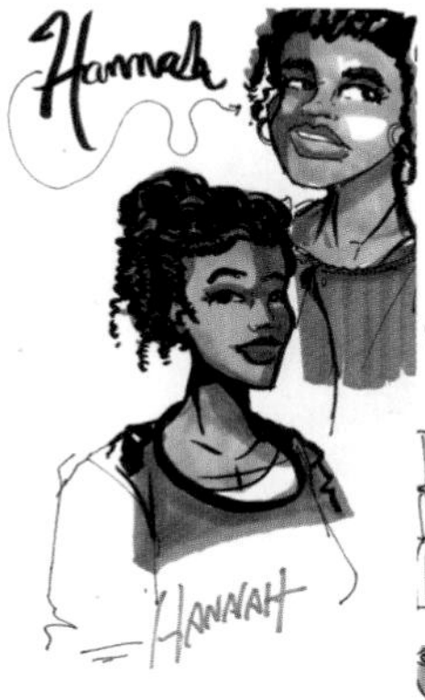
Hannah
HANNAH

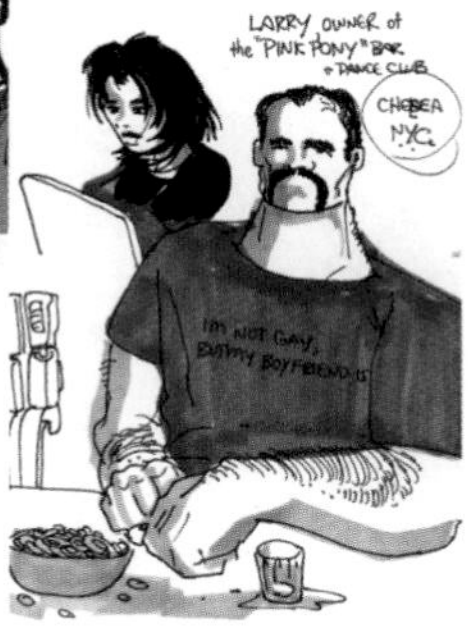
LARRY OWNER of the "PINK PONY" BAR & DANCE CLUB
CHELSEA NYC
I'M NOT GAY, BUT MY BOYFRIEND IS

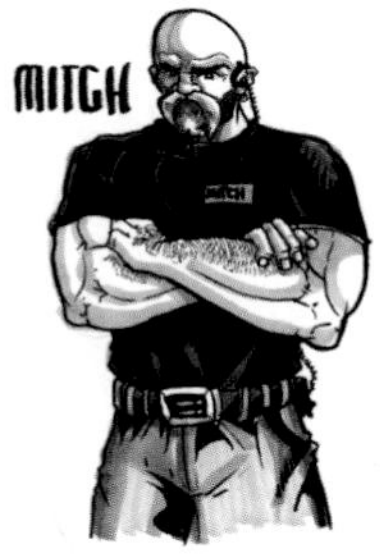
MITCH

MARK PAULIK www.wanderingpilot.com

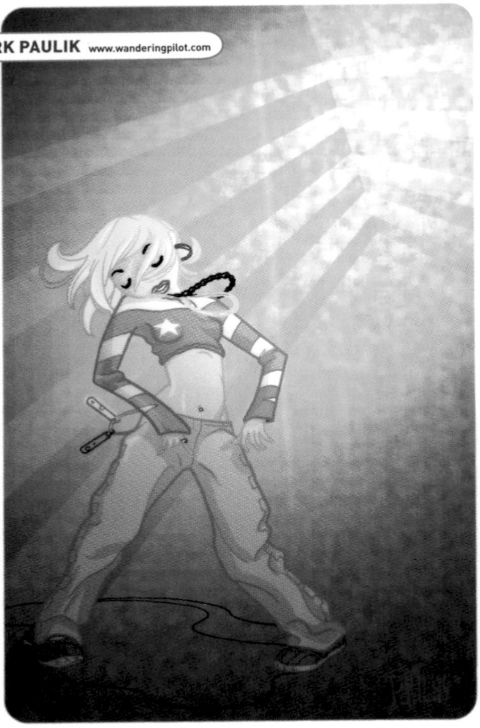

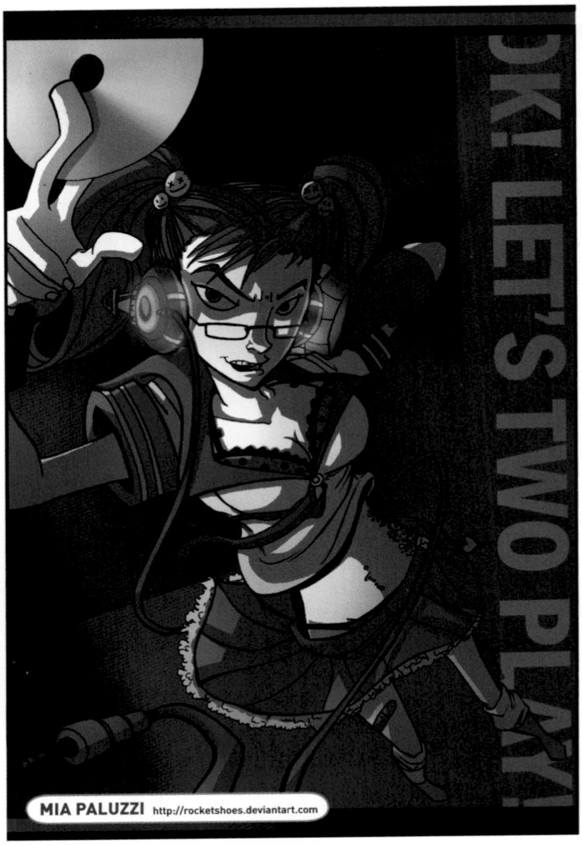
OK! LET'S TWO PLAY!

MIA PALUZZI http://rocketshoes.deviantart.com

KARL ALTSTAETTER www.hyperwerks.com

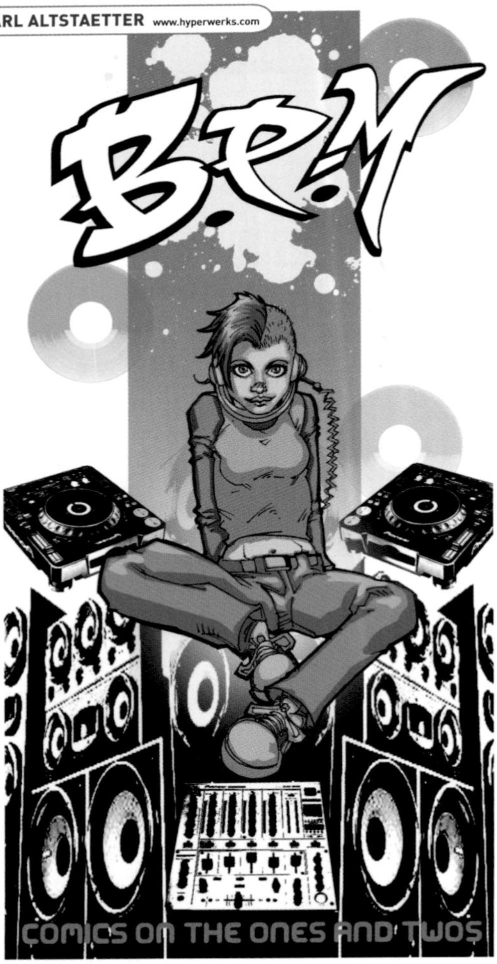
B.P.M
COMICS ON THE ONES AND TWOS

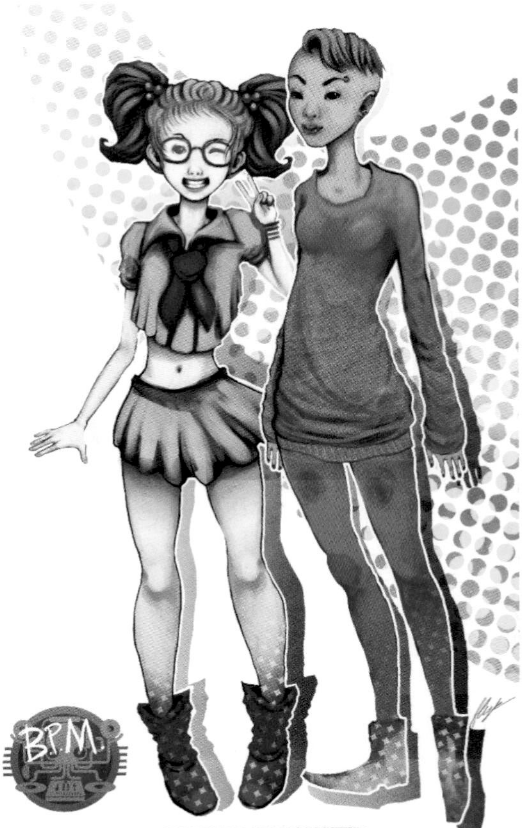
B.P.M.

SARA WILSON www.fly-k.net

B.P.M. SET LIST/SOUNDTRACK

The "soundtrack" of B.P.M. is actually more of a mixtape for the book, rather than a set list for a club night. Clocking in at nearly four hours, it could be a decent (and very diverse) night's set, but I selected these songs more to accompany the many moods and happenings of B.P.M., rather than be a real-time soundtrack. It also serves one of my greatest loves; exposing people to new music and letting them in on the diversity and energy of dance and electronic music. Like any good mixtape, it takes you on a journey through the familiar and the new.

You can sample, purchase and download all of this music through iTunes as four collected "iMixes" that I've created for this book. Go to www.paulsizer.com and click on the "B.P.M." link on the front page to find all the links to this music through iTunes, downloads of CD covers for the iMixes, B.P.M. wallpapers and more!

1. **WOWIE ZOWIE (FEATURING EDGY)** 4:57 SUPERCHUMBO
2. **PACIFIC 202** 5:38 808 STATE
3. **THIS MUST BE THE PLACE (NAIVE MELODY)** 4:57 TALKING HEADS
4. **DAEL** 6:40 AUTECHRE
5. **PUMP UP THE VOLUME** 4:07 M/A/R/R/S
6. **MUSIC IS THE VICTIM** 3:02 SCISSOR SISTERS
7. **BETTER THINGS** 4:14 MASSIVE ATTACK
8. **HIP HOP BE BOP (ORIGINAL VERSION)** 5:36 MAN PARRISH
9. **COME INTO MY WORLD** 4:32 KYLIE MINOGUE
10. **POISON ARROW (SINGLE VERSION)** 3:23 ABC
11. **ROCKIT** 5:27 HERBIE HANCOCK
12. **WALKING ON SUNSHINE (RADIO EDIT)** 4:51 ROCKERS REVENGE
13. **DARK BEAT (MURK MONSTER MIX)** 9:23 OSCAR G. & RALPH FALCON
14. **LOVE IS GONNA SAVE US** 5:05 BENNY BENASSI & THE BIZ
15. **WALKING WOUNDED** 6:05 EVERYTHING BUT THE GIRL
16. **HOW DOES IT MAKE YOU FEEL?** 4:38 AIR
17. **BOOGIE ON REGGAE WOMAN (1982 MUSIQUARIUM VERSION)** 4:56 STEVIE WONDER
18. **GROOVE IS IN THE HEART** 3:52 DEEE-LITE
19. **TRUE FAITH (THE MORNING SUN EXTENDED REMIX)** 9:01 NEW ORDER
20. **ATOMIC DOG [LP VERSION]** 4:46 GEORGE CLINTON
21. **ELEMENTS** 7:37 DANNY TENAGLIA
22. **GO (RADIO EDIT)** 3:38 MOBY
23. **DAYS GO BY** 7:08 DIRTY VEGAS
24. **MISSING YOU** 5:07 THE BELOVED
25. **HEY U** 4:54 BASEMENT JAXX
26. **RIZE UP** 4:09 THE CHEMICAL BROTHERS
27. **SAY HELLO** 4:35 DEEP DISH
28. **IN THIS WORLD** 4:03 MOBY
29. **HAPPY (SPIRITUAL SOUTH GO HAPPY IN RIO MIX)** 6:45 MAX SEDGLEY
30. **WORK TO DO** 10:52 SANDER KLEINENBERG
31. **MADSKILLZ-MIC CHEKKA** 5:36 BT
32. **THE DOWNTOWN LIGHTS** 6:31 THE BLUE NILE
33. **ONCE IN A LIFETIME (2006 VERSION)** 4:18 TALKING HEADS
34. **RAPTURE (ORIGINAL EXTENDED)** 6:50 IIO
35. **ROCK YOUR BODY, ROCK** 5:15 FERRY CORSTEN
36. **49 PERCENT (EWAN PEARSON GLASS HALF FULL REMIX)** 6:05 RÖYKSOPP
37. **NEW YORK CITY BOY [THE ALMIGHTY DEFINITIVE MIX]** 6:32 PET SHOP BOYS
38. **I FEEL LOVE (12" VERSION)** 8:17 DONNA SUMMER
39. **NEW YORK CITY** 3:03 THEY MIGHT BE GIANTS
40. **SHIVER (PLUMP DJS MIX)** 3:53 LEE COOMBS
41. **SLAVE TO THE RHYTHM** 4:21 GRACE JONES
42. **LOOKING FOR THE PERFECT BEAT (12" VOCAL VERSION)** 6:58 AFRIKA BAMBAATAA
43. **MUSIC MATTERS (AXWELL REMIX)** 8:31 FAITHLESS

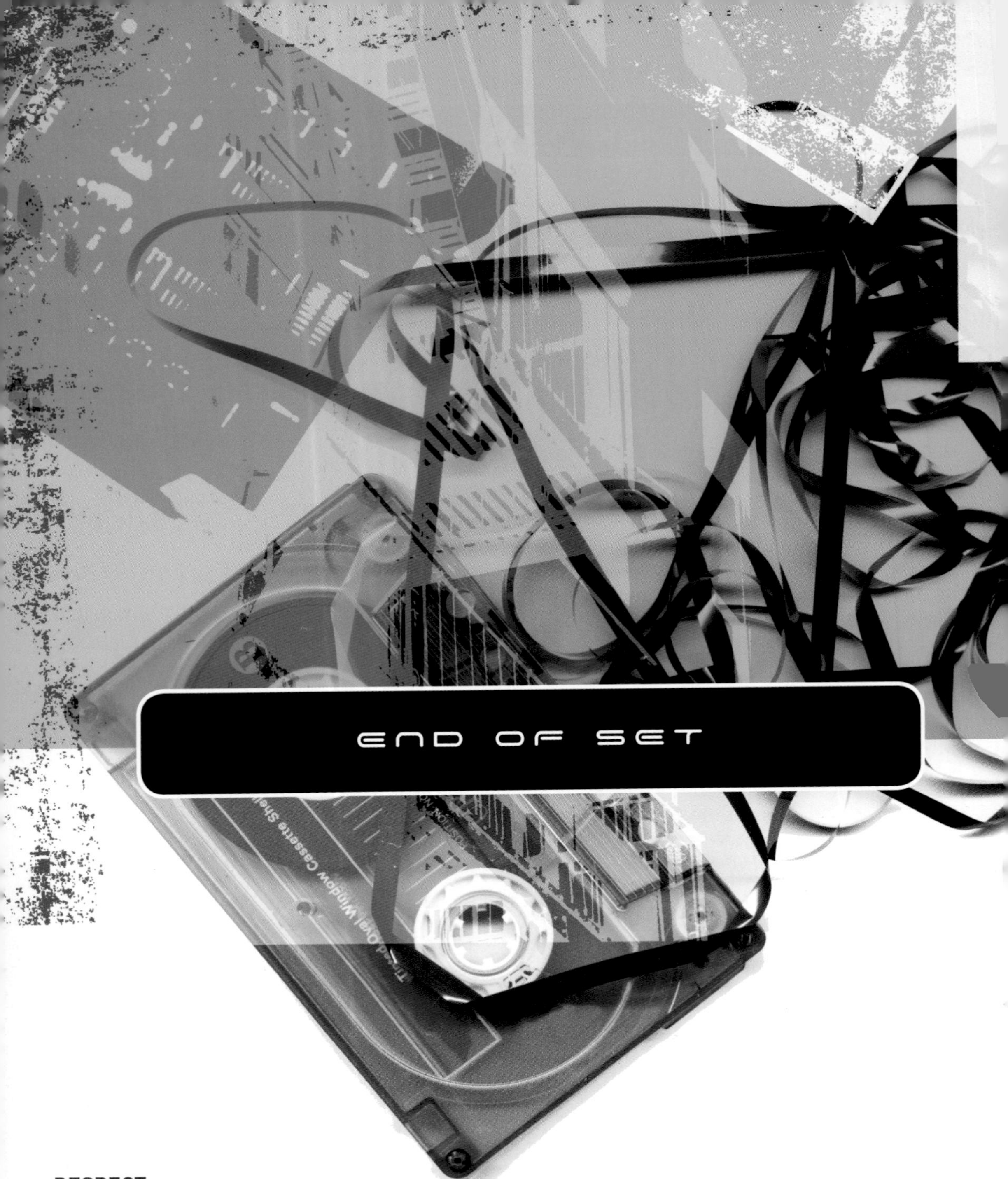
END OF SET

RESPECT

Kraftwerk, Afrika Bambaataa/Soul Sonic Force, Yello, Pet Shop Boys, Moby, Fluke, Underworld, Giorgio Moroder, Tim Simenon, Arthur Baker, John Robie, The Latin Rascals, Grandmaster Flash and the Furious Five, BT, ABBA, Autechre, B-52's, Basement Jaxx, William Orbit, Depeche Mode, Cabaret Voltaire, David Bowie, Vanessa Daou, Thomas Dolby, 808 State, New Order, Vince Clarke, Rollo and Sister Bliss, Front 242, Heaven 17/Human League, Madonna, Leftfield, Jam & Spoon, Massive Attack, Gary Numan, John Foxx, O.M.D., Prince, Sparks, Ryuichi Sakamoto, Sasha, Shep Pettibone, John Luongo, Phil Harding, Junior Vasquez, Claudia Brücken, Pascal Gabriel, David Byrne/Talking Heads, Brian Eno, Derrick May, Juan Atkins, Carl Craig, Kevin Saunderson, Laurie Anderson, David Sylvian, Adrian Sherwood, Al Jourgenson, Trent Reznor, Carl Cox, Severed Heads, Shriekback, Paul Oakenfold, Mark Moore/S'Express, Man Parrish, Plump DJs, Deep Dish, Stevie Wonder, and hundreds of others too long to list.

THANKS ABOVE AND BEYOND

Jane Irwin (I love you!), Johanna Draper Carlson, Dan Traeger, Mike Pfieffer, Karen "DJ Jackalope" Maeda, Mark Paulik, Mia Paluzzi, Sara Wilson, Karl Altstaetter, the staff of Rebel Rebel NYC, Dave Glide, Logan Kelly, Jamie Hewlett and Gorillaz, Becky Cooper, everyone at DeviantArt, Fist Full o' Comics, Fanfare, James Sime and Isotope, Kevin King, Tim O'Shea, Michael Goliver, Amanda Schwarz, Mark Smylie, and all the fans who have read my books or heard me play a record somewhere. Groove is in the heart.